Youth Violence and Delinquency

Youth Violence and Delinquency

Monsters and Myths

Volume 3

Juvenile Treatment and Crime Prevention

Edited by

MARILYN D. MCSHANE
AND FRANK P. WILLIAMS III

Praeger Perspectives

Criminal Justice, Delinquency, and Corrections

PRAEGER

Westport, Connecticut
London

Library of Congress Cataloging-in-Publication Data

Youth violence and delinquency : monsters and myths / edited by Marilyn
D. McShane and Frank P. Williams III.
    p. cm. — (Criminal justice, delinquency, and corrections, ISSN 1535-0371)
    Includes bibliographical references and index.
    ISBN 978-0-275-99112-8 (set : alk. paper) — ISBN 978-0-275-99113-5
(v. 1 : alk. paper) — ISBN 978-0-275-99114-2 (v. 2 : alk. paper) —
ISBN 978-0-275-99115-9 (v. 3 : alk. paper) 1. Juvenile delinquency—
United States. 2. Juvenile justice, Administration of—United States. 3. Victims of
juvenile crime—United States. 4. Juvenile delinquency—United States—Prevention.
I. McShane, Marilyn D., 1956- II. Williams, Franklin P.
    HV9104.Y6854 2007
    364.360973—dc22   2007003047

British Library Cataloguing in Publication Data is available.

Library of Congress Catalog Card Number: 2007003047
ISBN-10: 0-275-99112-1 (set)
        0-275-99113-X (vol. 1)
        0-275-99114-8 (vol. 2)
        0-275-99115-6 (vol. 3)

ISBN-13: 978-0-275-99112-8 (set)
        978-0-275-99113-5 (vol. 1)
        978-0-275-99114-2 (vol. 2)
        978-0-275-99115-9 (vol. 3)

ISSN: 1535-0371

First published in 2007

Praeger Publishers, 88 Post Road West, Westport, CT 06881
An imprint of Greenwood Publishing Group, Inc.
www.praeger.com

Printed in the United States of America

The paper used in this book complies with the
Permanent Paper Standard issued by the National
Information Standards Organization (Z39.48-1984).

10 9 8 7 6 5 4 3 2 1

Contents

Preface

The bright lights of the juvenile training center, a euphemism for a large prison for youths, glare across the horizon. It is only early summer, but the temperatures are already in the steamy range and evening activities are concluding. Groups of state wards file toward the living quarters, swarms that seem tense, loud, and expansive. The energy in the area as the population surges is particularly nerve-wracking. If it were to erupt, what would happen and, given the volatile nature of the elements, why doesn't it?

For visitors, the scene that plays out at the facility is frighteningly surreal. Across America hundreds of secure facilities house undereducated, angry, overmedicated youth bristling with testosterone, adorned with tattoos and scars, just waiting for release. Although many forms of treatment and services are legally mandated, they are often inappropriately and half-heartedly delivered and even less enthusiastically received.

Several of the youths we talk to are not optimistic about their release. Their families are entrenched in habits and activities that are destined to lead to their revocation. One of the confounding aspects of disproportionate minority confinement is the cyclical nature of crime in poor and immigrant families from neighborhoods characterized by social disorganization. How long can they remain out of the eye of authorities when cousins, uncles, brothers, and parents are continually drawn into the petty crimes and activities of the streets that bring the police and, inevitably, the juvenile authorities?

For too many years corrections officials have been paralyzed by public stinginess and vindictive tirades about why criminals should not get valuable services and programming that law-abiding poor are denied. The problem is in the false dichotomy—the poor should not be denied either. The problem is that none, least of all offenders, are able to obtain programming and services from the state. We have become a soulless machine that blames and punishes without humanitarian concern for the rehabilitation and improvement of the wayward. These are the people on whom we focused during early American civic development. Then, we took pride in our ability to reform and recycle offenders back into the fabric of a working citizenship. Today, there is only an unforgiving litany of just desserts and cold, hard consequences. Perhaps it is time to break the pattern of institutional defeatism, to abandon the system of complex processing that only serves to discard and abandon people, and to adopt a rehabilitation mindset.

To do so, we must break the cycles. Cycles of violence, cycles of abuse, and cycles of crime all lead us to question whether there is really any intervention or treatment that offers hope for delinquents today. Do we have the resources and the patience to develop more individualized treatment strategies that might result in more successful outcomes? The suggestions offered in this volume give us much to think about in terms not only of what types of programming would be most effective but also why programming itself is critical for the future of youth corrections.

For us to engage in effective youthful corrections, it only takes imagination. Imagine working in a system in which children are valued; one in which their needs are addressed in unique and individual ways. Imagine workers who are optimistic and upbeat, encouraging and caring. Workers who take the time to mentor and teach, discipline and listen, and work with families to repair and restructure themselves into healthy functioning units. Imagine healing lives and seeing progress and hopefulness, jobs and education, come together as a reality despite the struggle and resistance, complications, and setbacks. Imagine seeing it work. When someone asks, "what did you do today?" imagine what you would say.

CHAPTER 1

What Works with Juveniles? Intervention, Treatment, and Rehabilitation

Clete Snell and Beau Snell

In recent years, a number of federal and state initiatives have had the objective to identify "what works" with juvenile offenders. The result has been a number of reports concerning programs and practices to reduce juvenile crime, including *Diverting Children from a Life of Crime: Measuring Costs and Benefits; Investing in Our Children: What We Know and Don't Know about the Costs and Benefits of Early Childhood Interventions;* and *Preventing Crime: What Works, What Doesn't, What's Promising.* The overriding message in these reports is that a growing body of knowledge demonstrates that many programs work. Currie examined a number of programs that had crime-reduction potential and concluded, "the best of them work, and they work remarkably well given how limited and under-funded they usually are."[1] This chapter will focus on a number of innovative programs that have demonstrated effectiveness in preventing, treating, and rehabilitating juvenile offenders.

HOW DO WE KNOW WHAT WORKS?

Before discussing programs that work with juvenile offenders, an important question to consider is, how do we know what works? The programs and policies that will be discussed in the following sections underwent *evaluative designs.* The purpose of an evaluation is to determine whether a program was effective in accomplishing its goals. Experimental evaluative designs are an especially effective way of determining whether a program is working. It includes a *control group* of untreated juveniles. This makes it possible to compare the *treatment group,* the group receiving the intervention or program, with a group that does not receive the treatment. In this way, researchers can answer such questions as the following: is the treatment more effective than simply leaving juveniles alone or providing them with the typical services?

An extremely important component of experimental evaluative designs involves *random assignment* procedures, such that juveniles are randomly assigned to the treatment group or the control group. Random assignment gives researchers confidence that the treated and untreated groups are equivalent in important ways at the beginning of the program. If the purpose of a program is to reduce delinquency, random assignment should ensure that both groups are equal in their frequency of delinquent offenses before a program begins. Random assignment helps ensure that differences between the groups after a treatment or program are due to exposure to the program and not other factors. Because this type of research design rules out so many alternative explanations for differences in outcomes between treated and untreated groups, no other type permits as much confidence in linking treatments or program goals with results.

Unfortunately, for a variety of reasons, it is not always possible to randomly assign individuals to groups that receive a treatment or program intervention and those that do not. In these cases, researchers attempt to compensate by creating a comparison group that is nearly equivalent in important ways such as age, gender, race, and socioeconomic status.

Another important component of evaluation research is the inclusion of *follow-up measures*. Initial results of a program or treatment may show that the treatment group improved in some way, such as had lower delinquency rates or a decrease in drug use. Follow-up measures are important because they allow researchers to assess the stability of initial findings. Sometimes they show that initial findings remain essentially unchanged over time. On other occasions, follow-up measures may reveal that initial differences have disappeared. This result suggests that the program or treatment did not have a lasting impact.

Finally, evaluations of programs and treatments should be repeated in other settings and with different participants. This is called *replication*. As treatment hypotheses or program goals are repeated and similar results are reported, researchers gain confidence in the effectiveness of the treatment approach or the program.

In 1996, researchers at the University of Colorado developed the *Blueprints for Violence Prevention Program*. The sole goal of the program was to identify effective interventions to prevent or reduce juvenile delinquency. To be judged effective the following components had to be in place: (1) a strong evaluation design (generally using random assignment) had to be included; (2) the evaluation must show that the program had *significant* prevention effects (the difference in outcomes between the treatment group and control group cannot be so trivial that it does not justify the costs of the program); (3) the effect must be sustained over time, at least one year, with no evidence of loss of effectiveness; and (4) the program must be effective in more than one site. The researchers examined hundreds of programs and only found about a dozen model programs that meet all of these criteria. Those programs will be discussed in the following section. It's important, however, to first discuss why so many other interventions have fallen short.

Ellis and Sowers discussed what they consider the common characteristics of intervention failures with juveniles.[2] First, many programs are not sufficiently comprehensive. In other words, they focus on only one aspect or problem in the life of a juvenile offender. Other programs have failed because they used ineffective strategies to address specific problems. Many programs have suffered from a lack of trained, professional workers. High turnover or staff without basic knowledge and skills to aid offenders has plagued other programs. Similarly, quality of service delivery has been a frequent problem. In many cases, practitioners find it difficult to consistently provide the services they were trained to provide for many possible reasons, such as high caseloads. Many programs are ineffective because of a lack of family participation. In institutional settings, juveniles are frequently taken far away from their family. In other cases, where families could participate, many do not. Finally, other problems include inadequate follow-up to treatment and insufficient funding.

In contrast, successful interventions have a theoretical base, are highly structured, and are comprehensive in nature. Successful programs confront the known risk factors for delinquency, including breakdowns in parenting and the family, school failure, peer reinforcement of delinquency, lack of community involvement in the lives of youth, abuse and neglect, and early childhood aggression. Early intervention in the lives of children at risk of delinquency is a consistent theme among these programs. Another theme is that multiple channels or networks that reinforce prevention messages should be used. Drug prevention programs are somewhat overrepresented among the model programs. Why is that the case? The public health community has found successful prevention methods for gateway drugs such as tobacco, alcohol, and marijuana. Not only are these drugs gateways to illicit substance abuse, but also the use of these drugs is highly correlated with other forms of delinquency.

MODEL PROGRAMS

The Midwestern Prevention Project

The Midwestern Prevention Project (MPP) is a comprehensive, community-based, multifaceted program designed to prevent adolescent drug use. The MPP involves an extended period of programming. The program is initiated in a school setting, but unlike Drug Abuse Resistance Education (D.A.R.E.) and similar programs, it goes beyond the school to include family and community contexts.

The MPP is designed to bridge the transition from early adolescence to middle through late adolescence. Thus, programming starts with whole populations of 6th- or 7th-grade students. Studies consistently indicate that early adolescence is the first risk period for gateway drug use (i.e., alcohol, cigarettes, and marijuana). Research shows that youth who experiment with these drugs are more likely to abuse other illicit drugs later in life.

Recognizing the tremendous social pressures to use drugs, MPP provides training skills in how to avoid drug use and drug-use situations. These skills are initially learned in the school program. However, they are also reinforced through parents, the media, and community organizations.

The MPP message is distributed through a system of coordinated community-wide strategies that include mass media programming, a school program and school boosters, parent education, community organizations, and a means to work toward local policy changes regarding tobacco, alcohol, and other drugs. The primary component of the programming occurs in the school, but the other components are introduced sequentially to the community at a rate of one per year. The mass media message is distributed throughout all the years of the program.

The school program uses social learning techniques such as modeling, role-playing, and discussions with student peer leaders assisting teachers. The family gets involved when youth have homework assignments. Parents also get involved when they meet with the school program members through parent-principal committees. These committees review school drug policy and provide parent-child communications training. Mass media coverage, community organizations, and local health policy changes work together to deliver a consistent message that drug use is not the norm. Representatives from all of the program components meet regularly to review and refine programs.

Evaluations of the MPP have shown impressive results. Youth involved in MPP had a 40 percent reduction in daily smoking and a similar reduction in marijuana use compared with a control group of youth that did not receive these messages. Smaller reductions in alcohol use were achieved through grade 12. Long-term follow-ups have shown positive impacts on daily smoking, heavy marijuana use, and some hard drug use through early adulthood. Evaluations have shown that MPP has led to increased communications between parents and their children about drugs. The program has also helped to establish prevention programs, activities, and services among community leaders.[3]

The program costs approximately $175,000 over a three-year period. This includes the costs of teacher, parent, and community leader training and curriculum materials for the school-based program that serves 1,000 students.

Big Brothers Big Sisters of America

Mentoring programs have become extremely popular over recent years. Big Brothers Big Sisters of America (BBBSA) is a mentoring program that has been providing adult support and friendship to kids for almost a century. In 1991, BBBSA had a network of nearly 500 agencies across the country, with more than 70,000 youth and adults matched in one-to-one relationships.

The program typically involves youth ages 6 to 18 from single-parent homes. BBBSA delivers services by volunteers who meet regularly and engage in activities with a youth on a one-to-one basis. Managers, who follow through on each case from the participant's initial inquiry through closure, use a case management approach. The case manager screens adult and youth applicants, creates and supervises the matches, and terminates the match when eligibility requirements are no longer met, or either party decides not to participate fully in the relationship.

BBBSA has developed rigorous standards and procedures that other mentoring programs lack. Participants go through an initial *orientation* session. Volunteers are screened using background checks, an extensive interview, and a home visit. The screening process attempts to exclude volunteers who may inflict psychological or physical harm, do not have the capacity to form bonding relationships with children, or who are unlikely to honor time commitments. The youth assessment requires a written application by the parent, along with interviews of both the parent and child, and a home visit. It is intended to help the caseworker learn about the child so that the best possible match is made. Matches are based on a number of criteria including the needs of the child, the volunteer's abilities, parental preferences, and the capacity of program staff.

Program staff maintains supervision through an initial contact with the parent, the child, and the volunteer within two weeks of the match. Afterward, monthly telephone contact is made with the parent or child and the volunteer in the first year. Quarterly contact is then made with all parties for the duration of the match.

One evaluation of the BBBSA program found that after eighteen months, participants were 46 percent less likely to initiate drug use and 27 percent less likely to initiate alcohol use as compared with a control group. Participants were about one-third less likely than the control group youth to hit someone, and demonstrated better academic behavior, attitudes, and performance. Finally, participants were more likely to have better relationships with their parents and their peers as compared with the control group.[4] The cost of the program is approximately $1,000 per year for making and supporting each match.

Life Skills Training

The Life Skills Training (LST) program has been evaluated more than a dozen times and has consistently been found to dramatically reduce tobacco, alcohol, and marijuana use. Perhaps more impressive, these studies show that the program works with a diverse range of adolescents, produces long-lasting results, and is effective when taught by teachers, peer leaders, or health professionals.

Initially, LST is introduced in grades 6 or 7 depending on the school structure and continues through middle and high school for three years. Like the MPP, LST was designed to prevent or reduce gateway drug use. Generally, the program has been implemented in school classrooms and delivered by teachers. The program is delivered in 15 sessions in the first

year, 10 sessions in the second year, and 5 sessions in the final year. The
sessions generally last an average of 45 minutes and can be delivered once
a week or as an intensive minicourse.

The program consists of three major components that teach students
general self-management skills, social skills, and information and skill
development specifically related to drug use. Training techniques are fairly
diverse using instruction, demonstration, feedback, reinforcement, and
practice.

All evaluations of LST have revealed the program's effectiveness. Averages of the outcomes from more than a dozen evaluations of LST have
found that it cuts tobacco, alcohol, and marijuana use by 50 to 75 percent. Long-term program follow-ups (six years after the intervention) have
found that it reduces multiple drug use by 66 percent, pack-a-day smoking
by 25 percent, and use of inhalants, narcotics, and hallucinogens.[5] LST
can be implemented at a start-up cost of $2,000 per day for the initial
training (training lasts one or two days), and at a continuing cost of $7
per student per year.

Multisystemic Therapy

Multisystemic Therapy (MST) is an intervention that uses intensive case
management to target multiple problems with a juvenile offender and his
or her environment. The assessment and intervention approach of MST is
based on systems theory. Systems theory claims that individuals are integral
parts of several different and overlapping social systems. The behavior of
individuals affects the systems with which they interact and, in turn, the
behavior of the systems affects the individual. Thus, this theory suggests
that when juveniles commit crimes, it is in part due to choices the juvenile
made and, in part, influenced by factors in his or her environment.
According to this theory, for interventions to be lasting, they cannot focus
solely on the juvenile.

In MST, a therapist or case manager is assigned to individual juvenile
offenders. A team of other professionals assists the case manager, and they
are the source of all services to the offender and his or her family. This team
is available 24 hours per day and 7 days per week. The team identifies and
addresses multiple problems in the juvenile and throughout his or her social
systems. Caseloads are kept necessarily small. Specific interventions are used
for specific situations such as cognitive-behavioral therapy for the offender
and family. Other strategies may target other social systems, such as the
school, peer groups, and the community. The case management team has
frequent contact with the family throughout the early stages of the intervention. The number of contact hours gradually decreases as prosocial competence in the offender grows and problems are solved.

There have been several outcome evaluations of MST. One of the
strengths of this program is that it has been used with several different
offender groups, including sex offenders, substance abusers, neglectful and
abusive families, and inner-city offenders. All evaluation studies have demonstrated positive results.

Evaluations have shown that serious juvenile offenders who participated in MST had reductions of 25 to 70 percent in long-term rates of rearrest and reductions of 47 to 64 percent in out-of-home placements. Additionally, MST participants experienced measurable improvement in family functioning and significantly fewer mental health problems than serious offenders receiving standard treatment.[6]

MST has achieved these results at a much lower cost than the usual mental health and juvenile justice services, such as incarceration and residential treatment. At a cost of $4,500 per youth, a recent policy report concluded that MST was the most cost-effective option of a wide range of intervention programs aimed at serious juvenile offenders.

Nurse-Family Partnership

Nurse-Family Partnership (Formerly Prenatal and Infancy Home Visitation by Nurses) was designed to serve low-income, at-risk pregnant women who are having their first child. Nurses visit the mother's home throughout her pregnancy and during the first two years of the child's life. The primary mode of service delivery is home visitation. However, the program also uses a variety of other health and human services to achieve its positive effects.

There are several goals of the program. One goal is to help women improve their prenatal health and the outcomes of pregnancy. The program attempts to improve women's personal development, planning for future pregnancies, development of education goals, and job placement. Finally, to improve the health and development of children, the program attempts to improve the care provided to infants and toddlers. Generally, a nurse visitor is assigned to a family and works with that family throughout the length of the program. The program has been applied in urban and rural areas and has supported white and African American families.

Evaluations of the program have found positive results for all program goals. For example, an evaluation was conducted of primarily white families in Elmira, New York. Program recipients were low-income, unmarried women who were provided a nurse home visitor. Women in the program had 79 percent fewer verified reports of child abuse or neglect than a matched comparison group. Program recipients had 31 percent fewer subsequent births, averaged intervals more than two years greater between the birth of their first and second child, and received 30 months less of Aid to Families with Dependent Children. In terms of criminal and behavioral issues, program recipients had 44 percent fewer behavioral problems caused by alcohol and drug abuse and 69 percent fewer arrests. Some of the program participants were young teenage women. Among 15 year olds in the program, there were 60 percent fewer instances of running away, 56 percent fewer arrests, and 56 percent fewer days of alcohol consumption than in the comparison group.[7]

In 1997, the program was estimated to cost $3,200 per year per family during the first three years of program operation. Once the nurses were completely trained and working at full capacity, the cost drops to $2,800 per family per year. Actual costs vary according to community-health nurse salaries. Many communities involved in the program have used a variety of local, state, and federal funding sources, including Medicaid, welfare-reform, maternal and child health, and child abuse prevention dollars.

Multidimensional Treatment Foster Care

Multidimensional Treatment Foster Care (MTFC) was created for youth diagnosed with antisocial personality disorder, emotional disturbances, and delinquency. It is a cost-effective alternative to group or residential treatment, incarceration, and hospitalization for youth with serious and chronic behavioral problems and for youth with histories of severe criminal behavior who are at risk of incarceration.

Community families are recruited, trained, and closely supervised to provide MTFC youth with treatment and intensive supervision at home, in school, and in the community. MTFC parents must complete a preservice training session before placement. Afterward, MTFC parents attend a weekly group meeting run by a program case manager. Supervision and support of MTFC parents continues through daily telephone calls to check on youth progress and problems.

The training provided to MTFC parents emphasizes numerous behavior management techniques, including the following: clear and consistent limits with appropriate follow-through on consequences, positive reinforcement for appropriate behavior, a relationship with a mentoring adult, and separation from delinquent peers. The goal is to provide troubled youth with a structured living environment.

MTFC recognizes that the program cannot make changes with the adolescents it serves without also making changes to their home life. Therefore, family therapy is provided for the youth's biological (or adoptive) family. The ultimate goal is return the adolescents to their homes. The parents are taught the same behavioral approaches and structure that is being used in the MTFC home. Parents are encouraged to maintain contact with the MTFC case manager and get information about their child's progress in the program. The MTFC case manager also maintains contact and coordinates with the youth's probation officer, school officials, employers, and other adults in the youth's life. Evaluations of MTFC have found that program youth have made impressive strides in comparison to youth in control groups. One year after completing the program, MTFC participants spent 60 percent fewer days incarcerated, had significantly fewer rearrests, were three times less likely to run away from home, and were much less likely to abuse hard drugs.[8] The cost of the program per youth is $2,691 per month, and the average length of stay is seven months.

Olweus Bullying Prevention Program

The Olweus Bullying Prevention Program has the goal of reducing and preventing bully-victim problems. The program is provided in a school setting, and school staff are primarily responsible for introducing and implementing the program.

Because bullying behavior generally develops at a young age, the program targets students in elementary, middle, and junior high schools. Although all students in a particular school participate in the program, other individual interventions are directed to students who are identified as bullies or victims of bullying.

The program is implemented at the school level, class level, and individual level. First, at the school level, an anonymous questionnaire is administered to assess the nature and prevalence of bullying at each school. Additionally, a school conference day is held to discuss bullying at school and develop interventions. One intervention is a Bullying Prevention Coordinating Committee to manage all aspects of the program and to supervise areas of the school where bullying typically takes place.

Within the classroom, class rules are created and enforced concerning bullying, and regular class meetings are held. Interventions are provided for particular children identified as either bullies or victims and include these children's parents. Counselors and other school-based mental health experts may assist teachers. The Olweus Bullying Prevention Program has been found to achieve its primary goal—that is, to substantially reduce bullying and victimization among boys and girls. The program has had the added benefit of reducing other problem behaviors, such as vandalism, fighting, theft, and truancy. Students who participate report improved order and discipline in the classroom, more positive social relationships with peers, and a better attitude toward school and academics.[9] Costs for an on-site program coordinator vary from site to site. Other program expenses are approximately $200 per school to administer the survey and $65 per teacher for the costs of classroom materials.

Promoting Alternative Thinking Strategies

The primary goals of Promoting Alternative Thinking Strategies (PATHS) are to promote emotional and social competencies among elementary-age children and reduce aggression and behavior problems. The curriculum attempts to enhance the educational process in the classroom. Educators and counselors deliver the program over several years throughout an entire elementary school. The program was developed to be delivered at the entrance to schooling and continue through the 5th grade.

PATHS has been field tested and researched with children in typical classroom settings, but it has been used with a variety of special needs students. The PATHS Curriculum is delivered three times per week for a minimum of 20 to 30 minutes per day. It provides teachers with developmentally based lessons, materials, and instructions for teaching their students emotional literacy, self-control, social competence, positive peer relations, and interpersonal problem-solving skills. Teachers who participate receive training in a two- to three-day workshop and in biweekly meetings with a curriculum consultant.

One of the primary objectives of promoting these developmental skills is to prevent or reduce behavioral and emotional problems. Students who receive PATHS lessons are taught to identify and label their feelings, express feelings, assess the intensity of feelings, and manage their feelings. They are taught the difference between feelings and behaviors, and how to delay gratification, control impulses, and read and interpret social cues. Finally, the curriculum teaches students how to understand the other's perspectives, problem-solve, develop a positive attitude toward life, and use both nonverbal and verbal communication skills.

The PATHS Curriculum has been shown to reduce behavioral risk factors. Evaluations have demonstrated significant improvements for program youth, including special needs students, as compared with control youth in several important areas. Youth who participate in the program have been found to improve self-control, improve understanding and recognition of emotions, increase the ability to tolerate frustration, use more effective conflict-resolution strategies, and improve thinking and planning skills. Special needs students were more likely to experience less anxiety and conduct problems, symptoms of sadness, and depression. Finally, there were fewer reports of conduct problems, including aggression, among program participants.[10]

Program costs over a three-year period range from $15 to $45 per student per year. The higher cost would include hiring an on-site coordinator, while the lower cost would include redeploying current staff.

The Incredible Years

The Incredible Years is similar to PATHS in the sense that it has the goals of promoting emotional and social competence, as well as preventing, reducing, and treating behavior and emotional problems in young children. The program targets youth ages two to eight who are at risk or already engaging in conduct problems such as aggression, defiance, and oppositional and impulsive behaviors. The program is designed to promote the social adjustment of high-risk children in preschool programs, such as Head Start; at-risk, elementary-age youth through grade three; and other children who have begun to demonstrate conduct problems.

The Incredible Years includes a series of programs that address multiple risk factors across settings related to the development of conduct disorders in children. Facilitators use videotape scenes to encourage group discussion, problem-solving, and sharing of ideas for parents, teachers, and students. The BASIC parent series is a necessary component of the prevention program, while the parent training, teacher training, and child components are strongly recommended with particular types of kids and parents.

The Incredible Years parenting series includes three distinct programs for parents of high-risk children or for parents with children displaying behavior problems. The BASIC program introduces parenting skills known to encourage children's social competence and reduce behavior problems.

These skills include learning how to play with children, helping children learn, using reinforcement through praise and incentives, setting limits, and applying strategies to handle misbehavior.

The ADVANCE program emphasizes parent interpersonal skills, such as effective communication, anger management, problem-solving between adults, and ways to give and get support. Another program, termed SCHOOL, helps parents promote their child's academic success and emphasizes reading skills, development of homework routines, and building good working relationships with teachers.

Incredible Years Training for Teachers emphasizes effective classroom management skills. Some of these skills include use of teacher attention, praise and encouragement, incentives for difficult behavior problems, and proactive teaching strategies. The training provides instruction about how to manage inappropriate classroom behaviors, the importance of building positive relationships with students, and how to teach empathy, social skills, and problem solving in the classroom.

The final area of the Incredible Years involves training for children. The Dinosaur Curriculum emphasizes training children in such skills as emotional literacy, empathy or taking the perspective of another, friendship skills, anger management, interpersonal problem-solving, adherence to school rules, and success at school. The program is used for small groups of children identified as displaying conduct problems. There have been six randomized control group evaluations of the parenting series. These evaluations have shown that parents who participated in the program increased the use of positive praise and reduced the use of criticism and negative commands. Parents also increased their use of effective limit-setting, replaced spanking and harsh discipline with nonviolent discipline techniques, and increased monitoring of children. There were reductions in parental depression and increases in parental self-confidence. Families that participated experienced increased positive family communication and problem-solving. They also were able to reduce conduct problems in their children and gain greater compliance to parental commands.[11] Two randomized control group evaluations found that teachers who participated in the program increased their use of praise and encouragement and reduced their use of criticism and harsh discipline. These teachers experienced greater cooperation among their students, found that their students had more positive interactions with peers, and saw that their students were more engaged with school activities. Importantly, they also reported greater reductions in peer aggression in the classroom.[12] Two randomized control group evaluations of the child training series found that children who participated in the program significantly increased their ability to solve problems and were better able to manage conflict with their peers.[13] These youth also reduced their conduct problems at home.

The costs of curriculum materials (including videotapes, comprehensive manuals, books, and other teaching aids) for the Parent Training Program are $1,300 for the BASIC program, $775 for the ADVANCE program, and $995 for the SCHOOL program. The Teacher Training Program costs $1,250, and the Child Training Program costs $975.

Project Towards No Drug Abuse (Project TND)

Project TND is an effective drug abuse and violence prevention program that targets high school youth from all types of demographic backgrounds at both traditional and alternative schools.

Project TND consists of 12 in-class interactive sessions that provide motivation skills and decision-making material targeting cigarette, alcohol, marijuana, and hard drug use, and violence-related behavior. The topics of the sessions include the following: (1) active listening; (2) stereotyping; (3) myths and denials; (4) chemical dependency; (5) talk show; (6) marijuana panel; (7) tobacco use cessation; (8) stress, health, and goals; (9) self-control; (10) positive and negative thought and behavior loops; (11) perspectives; and (12) decision making and commitment.

Each classroom lesson is approximately 40 to 50 minutes in length and designed to be implemented over a four-week period. The instruction to students provides motivation enhancement activities to not use drugs, detailed information about the social and health consequences of drug use, and correction of common misperceptions about drugs. The instruction addresses a variety of topics, including active listening, effective communication skills, stress management, coping skills, tobacco cessation techniques, and self-control to counteract risk factors for drug abuse relevant to older teens.

Project TND has been tested in three experimental field trials. Approximately 3,000 youth from 42 schools participated across the three trials. In comparison with youth who received traditional antidrug education, after one year participants were 27 percent less likely to use cigarettes in the past 30 days, 22 percent less likely to use marijuana in the past 30 days, 26 percent less likely to use hard drugs, 9 percent less likely to be baseline drinkers, and 6 percent less likely to be a victim of violence.[14]

The Project TND Teacher's Manual costs $70, and student workbooks cost $50 for a set of five. A two-day training session, which includes the trainer's fee and travel, is $2,500.

The Perry Preschool Program and Head Start

The *Blueprints for Violence Prevention Program* mentioned several programs that it considered promising for reducing problem behaviors but that failed to make their list because they were not supported by rigorous studies. One of those programs is the Perry Preschool Program. Although it was an "honorable mention," so to speak, it's a unique program that has been widely discussed for many years because of its effectiveness.

Many young children from disadvantaged neighborhoods and low-income families come to school unprepared. Their language skills are often less developed, and their motivation to achieve and self-confidence are lower than that of middle-class children. Essentially, they begin school at a tremendous disadvantage. Delinquency studies tell us that school failure frequently leads to a host of problems later in life. Beginning in the 1960s, educators and researchers began creating developmentally focused preschool programs.

In 1962, a psychologist named David Weikart developed the Perry Preschool Program. Among the early preschool programs, it was one of the few created specifically to prevent delinquency later in life. Dr. Weikart recruited 123 African American children ages three and four from low-income families in Ypsilanti, Michigan. All families had incomes below the poverty line. Children were randomly assigned to either the experimental preschool program or to a control group. Perry Preschool instruction lasted two-and-a-half hours per day for two school years. The program included many important features, such as a high teacher-to-student ratio (1 to 5), team teaching, weekly home visits lasting about one-and-a-half hours, and student participation in planning classroom activities.

Evaluations of the program have revealed some impressive results.[15] By the age of 19, program participants were more likely than the control group to have graduated from high school, and were more likely to have a job, attend college, or pursue further training. More important from the perspective of delinquency prevention, the rates of arrest for Perry participants were 40 percent lower than the control group. The rate of teen pregnancy was 42 percent lower among the Perry group as compared with the control group. A cost-benefit analysis of the Perry Preschool Program indicated that the program costs about $5,000 per child, but that a two-year program will yield $3 for every $1 invested.

The Perry Preschool Program and similar initiatives provided the foundation for Project Head Start, which is widely considered to be one of the most ambitious antipoverty programs in American history. Head Start was designed as a comprehensive program designed to eliminate the physical, intellectual, and social barriers to success in school. Evaluations of Head Start and similar programs have found that participants were less likely to be held back a grade or placed in special education during middle and high school than comparison students. Most important, however, Head Start reached only 20 percent of children in need in 1990. Congress has increased funding of Head Start, but researchers question whether the program has the resources needed to be effective. Unlike the Perry Preschool Program, most Head Start programs spend about 60 percent less per child and do not employ professional staff.[16]

ARE WE PRACTICING WHAT WORKS?

The 1980s and 1990s will long be remembered as a time when we "got tough" on juvenile offenders. A large increase in juvenile violence in the late 1980s and early 1990s led to much tougher measures to decrease juvenile crime. In terms of community corrections, there has been a greater use of juvenile boot camps, intensive probation, and scared straight programs.

There has also been a tremendous increase in the frequency of juveniles waived to adult courts. That is, the juvenile court either voluntarily released jurisdiction over youth or were required to by legislators or prosecutors. The result is that many youth are prosecuted as adults and receive adult punishment. Some states have passed habitual juvenile offender laws, much like three-strikes laws, for youth who commit several acts of delinquency. Finally, until last year when the Supreme Court overruled itself, the death penalty was an option for juveniles age 16 or above. All of these policies have been evaluated for their effectiveness as well. Worrall states, "The verdict for juvenile crime control, as opposed to prevention, is not a favorable one. With the possible exception of restitution and treatment, most of the popular methods of addressing juvenile crime after it has been committed do not appear to work."[17]

Not only do they not work, but also they are much more expensive than the prevention and intervention programs discussed above. They cost more fiscally, and they certainly cost more in the loss of productive youth. Blumstein observes, "If you intervene early, you not only save the costs of incarceration, you also save the costs of crime and gain the benefits of an individual who is a taxpaying contributor to the economy."[18] "Getting tough" may actually have the opposite effect of specific deterrence from a life of crime. Most of those juvenile offenders sentenced to long terms in adult prisons will be released, and many will come out bitter, disillusioned, and lacking basic skills to succeed. Instead of getting tough on juvenile crime, it's time to get smart and innovative. We have a good working knowledge of what works, we just need to do it.

NOTES

1. Currie, 1998, p. 81.
2. Ellis & Sowers, 2001.
3. Pentz, Mihalic, & Grotpeter, 1998.
4. McGill, Mihalic, & Grotpeter, 1998.
5. Botvin, Mihalic, & Grotpeter, 1998.
6. Henggeler, Mihalic, Rone, Thomas, & Timmons-Mitchell, 1998.
7. Olds, Hill, Mihalic, & O'Brien, 1998.
8. Chamberlain & Mihalic, 1998.
9. Olweus, Limber, & Mihalic, 1999.
10. Greenberg, Kusché, & Mihalic, 1998.
11. Webster-Stratton et al., 2001.
12. Webster-Stratton et al., 2001.
13. Webster-Stratton et al., 2001.
14. Sussman, Rohrbach, & Mihalic, 2004.
15. Berrueta-Clement, Schweinhart, Barnett, Epstein, & Weikart, 1984; Schweinhart & Weikart, 1980.
16. Bright, 1992.
17. Worrall, 2006, p. 325.
18. Blumstein as quoted in Butterfield, 1996, p. A24.

REFERENCES

Berrueta-Clement, J. R., Schweinhart, L. J., Barnett, W. S., Epstein, A. S., & Weikart, D. P. (1984). *Changed lives: The effects of the Perry preschool program on youths through age 19*. Ypsilanti, MI: The High/Scope Press.

Botvin, G. J., Mihalic, S. F., & Grotpeter, J. K. (1998). *Blueprints for violence prevention, book five: Life skills training.* Boulder, CO: Center for the Study and Prevention of Violence.

Bright, J. (1992). *Crime prevention in America: A British perspective.* Chicago: Office of International Criminal Justice, University of Illinois at Chicago.

Butterfield, F. (1996, June 23). Intervening early costs less than 3-strikes' laws, study says. *The New York Times,* p. A24.

Chamberlain, P., & Mihalic, S. F. (1998). *Blueprints for violence prevention, book eight: Multidimensional treatment foster care.* Boulder, CO: Center for the Study and Prevention of Violence.

Currie, E. (1998). *Crime and punishment in America.* New York: Metropolitan Henry Holt.

Ellis, R. & Sowers, S. (2001). *Juvenile justice practice: A cross-disciplinary approach to intervention.* Belmont, CA: Wadsworth/Thomson Learning.

Greenberg, M. T., Kusché, C., & Mihalic, S. F. (1998). *Blueprints for violence prevention, book ten: Promoting alternative thinking strategies (PATHS).* Boulder, CO: Center for the Study and Prevention of Violence.

Henggeler, S. W., Mihalic, S. F., Rone, L., Thomas, C., & Timmons-Mitchell, J. (1998). *Blueprints for violence prevention, book six: Multisystemic therapy.* Boulder, CO: Center for the Study and Prevention of Violence.

McGill, D. C., Mihalic, S. F., & Grotpeter, J. K. (1998). *Blueprints for violence prevention, book two: Big brothers and big sisters of America.* Boulder, CO: Center for the Study and Prevention of Violence.

Olds, D., Hill, P., Mihalic, S., & O'Brien, R. (1998). *Blueprints for violence prevention, book seven: Prenatal and infancy home visitation by nurses.* Boulder, CO: Center for the Study and Prevention of Violence.

Olweus, D., Limber, S., & Mihalic, S. F. (1999). *Blueprints for violence prevention, book nine: Bullying prevention program.* Boulder, CO: Center for the Study and Prevention of Violence.

Pentz, M. A, Mihalic, S. F., & Grotpeter, J. K. (1998). *Blueprints for violence prevention, book one: The midwestern prevention project.* Boulder, CO: Center for the Study and Prevention of Violence.

Schweinhart, L. J., & Weikart, D. P. (1980). *Young children grow up: The effects of the Perry preschool program on youths through age 15.* Ypsilanti, MI: The High/Scope Press.

Sussman, S., Rohrbach, L., & Mihalic, S. (2004). *Blueprints for violence prevention, book twelve: Project towards no drug abuse.* Boulder, CO: Center for the Study and Prevention of Violence.

Webster-Stratton, C., Mihalic, S., Fagan, A., Arnold, D., Taylor, T., & Tingley, C. (2001). *Blueprints for violence prevention, book eleven: The incredible years.* Boulder, CO: Center for the Study and Prevention of Violence.

Worrall, J. L. (2006). *Crime control in America: An assessment of the evidence.* Boston: Pearson.

CHAPTER 2

Delinquency Programs That Failed

Pamela J. Schram

This chapter provides an overview of three nationally recognized programs for juveniles that have been considered "failures." Before focusing specifically on these three programs, however, it is essential to understand how a program is considered "successful" or "unsuccessful." To appreciate how programs are deemed successful or unsuccessful, one needs to understand the importance of conducting evaluation research. This chapter begins with a general discussion of evaluation research as well as key issues pertaining to this type of research. This chapter next provides a general overview of three juvenile programs that have been deemed failures: the Juvenile Awareness Project ("Scared Straight"), Drug Abuse Resistance Education (D.A.R.E.), and boot camps.

IS THE PROGRAM A SUCCESS OR FAILURE?

Evaluation Research

Compared with other types of research, such as experimental or survey, evaluation research is not so much a research *design* as it is a research *purpose*. Specifically, the purpose of evaluation research is to provide scientific evidence that guides public policy or programs. Designs used in basic research are easily adapted for implementation in evaluation research.[1] Evaluation research attempts to answer such questions as the following: "Do the programs work?" "Do the programs produce the intended result?" "Do the programs provide enough benefits to justify their costs?" and "Should the programs be sustained or discontinued?" Thus, "evaluation research can be defined as measurement of the effects of a program in terms of its specific goals, outcomes, or particular program criteria."[2]

There are two general types of evaluation research—process evaluation and impact evaluation. Process evaluation focuses on the relationship between the results of program participation (such as the number of arrests) and the program inputs and activities (such as the selection of participants and program delivery). Impact evaluation examines the relationship between outcomes (such as crime reduction) and inputs, activities, and program results. Other approaches to learning about a program include assessment and monitoring. Assessment, or needs assessment, attempts to identify an activity or resource for a particular area or organization. Monitoring examines whether the plans for program implementation have been met; for instance, do the program activities correspond to the program inputs?[3]

To further illustrate what is meant by evaluation research, Rossi and Freeman maintained that *comprehensive evaluations* consist of three general groups of activities. These activities are listed below along with examples of questions associated with these activities:[4]

- *Program conceptualization and design:* What is the extent and distribution of the target problem and/or population? What are projected or existing costs and what is their relation to benefits and effectiveness?
- *Monitoring and accountability of program implementation:* Is the program reaching the specified target population or target area? Are the intervention efforts being conducted as specified in the program design?
- *Assessment of program utility:* Is the program effective in achieving its intended goals? Is the program having some effects that were not intended?[5]

Key Issues Pertaining to Evaluation Research

It is essential to appreciate that evaluation research is not conducted in a "vacuum." Rather, this type of research is conducted in the field. Thus, various factors, intended as well as unintended, can have an effect on the research project. Some of these issues include implementing an experimental design, defining success, identifying the interest of stakeholders, and understanding the political climate.

The Experimental Design

Some maintain that one of the most rigorous methods used to evaluate a program is the experimental design. This type of design randomly assigns the research subjects into an experimental or a control group; the experimental group would receive some type of stimulus or treatment whereas the control group would not receive this stimulus or treatment. With respect to relevant factors, however, these two groups would be equivalent (e.g., age, gender, prior criminal history).

Other situations in which the research subjects are randomly assigned to either an experimental or control group can raise legal, ethical, and practical issues. For instance, some may argue that to deny individuals treatment only because they were randomly placed in a control group is unethical. Researchers also face practical issues when conducting an evaluation. For example, some programs may have difficulty identifying enough individuals for a program; thus, those individuals who were designated for the control group may be placed into the program. This could be a major issue if agencies need to "justify" the funding for the program by assessing the cost of the program *per* participant. Maintaining the integrity of the research design can also be problematic. For instance, if agency personnel are responsible for identifying individuals in the experimental or control group, as opposed to research staff, the criteria used for random assignment may be compromised and thereby increase the probability of biasing the groups.[6]

Defining Success

Traditionally, within a criminal justice paradigm, program success has been determined in terms of recidivism. As mentioned previously, this is primarily due to the perspective that comparison group studies, or *true* experimental designs, are the most robust type of research design. Furthermore, in an experimental study, some comparable outcome measure must relate to the goal of the program. In criminal justice, the primary goal of any program or intervention strategy tends to rely on the basic criterion of reducing future recidivism. As a result, recidivism usually is the preferred variable to determine program success. Although there is little disagreement that the goal of any criminal justice program should be to curtail future offending, there is a great deal of dissension as to the best approach to achieve that goal.

Difficulty in measuring program success in terms of recidivism was highlighted by Clear and Dammer.[7] They noted that a common criterion for measuring effectiveness (such as probation) is recidivism, or the return to criminal behavior:

> Recidivism in probation can be measured in at least four different ways: (1) violations of the conditions of probation, (2) arrests for new offenses committed by probationers, (3) convictions for new offenses, and (4) revocations of probation. Any one of these or a combination may display some level of recidivism.[8]

They continued by noting that this issue is further complicated by the amount of discretion used by the probation officer. For instance, if a probation officer considers the offender's behavior to be insignificant, such as a minor violation of the probation contract, then the officer might not consider any of the abovementioned actions as recidivism while on probation. Thus, although recidivism initially appears to be a logical goal of a program for probationers, the measurement of recidivism is not necessarily so simple.

Stakeholders

When evaluating a program, one should realize that many individuals may have an interest in the program as well as the results of the program evaluation. These interested individuals have been designated as *stakeholders*.[9] When conducting an evaluation, researchers may work with some stakeholders who are supportive of such a study; other stakeholders may be less supportive to the extent of opposing such an evaluation; and yet other stakeholders may be indifferent.

Kemshall and Ross provided a model for conducting an evaluation of a project that involves different agencies or stakeholders. They emphasize the importance of developing and maintaining partnerships. Further, they note that—

> [a]s resources continue to shrink and community organizations compete for relatively small sums of money which are nevertheless essential to their survival and the retention of staff, [agencies] will face increasingly difficult decisions on funding. Value for money, evaluation of desirable outcomes, and quality will be essential components of such decisions.[10]

In an attempt to understand the various barriers to conducting rigorous outcome evaluation, Petrosino conducted in-person interviews with research and evaluation managers working in different agencies in one state. When asked as to why, among the thousands of programs administered by these agencies, no randomized experiment had been conducted, three such reasons were given, including (1) we know our programs work (why evaluate them?); (2) we know they are not harming anyone; and (3) if the program helps a single child, it's worth it (again, why evaluate?).[11]

As mentioned at the beginning of this section, evaluation research is not conducted in a vacuum, devoid of other factors and influences. As Kemshall and Ross note, other issues are also at play, including funding and program retention. Another interrelated aspect to stakeholders is political climate.

Political Climate

The political climate can influence, directly or indirectly, not only the evaluation but also the continuation of a program. For instance, a "get tough on crime" perspective could influence funding for a more punitive-type program as opposed to a more rehabilitative-type program. As Maxfield and Babbie argue, "[p]olitical preferences and ideology may also influence criminal justice research agendas by making funds available for some projects but not others."[12] This issue is illustrated with the various programs that are discussed in this chapter.

Furthermore, when combining the issues of political climate and stakeholders, Seiter maintained that—

> [a]lthough determination of policy from program evaluation seems logical, criminal justice programs are often started and continued even when the

program is not accomplishing its stated objectives. However, this seemingly inefficient management is not solely the responsibility of the program admin-istrator; the pressures under which he [or she] operates must also be exam-ined. Within the "fish bowl" operations of public programs, it is more difficult to accept failure and make changes than in the private sector.[13]

Thus, when determining whether a program is successful or unsuccessful, one needs to appreciate the various factors that influence not only pro-gram implementation but also the evaluation of that program. Having pre-sented some of these issues, below are four programs that have been deemed so-called failures. It is essential, however, to consider such issues as implementing an experimental design, defining success, identifying stakeholders, and understanding the political climate.

JUVENILE PROGRAMS

Juvenile Awareness Project

One of the most well-known and controversial prison-based programs to scare juveniles straight was the Juvenile Awareness Project ("Scared Straight") at Rahway State Prison in New Jersey. The Scared Straight Pro-gram in New Jersey received a great deal of media coverage, especially given the Academy Award–winning documentary and academic debate over the program's effectiveness on juveniles' subsequent delinquent behavior.[14] Approximately 15 years earlier, however, a similar program was implemented at the Michigan Reformatory in Ionia, Michigan. An evaluation of the Michigan Reformatory Visitation Program revealed that of those juveniles who participated in the program, 43 percent subsequently received a proba-tion violation or a court petition compared with 17 percent of the juveniles who were in the control group.[15]

History of the Juvenile Awareness Project (Scared Straight)

The Juvenile Awareness Project was originated by a group of prisoners serving sentences of 25 years or more in New Jersey's Rahway State Prison. In late 1975, this group of prisoners, identifying themselves as the Lifers' Group, was formed in part to address what they considered the general public's stereotyped, Hollywood image of prisons and prisoners. The Lifers maintained that this image portrayed prisoners as immoral and inhuman. Thus, they wanted to dispel these images and demonstrate that they were productive and worthwhile individuals.

One of the committees formed within the Lifers' Group was the Juve-nile Intervention Committee. Richard Rowe, president of the Lifers, was instrumental in developing the Scared Straight Program. Because of con-cern over his then–12-year-old son who was getting into trouble, Rowe wanted to implement a program that could divert juveniles from further involvement in the criminal justice system. Furthermore, the Lifers realized that groups of college students were eligible to visit the prison for tours;

thus, if college students could tour the prison, why not juveniles? A significant difference, however, was that the college tours were focused on education, whereas the juvenile visits were designed "to deter or scare delinquency out of the kids."[16]

To put their idea into action, the Lifers had to first obtain permission from the superintendent of the prison, Robert S. Hatrak, to allow these juveniles to tour the prison and meet with the prisoners; second, they had to obtain the cooperation of an official or agency to bring the youths to Rahway. Rowe's wife contacted the local police chief and juvenile court judge for their support. Subsequently, they convinced Hatrak to permit such a program. In September 1976, the first group of juveniles toured the prison and met with the prisoners.[17]

Program Implementation

Deterrence theory is a fundamental aspect of Scared Straight. Essentially, deterrence theory proposes that the fear of punishment *deters* individuals from engaging in criminal activity. According to deterrence theory, a juvenile will rationally calculate the potential consequences of various actions. A key aspect to this rational calculation is the youth's perception of the speed, certainty, and severity of the punishment associated with engaging in certain illegal behaviors. Research has revealed that—

> youngsters were not so much concerned with how quickly or harshly they might be punished, but they did show some concern for how certain it would be that they would be punished.[18]

The Scared Straight Program centered around the concept that the fear of severe punishment inhibits juveniles from engaging in delinquent activity.

Intensive confrontation sessions were thought to be one approach to alter juveniles' perceptions of the severity of punishment. Initially, "[t]here was no overt attempt to intimidate or terrorize the youths … but this later became a more prominent and dramatic feature of the project."[19] Thus, at the beginning, the program was not as confrontational. A correctional officer met each group of youths. These youths were given a brief overview of the program and then were processed through prison security. Next, the prisoners talked to the juveniles about prison life, including the harsh realities such as assaults, rapes, and suicides. The juveniles were given the opportunity to ask the prisoners questions about prison life. Subsequently, the youths were given a tour of the institution. During the beginning stages, a large number of youths participating in the program admitted to being neither delinquents nor predelinquents (i.e., demonstrating some indications of potential delinquency or at-risk factors).[20]

The prisoners, however, soon realized that this "big-brother" approach was not reaching the youths. Thus, a more confrontational and shocking approach was soon adopted.[21] The more well-known version of Scared Straight—in-your-face, intimidating, and harsh language—soon emerged.[22] It was this version of Scared Straight that received a great deal of media coverage. With this approach, when sharing their experiences of prison life, the prisoners would shout, swear, and make threats of physical abuse. The following are examples of statements directed at the youths by the prisoners:[23]

> "I'm gonnna hurt you."
> "You take something from me and I'll kill you."
> "You see them pretty blue eyes of yours? I'll take one out of your face and squish it in front of you."
> "Do you know what we see when we look at you—we see ourselves."
> "If someone had done this to me I wouldn't be here."

Some contend that this confrontational approach may have gone beyond taunts and threats. The Juvenile Awareness Program implemented two primary techniques: exaggeration and manhandling. The latter technique has likely led to certain incidents that generally are unknown by the public. For instance, there were allegations of various youths being "culled about, lifted by the head and shaken, 'goosed' or pinched in their behind."[24]

Evaluation of the Juvenile Awareness Project

Professor Finckenauer initially planned to evaluate the Juvenile Awareness Project by implementing an experimental design with random assignment. The successful implementation of this random assignment was strongly determined by the cooperation of the agencies who referred youth to the program. For various reasons, however, some of these agencies did not follow the protocol established for selecting youths for the experimental and the control groups. As a result, the research was modified in two important ways: (1) the sample size was reduced from 50 juveniles in each group to 46 in the Rahway group (i.e., experimental group) and 35 in the control group; and (2) the experimental design was changed to a quasi-experimental design (i.e., random assignment to the two groups was discontinued).[25]

A six-month follow-up period was established to track each youth's court record: six months after the prison visit for the Rahway group and six months after the pretesting for the control group. A major finding from this evaluation was that a significantly higher proportion of youths who did *not* participate in the program did better with respect to subsequent delinquent behavior compared with the Rahway group. Specifically, among the control group, 88.6 percent had no new recorded offense compared with 11.4 percent who did have a new recorded offense; among the Rahway group, 58.7 percent had no new recorded offense compared with 41.3 percent who did have a new recorded offense.[26]

Finckenauer's research revealed that among the Rahway group, 6 of the 19 youths (31.6 percent) with no prior record subsequently engaged in delinquent behavior. He noted that there could be various explanations for this outcome:

> First, there is something about the project that actually stimulates rather than prevents or deters delinquency. Or second, these kids were simply

hidden, closet delinquents who happened to get caught after attending the project.[27]

Additional analyses revealed that the Rahway group did significantly *worse* than the control group.

These findings are consistent with other programs similar to Scared Straight. Petrosino, Turpin-Petrosino, and Finckenauer conducted a systematic review of nine randomized experiments of the Scared Straight Program or similar prison visitation programs. Seven of these programs, including Finckenauer's evaluation of the Rahway State Prison Program and the 1967 evaluation of the program at the Michigan Reformatory, reported first effects in a negative direction. These researchers concluded that the results of the systematic review are sobering. Furthermore, these findings indicate that, despite the best intentions, the programs not only failed to met their objectives but also backfired, resulting in more harm than good. Given this potential to cause harm, the government has an ethical responsibility to rigorously evaluate, on a continual basis, the policies, practices, and programs it implements.[28]

An interesting aspect to the Scared Straight Program is the public response to the project. Finckenaeur noted that the release of his findings resulted in an "uproar" with a storm of response. He detailed the various types of reactions he received, including the following portions of a letter to Golden West Television from a juvenile court judge in Indiana:

> The Rutgers report and the ensuring criticism calls to my mind Walt Kelly's line in *Pogo*: "We have met the enemy and it is us." I am convinced that if Jesus Christ appeared tomorrow, then certainly some professor or college institute or government bureaucrat would quickly release a study, complete with statistics, to clearly prove that what we know to be true was false.[29]

Furthermore, the media coverage of the Scared Straight Program illustrates how the political climate can influence the public's perceptions of a program's effectiveness as well as reflect society's ideology about crime and criminals.

In March 1979, the documentary *Scared Straight* was nationally broadcasted in more than 200 markets. After airing the documentary, television stations were flooded with phone calls and letters praising the project.[30] The documentary, however, amplified or exaggerated its effectiveness. First, is amplified the extent of delinquency involvement among the juveniles participating in the documentary; at the worst, most of the youths had committed status offenses. Second, the documentary amplified the effectiveness of the program on subsequent delinquent behavior. Third, the documentary amplified the dramatic brutality of prison life; although rapes and assaults do occur in prison, the major problem prisoners deal with is boredom.[31]

Cavender argued that Scared Straight was a media-generated phenomenon:

> The media lured the public with crime statistics and success figures and manipulated and/or reinforced stereotyped perceptions of crime and

criminals. Based on the distorted reality, the film offered a solution to crime, one that was kept before the public with supportive media coverage....[32]

The Juvenile Awareness Project, and the mass media coverage of this project, revealed an interesting relationship between mass media portrayals of crime and criminals and public perceptions about crime and criminals. This relationship, however, did not develop during the Scared Straight Program. For instance, during the late-nineteenth century, reformers such as the "child-savers" informed the public of the problems of lower-class urban youth, which resulted in the establishment of the juvenile justice system.[33]

D.A.R.E.

The Drug Abuse Resistance Education (D.A.R.E.) Program is a school-based drug prevention program that focuses on educating youths about the consequences of using and abusing tobacco, alcohol, and other drugs. Compared with other school-based programs, D.A.R.E. has various unique features:

- The program is implemented by law enforcement officers, whereas other programs are usually implemented by teachers.
- D.A.R.E. officers complete approximately two weeks of intensive training whereas more drug prevention program training is shorter in length.
- D.A.R.E. officers are strongly encouraged to deliver the curriculum in sequence rather than departing from the lesson plans, whereas teachers in other drug prevention programs can modify their curricula.
- The officers' performance is usually monitored and evaluated in a more structured manner compared with others who implement drug prevention programs.
- The mission of D.A.R.E. officers is exclusively on drug prevention, whereas other programs also incorporate issues in addition to drug prevention.[34]

History of D.A.R.E.

The D.A.R.E. Program was originated in 1983 by the Los Angeles Police Department in collaboration with the Los Angeles Unified School District (LAUSD). The original core curriculum was developed by Dr. Ruth Rich, a health education specialist of the LAUSD. This core curriculum was based on an examination of various drug prevention programs with a specific focus on Project SMART (Self-Management and Resistance Training). D.A.R.E. was developed as a continuing drug education program for youths in kindergarten through high school. The junior high and senior high curricula were subsequently developed in 1986 and 1988, respectively. The D.A.R.E. Program designed a parent curriculum to instruct and inform parents how to recognize as well as prevent drug use among their children.[35]

During the first year of implementation, 10 officers were responsible for teaching the D.A.R.E. curriculum in 50 Los Angeles elementary schools. Currently, D.A.R.E. has been adopted throughout the United States as well as in some countries in Europe and Asia. The D.A.R.E. organization claims that 36 million school children around the world have participated in D.A.R.E. with approximately 26 million in the United States (D.A.R.E., n.d.). Thus, some have designated the D.A.R.E. program to be the largest as well as the most popular drug prevention program in the United States.[36]

Program Implementation

Some have maintained that the D.A.R.E. Program is "atheoretical,"[37] but others contend that it is grounded in both theory and research.[38] The D.A.R.E. Program is founded in the social skills and social influence model of drug education. Specifically, this "psychosocial" approach incorporates such factors as psychological inoculation (a psychological "vaccine" such as simulated temptations and pressures to use drugs), resistance skills training (teaching and learning skills to resisting negative social influences to use drugs), and personal and social skills training (general skills focusing such as socially learned behaviors and attitudes that are considered to be associated with substance abuse).[39]

The D.A.R.E. curriculum is modified to fit the varying grade levels: early elementary (kindergarten through 4th grade), elementary core curriculum (5th through 6th grade), middle school (7th through 8th grade), and high school (9th through 12th grade). The overall purposes of all the D.A.R.E. curricula include the following:

- Teach students to recognize pressures to use drugs from peers and from the media
- Teach students the skills to resist peer inducements to use drugs
- Enhance students' self-esteem
- Teach positive alternatives to substance use
- Increase students' interpersonal, communication, and decision-making skills[40]

The curriculum for each of the different grade level groups is periodically revised and updated.

Regarding D.A.R.E. officers and their training, law enforcement agencies are primarily responsible for identifying those officers who are designated as D.A.R.E. officers. Overall, these officers must be full-time, uniformed officers with at least two years of experience. It is recommended that agencies consider such factors as the officer's ability to interact with children, his or her organization skills, and the officer's ability to handle unexpected situations. Furthermore, potential D.A.R.E. officers need to be exemplary role models and must avoid making sexual, racial, stereotypical, or inappropriate remarks.

As mentioned previously, those selected officers are required to complete two weeks of intensive training. This training includes learning the core curriculum as well as practice lessons with peers and in the actual classroom environment; additional training includes public speaking, teaching skills, and classroom management. During this training, officers are evaluated and critiqued by mentors who are specifically trained in the D.A.R.E. Program. Additional speakers and consultants are involved in this training to assist the officers in areas that may require special expertise, such as a psychologist providing information on the various stages of child development.

A key feature of D.A.R.E. is how this program combines drug education efforts and community policing. Carter highlights the ways that implementing D.A.R.E. Programs complement the community policing component of law enforcement. Some of these complements include the following: (1) D.A.R.E. "humanizes" the police so that youths can relate to officers as people rather than see them only in terms of uniforms or part of an institution; (2) D.A.R.E. allows students to perceive police officers in a helping role, not just in an enforcement role; (3) D.A.R.E. provides a source of feedback to the police department to communicate the fears and concerns of youths; (4) D.A.R.E. can serve as a stimulus for youths to become more involved in other responsible activities, such as the Police Explorers, Police Athletic League, or other such programs; and (5) exposure to life in the public schools can enhance officers' perspectives on, and understanding of, community concerns and issues.[41]

Evaluation of D.A.R.E.

In the 1990s, there was a growing debate between D.A.R.E. advocates and the research community pertaining to demonstrated effectiveness of the program through rigorous scientific research. Interestingly, D.A.R.E. is one of the most extensively studied drug prevention programs in the world. These numerous studies, however, vary with respect to their methodological rigor. The two most rigorous longitudinal studies of the program revealed no overall effects on drug use after 6 and 10 years.[42]

One study, sponsored by the National Institute of Justice was conducted by the Research Triangle Institute.[43] This study conducted two types of assessments. First, the researchers examined the implementation of the program such as the structure and operations as well as how the program is perceived by program coordinators at the school-district level. Second, the researchers assessed the outcomes or effectiveness of the program by conducting a meta-analysis. A meta-analysis follows a research approach or analysis that synthesizes the results of previous studies to assess the short-term effectiveness of a program's core curriculum. This evaluation study compared the effectiveness of D.A.R.E. to other school-based substance abuse prevention programs.

In reference to "user satisfaction," the research supported previous assertions as far as the prevalence, popularity, and support for the D.A.R.E. Program among students, school staff, parents, community representatives, and law enforcement agencies. In terms of effectiveness, the findings were not as positive:

> [A]s our findings confirm D.A.R.E.'s prevalence and popularity, they also suggest that the original D.A.R.E. core curriculum has not been as successful in accomplishing its mission to prevent drug use among fifth- and sixth-graders as have interactive programs. Review of the rigorous evaluations of the original core curriculum, the heart of D.A.R.E., showed that D.A.R.E. has only limited immediate effects on students' drug use.[44]

Specifically, the meta-analysis revealed that the D.A.R.E. Program did enhance students' knowledge about substance abuse as well as their social skills. However, the short-term effects of substance use among 5th- and 6th-graders were small. The only significant short-term effect among this group was tobacco use.[45]

Based on research implementing rigorous methodological approaches to evaluating D.A.R.E., Rosenbaum summarized what is known about the effectiveness of the program as follows:

- D.A.R.E. has some immediate beneficial effect on students' knowledge and attitudes about drugs.
- These effects are short-lived and usually dissipate within one or two years.
- D.A.R.E.'s effect on drug use behaviors are extremely rare, and when found, they are small in size and dissipate quickly.[46]

In their 1998 review of the literature evaluating D.A.R.E. Programs, Rosenbaum and Hanson noted an inverse relationship between the strength of the methodological design of the study and the possibility of revealing positive outcomes. Thus, "[t]he stronger the research design, the less impact researchers have reported on drug use measures."[47]

Given the questionable effectiveness of the D.A.R.E. Program on subsequent substance use, Wysong, Aniskiewicz, and Wright attempted to explain why D.A.R.E. has emerged as a popular programmatic policy response. First, this type of response focuses attention on the role and interests of political elites and the media in constructing the drug war and, in turn, promoting antidrug policies to address this problem.

Second, this type of response alerts the public of the importance of symbolic dimensions of ameliorative social programs in generating political and public support:

> The latter point refers to the idea that the public reassurance features of such programs are likely to be more important in generating political and public support than their actual substantive effects. Furthermore, the reassurance value of such programs can be viewed as linked to the extent to which they are grounded in widely respected and legitimate institutions and cultural traditions.[48]

Thus, this illustrates how the political climate can influence the implementation and continuation of a program. For instance, Wysong, Aniskiewicz, and Wright maintained that this type of program provides symbolic qualities, such as D.A.R.E.'s relationship with the schools and the police, that provide widespread acceptance regardless of effectiveness.

Boot Camps

In an attempt to define what is meant by a boot camp, the Office of Justice Programs outlined common elements of boot camps that include the following: (1) participation by nonviolent offenders only; (2) a residential placement of six months or less; (3) a regimented schedule emphasizing discipline, physical training, and hard labor; (4) participation among inmates in various education opportunities, job training, and substance abuse counseling or treatment; (5) and availability of aftercare services that are coordinated with the program during the time of confinement. In reference to boot camps for juveniles, the program guidelines included the following: (1) education, job training, and placement; (2) community service; (3) substance abuse counseling and treatment; (4) health and mental health care; (5) individualized case management; and (6) intensive aftercare services.[49]

History of Boot Camps

During the late 1800s, inmates spent a large part of their time involved in some type of trade or labor for manufacturing retail goods. These goods were subsequently sold at a much lower price because the manufacturers used inmate labor. Thus, these products undercut the prices of their competitors. Both the unions and the manufacturers argued that this competitive inmate labor was unfair and called for some type of legislative action. In 1905, President Theodore Roosevelt signed an executive order that banned the use of inmate labor on federal projects. In 1929, Congress passed the Hawes-Cooper Act, which allowed states to prohibit the importation of inmate products from other states.[50]

Because of these changes in the use of inmate labor, prison administers needed to find other activities that would occupy inmates' time. The New York Reformatory was one of the first prisons to consider some form of military-style training. In 1888, Elmira incorporated military organizational components into various aspects of the facility. Administrators thought that this approach had numerous benefits, such as helping inmates to reform their behavior and to learn honest skills. In the early 1900s, there was a major change in correctional ideology and practice. The militarization of facilities was replaced by a more therapeutic approach to helping inmates. In the 1970s, however, the therapeutic programming and rehabilitation approach was questioned and soon another major shift developed in correctional ideology and practice. This shift was a "get-tough" approach.[51]

This get-tough perspective revitalized military-style facilities:

One of the primary factors in revitalization and subsequent proliferation of boot camp programs throughout the United States was that the harsh, physical nature of discipline and activity in these types of programs was in tune with the emerging political climate.[52]

In 1983, Georgia and Oklahoma were the first states to establish correctional boot camps for adults. For instance, to avoid federal takeover of their overcrowded state prison system, Georgia developed a 50-bed, 90-day program. Boot camps for young adult offenders continued to grow in the 1980s.[53] The first juvenile boot camp was established in Orleans Parish, Louisiana, in 1985.[54] In the 1990s, the number of boot camps for juveniles continued to increase. A 1995 survey of state and local correctional officials revealed that a majority of the 37 boot camp programs were established after 1993, most of which were in response to the 1994 Crime Act.[55]

The earliest boot camps have sometimes been referred to as "first-generation" camps. These camps emphasized military-based program activities; they did not provide much treatment or aftercare programming. The "second-generation" boot camps were characterized as toning down the military emphasis and increasing programming such as substance abuse, education, and cognitive training; these boot camps enhanced post-release supervision and services. Some have argued that a "third generation" of boot camps has been developed. These boot camps establish daily regimens that move away from a military emphasis toward a greater emphasis on programming and treatment. However, "[t]hese latter programs are still quite uncommon, and especially so in relation to boot camps for adults."[56]

Program Implementation

One example of how juvenile boots camps are implemented comes from an evaluation of three demonstration programs funded by the Office of Juvenile Justice and Delinquency Prevention (OJJDP) and the Bureau of Justice Assistance. The three demonstration cites were Cleveland, Ohio; Denver, Colorado; and Mobile, Alabama. As mentioned previously, these juvenile boot camps were similar in implementation to the adult boot camps, but the camps for juveniles also emphasized treatment and rehabilitation. Interestingly,

> [s]taff ... reported that the programs had some difficulty achieving a healthy balance between adhering to the strict requirements of a military model and addressing the unique correctional needs of juveniles. Instructors and counselors with military backgrounds, for example, cited the frustration of trying to adjust to youths who were younger, more defiant, and less accustomed to structure than military recruits ... staff without military experience were not familiar with military procedures and drills, and many favored rehabilitation over the military model.[57]

The program goals included the following: (1) serve as a cost-effective alternative to institutionalization; (2) promote discipline through physical conditioning and teamwork; (3) instill more values and a work ethic;

(4) promote literacy and increase academic achievement; (5) reduce drug and alcohol abuse; (6) encourage participants to become productive, law-abiding citizens; and (7) ensure that offenders were held accountable for their actions.[58]

The youths selected for these boot camps were males, between the ages of 13 and 18 years old. Most of these juveniles had committed a property, drug, or other felony offense involving no injury or a small dollar amount. All three sites implemented a 90-day residential program that included military drills and physical conditioning as well as rehabilitative activities. Other common features included the following: (1) Spartan facilities located on the grounds of an existing correctional facility; (2) on-site drill instructors, teachers, and case managers as well as staff with military backgrounds; (3) military-style uniforms for youths and drill instructors and use of military jargon, customs, and courtesies; (4) a daily routine, starting at 5:30 or 6:00 A.M. and ending around 9:00 or 10:00 P.M.; (5) punishment for minor breaches of rules and a progression of sanctions; and (6) a public graduation ceremony.[59]

In terms of boot camps in general, however, it is essential to emphasize that juvenile boot camp programs vary on such facets, including the following: (1) adherence to the original military model; (2) the background and age of the youths; (3) the length of stay at the camps; (4) the cost per juvenile; and (5) the amount and type of aftercare. Furthermore, there are varying positions as to whether these programs should be continued, discontinued, or enhanced.[60]

Evaluation of Boot Camps

The effectiveness of juvenile boot camps, in terms of recidivism, has not been encouraging. The OJJDP study, mentioned in the previous section, implemented an experimental design by randomly selecting youths for participation in one of the three boot camps (i.e., Cleveland, Ohio; Denver, Colorado; and Mobile, Alabama) between April 1992 and December 1993.[61] The control group consisted of matched youths sentenced to traditional incarceration and parole. Recidivism was defined as a new offense that subsequently resulted in a court action. For those youth in Cleveland, 72 percent of the participants were adjudicated for a new offense compared with 50 percent of the youths in the control group. In Denver, the experimental group also had a higher recidivism rate but the difference was much smaller (i.e., 39 percent and 36 percent, respectively). In Mobile, however, the boot camp participants had a lower recidivism rate than the control group, but this difference was small. Youths participating in all three boot camp sites reoffended in less time than the control group. For instance, in Mobile the average length of time to reoffend among the participants was 156 days compared with 232 days among the control group.

In 1994, Salerno maintained that although boot camps have been a fast-growing alternative sanction for adults, as well as juveniles, these programs are doomed to fail. Thus, boot camps should be phased out immediately. He had three significant criticisms. First, screaming at some-one to prepare for combat may be necessary to accomplish some type of goal, but what is the goal when yelling at a juvenile offender? Second, why would a military-type program help offenders when these individuals are rejected for military service? One possible reason for this is the relation between criminality and character disorder and the problems of authority often associated with criminals. Third, participating in a military-type pro-gram is not necessarily voluntary. Thus, a continuing problem is associated with these types of programs—that is, the value of coerced treatment.[62] However, a study by MacKenzie, Wilson, Armstrong, and Gover revealed that, compared with juveniles in traditional facilities, juveniles in boot camps perceived their environment to be more positive or therapeutic, as well as less hostile and dangerous, and to provide more structure.[63]

In their survey of the literature on juvenile boot camps, Tyler, Darville, and Stalnaker provided various insightful conclusions regarding these pro-grams. First, shock incarceration programs, such as juvenile boot camps, have done little to reduce recidivism. However, these programs seem to be more popular among the general public. Thus, "we let superficial short-term results, the needs of political power and public demand for increased vigilance against delinquency color our perspective of a pro-gram's effectiveness."[64] Second, national recidivism rates for juvenile boot camp graduates are often high, with few exceptions. Third, although some evaluations have revealed that the long-term impact of juvenile boot camp programs is similar to traditional sanctions, the latter are usually less costly than boot camps. Fourth, boot camps are not "stand-alone" solutions. Specifically, it is naïve to presume that participation in a program for a few months will subsequently make permanent changes in these youths' lives.[65]

CONCLUSION

This chapter first provided a general overview of evaluation research with a particular emphasis on specific issues pertaining to this type of research. Subsequently, three programs that have been deemed "failures" were discussed in reference to their history, program implementation, and evaluation. Furthermore, these three programs illustrated how those spe-cific issues pertaining to evaluation research (i.e., implementing an experi-mental design, defining success, the interest of stakeholders, and the political climate) were factors when evaluating the effectiveness, as well as the continuation, of these program.

The primary purpose of this chapter, however, is not necessarily to focus on these three programs. Rather, by using these three programs as examples, the purpose is to illustrate how those specific issues pertaining to evaluation research can influence any criminal justice policy or program. Thus, researchers, practitioners, policy makers, and the general public, should consider these issues when assessing the effectiveness of any policy or program.

NOTES

1. Maxfield & Babbie, 2006, p. 296.
2. Hagan, 1993, p. 372.
3. Schneider, A. L., Schneider, P. R., Wilson, L. A., Griffith, W. R., Medler, J. F., & Feinman, H. F. 1978; see also Hagan, 1993.
4. Rossi & Freeman, 1982.
5. Rossi & Freeman, 1982, pp. 32–40.
6. Maxfield & Babbie, 2006.
7. Clear & Dammer, 2000.
8. Clear & Dammer, 2000, p. 171.
9. Rossi, Freeman, & Lipsey, 1999.
10. Kemshall & Ross, 2000, p. 563.
11. Petrosino, 1998.
12. Maxfield & Babbie, 2006, p. 304.
13. Seiter, 1978, pp. 3–4.
14. Lundman, 1993, p. 151.
15. Michigan Department of Corrections, 1967.
16. Finckenauer, 1982, p. 68.
17. Finckenauer, 1982, pp. 68–69.
18. Finckenauer, 1982, p. 34.
19. Finckenauer & Gavin, 1999, p. 21.
20. Finckenauer, 1982.
21. Finckenauer & Gavin, 1999.
22. Scheidegger, 2003, p. 330.
23. Lundman, 1993, p. 154.
24. Lundman, 1993, p. 155.
25. Lundman, 1993, pp. 155–156.
26. Finckenauer, 1982.
27. Finckenauer, 1982, p. 136.
28. Petrosino, Turpin-Petrosino, & Finckenauer, 2000, p. 371.
29. Finckenaeur, 1982, p. 183.
30. Cavender, 1981, p. 434.
31. Heeren & Shichor, 1984.
32. Cavender, 1981, p. 437.
33. Heeren & Shichor, 1984.
34. Ringwalt, et al., 1994, n. p.
35. Ringwalt et al., 1994.
36. Rosenbaum, 2003.
37. Winfree, Esbensen, & Osgood, 1996.
38. Rosenbaum & Hanson, 1998.
39. Botvin, 1990.
40. Ringwalt et al., 1994, n. p.
41. Carter, 1995, pp. 5–7.
42. Rosenbaum, 2003, p. 106.
43. Ringwalt et al., 1994.
44. Ringwalt et al., 1994, n. p.
45. See also National Institute of Justice, 1994.
46. Rosenbaum, 2003, p. 106.
47. Rosenbaum & Hanson, 1998, p. 386.
48. Wysong, Aniskiewicz, & Wright, 1994, p. 461.
49. Peters, Thomas, & Zamberlan, 1997, p. 3.

50. Armstrong & MacKenzie, 2003, p. 29.
51. Armstrong & MacKenzie, 2003, p. 29.
52. Armstrong & MacKenzie, 2003, p. 29.
53. Bourgue, et al., 1996.
54. Tyler, Darville, & Stalnaker, 2001.
55. MacKenzie, Brame, McDowell, & Souryal, 1995.
56. Austin, et al., 2000, pp. 4–5.
57. Bourque et al., 1996, p. 5.
58. Bourque et al., 1996, p. 2.
59. Bourque et al., 1996, p. 4.
60. Tyler et al., 2001.
61. Peters et al., 1997.
62. Salerno, 1994, pp. 151–154.
63. MacKenzie, Wilson, Armstrong, & Gover, 2001.
64. Tyler et al., 2001, p. 457.
65. Tyler et al., 2001, pp. 456–457.

REFERENCES

Armstrong, G. S., & MacKenzie, D. L. (2003). Boot camps. In M. D. McShane & F. P. Williams, III (Eds.), *Encyclopedia of juvenile justice* (pp. 329–332). Thousand Oaks, CA: Sage Publications.

Austin, J., Camp-Blair, D., Camp, A., Castellano, T., Adams-Fuller, T., Jones, M., Kerr, S., Lewis, R., & Plant, S. (2000). *Multi-site evaluation of boot camp programs* (Final report). Washington, D.C.: U.S. Department of Justice.

Botvin, G. J. (1990). Substance abuse prevention: Theory, practice and effectiveness. In M. Tonry & J. Q. Wilson (Eds.), *Drugs and crime* (pp. 461–519). Chicago: University of Chicago Press.

Bourgue, B. B., Cronin, R. C., Felker, D. B., Pearson, F. R., Han, M., & Hill, S. M. (1996). *Boot camps for juvenile offenders: An implementation evaluation of three demonstration programs* (Research Brief). Washington, D.C.: U.S. Department of Justice.

Carter, D. (1995). *Community policing and D.A.R.E.: A practitioner's perspective.* Washington, D.C.: U.S. Department of Justice, Bureau of Justice Assistance.

Cavender, G. (1981). "Scared Straight": Ideology and the media. *Journal of Criminal Justice, 9,* 431–439.

Clear, T., & Dammer, H. (2000). *The offender in the community.* Belmont, CA: Wadsworth.

Finckenauer, J. (1982). *Scared Straight! and the panacea phenomenon.* Englewood Cliffs, NJ: Prentice Hall.

Finckenauer, J. O., & Gavin, P. W. (1999). *Scared Straight: The panacea phenomenon revisited.* Prospect Heights, IL: Waveland Press.

Hagan, F. E. (1993). *Research methods in criminal justice and criminology* (3rd ed.). New York: Macmillan Publishing Company.

Heeren, J., & Shichor, D. (1984). Mass media and delinquency prevention: The case of "Scared Straight," *Deviant Behavior, 5,* 375–386.

Kemshall, H., & Ross, L. (2000). Partners in evaluation: Modelling quality in partnership projects. *Social Policy & Administration, 34,* 551–566.

Lundman, R. J. (1993). *Prevention and control of juvenile delinquency* (2nd ed.). New York: Oxford University Press.

MacKenzie, D. L., Brame, R., McDowell, D., & Souryal, C. (1995). Boot camp prisons and recidivism in eight states. *Criminology, 33,* 327–357.

MacKenzie, D. L., Wilson, D. B., Armstrong, G. S., & Gover, A. R. (2001). The impact of boot camps and traditional institutions on juvenile residents: Perceptions, adjustment, and change. *Journal of Research in Crime and Delinquency, 38,* 279–313.

Maxfield, M. G., & Babbie, E. (2006). *Basics of research methods for criminal justice and criminology.* Belmont, CA: Wadsworth.

Michigan Department of Corrections. (1967). *A six-month follow-up of juvenile delinquents visiting the Ionia Reformatory* (Research Report #4). Lansing, MI: Michigan Department of Corrections, Program Bureau.

National Institute of Justice. (1994). The D.A.R.E. Program: A review of prevalence, user satisfaction, and effectiveness. *National Institute of Justice Update.* Washington, D.C.: U.S. Department of Justice.

Peters, M., Thomas, D., & Zamberlan, C. (1997). *Boot camps for juvenile offenders: Program summary.* Washington, D.C.: Office of Juvenile Justice and Delinquency Prevention.

Petrosino, A. (1998). *Improving the evaluation of state-administered programs.* Unpublished manuscript.

Petrosino, A., Turpin-Petrosino, C., & Finckenauer, J. O. (2000). Well-meaning programs can have harmful effects! Lessons from experiments of programs such as Scared Straight. *Crime & Delinquency, 46,* 354–379.

Ringwalt, C. L., Greene, J. M., Ennett, S. T., Iachan, R., Clayton, R. R., & Leukefeld, C. G. (1994). *Past and future directions of the D.A.R.E. Program: An evaluation review.* Washington, D.C.: U.S. Department of Justice.

Rosenbaum, D. P. (2003). DARE (Drug Abuse Resistance Education). In M. D. McShane & F. P. Williams, III (Eds.), *Encyclopedia of juvenile justice* (pp. 105–107). Thousand Oaks, CA: Sage Publications.

Rosenbaum. D. P., & Hanson, G. D. (1998). Assessing the effects of school-based drug education: A six-year multilevel analysis of Project D.A.R.E. *Journal of research in crime and delinquency, 35,* 381–412.

Rossi, P. H., & Freeman, H. E. (1982). *Evaluation: A systematic approach.* Beverly Hills, CA: Sage Publications.

Salerno, A. W. (1994). Boot camps: A critique and a proposed alternative. *Journal of Offender Rehabilitation, 20*(3–4), pp. 147–158.

Scheidegger, A. R. (2003). Scared Straight. In M. D. McShane & F. P. Williams, III (Eds.), *Encyclopedia of juvenile justice* (pp. 329–332). Thousand Oaks, CA: Sage Publications.

Schneider, A. L., Schneider, P. R., Wilson, L. A., Griffith, W. R., Medler, J. F., & Feinman, H. F. (1978). *Handbook of resources for criminal justice evaluators.* Washington, D.C.: U.S. Department of Justice.

Seiter, R. P. (1978). *Evaluation research as a feedback mechanism for criminal justice policy making: A critical analysis.* San Francisco, CA: R&E Research Associates, Inc.

Tyler, J., Darville, R., & Stalnaker, K. (2001). Juvenile boot camps: A descriptive analysis of program diversity and effectiveness. *The Social Science Journal, 38,* 445–460.

Winfree, L. T., Esbensen, F-A., & Osgood, D. W. (1996). Evaluating a school-based gang-prevention program. *Evaluation Review, 20,* 181–203.

Wysong, E., Aniskiewicz, R., & Wright, D. (1994). Truth and DARE: Tracking drug education to graduation and as symbolic politics. *Social Problems, 41,* 448–472.

CHAPTER 3

The Role of Police in School Safety

Julie Kiernan Coon and Lawrence F. Travis III[1]

Crime and safety in schools has been a concern for at least the past 30 years, but recently it has been the subject of increased attention. Reports of violent incidents in schools—such as those that occurred in Red Lake, Minnesota; Littleton, Colorado; Jonesboro, Arkansas; Pearl, Mississippi; and West Paducah, Kentucky—have led to a range of efforts to reduce crime in schools. One common strategy has been to increase law enforcement involvement in schools. The current role of police in schools, however, has yet to be adequately explained nor has the role of police in public schools been determined.

This chapter presents findings from a national survey of public schools that was designed to learn about the role of law enforcement in schools. First, we briefly discuss prior research about school safety. We explain what was known, and not yet known, about the role of police in schools. Furthermore, we identify a wide range of activities police may participate in at schools, and then describe what we learned about the level and frequency of police involvement in these activities. The results presented are based on responses to a 2002 survey of more than 1,300 public school principals.

WHAT WAS KNOWN

Growing Interest

School safety was a major concern for many years and media reporting of high-profile cases of school violence captured the attention of parents, school administrators, and law enforcement. This growing interest in school safety was reflected by government sponsored research during the

1970s and 1980s. Some examples include the National Institute of Education's (1978) study, *Violent Schools-Safe Schools: The Safe School Study Report to the Congress*, and a special issue of *Crime and Delinquency* (1978) that specifically focused on the topic of school crime. Furthermore, the U.S. Department of Justice presented results from a national study of crime in schools in *Reducing School Crime and Student Misbehavior: A Problem Solving Strategy* (1986).[2] School crime became known as a special type of criminality,[3] and schools and government agencies sought effective responses to crime in schools.

Media coverage of school shootings during the 1990s created a sense of urgency about school crime. Early in this period, the problem was often specifically defined as school violence, rather than the broader issue of safety in schools.[4] Several federal projects and scholarly efforts attempted to address what was perceived to be a crisis in school safety. The Office of Juvenile Justice and Delinquency Prevention published numerous reports aimed at helping schools and youth-serving organizations reduce crime.[5] Furthermore, projects sponsored by the U.S. Department of Education and the U.S. Department of Justice—such as *Indicators of School Crime and Safety; School and Staffing Survey 2003-04; Safe School Initiative; Annual Report on School Safety 2000;* and *Principal/School Disciplinarian Survey on School Violence 1996-97*—examined school problems with the intention of helping to prevent school violence. Schools were encouraged to adopt "zero-tolerance" policies regarding drugs or weapons on campus, and programs aimed at prevention and heightened security at schools became commonplace.

Factors Related to School Safety

Studies of school crime tend to indicate that many factors are related to school safety. For example, research suggests that crime is most common in "poor" schools.[6] Gottfredson and Gottfredson contend that location and community characteristics, school population makeup, school size, school resources, school rules, as well as practices and perceptions of the school environment are related to disorder in schools.[7] Additionally, Cantor and Wright found that high schools with the greatest violence problems tended to be large urban schools (average of 1,060 students), had a high percentage of minority students, and were located in disadvantaged neighborhoods that lacked residential stability. These researchers also noted that it was not solely urban schools that were violent, indicating that violence occurs across a variety of settings.[8] Furthermore, Lab and Clark reported that school safety levels were affected by styles of discipline in school, and the National Institute of Education's *Safe Schools Study* found that perceptions of safety were related to management styles.[9]

Clearly, numerous factors may influence actual and perceived levels of school security. It is apparent that, despite its relative rareness, the potential for violence in schools affects both students and teachers.[10] Schools may be able to reduce levels of crime and fear using security products,[11] improvements in policies and training,[12] social skills development,[13] and law enforcement involvement in schools.

Myths about School Crime

Although concern about school crime and violence appeared to be escalating, research suggests that school safety had not changed significantly over this time period.[14] For example, the introduction to the *2000 Annual Report on School Safety* states, "The vast majority of America's schools continue to be safe places."[15] Overall, the rate of student victimization at schools decreased from 1993 to 2003, but there were no significant changes from 2002 to 2003 in total victimization, violent victimization, and theft.[16] Despite these crime trends, awareness and fear of school violence seemed to have increased.

Joint Efforts to Address School Safety

There has been a widespread call for preventive measures to address school safety problems. It is generally agreed that school safety is a community concern, which can be best addressed through joint efforts involving the entire school community. The *Safe Schools/Healthy Students* initiative of the U.S. Departments of Justice, Education, and Health and Human Services encourages extensive community involvement in promoting school safety. For example, officials from law enforcement, juvenile justice, social service, and mental health organizations may work with schools to form partnerships.[17] Furthermore, the federal government has shown a commitment to supporting such school safety efforts. During 2005, this initiative provided more than $76 million in grants toward reducing school violence and substance abuse in schools.[18]

Role of Law Enforcement in School Safety

Law enforcement agencies may be involved with schools in many different ways. Reporting on police partnerships with youth servicing agencies, Chaiken found that "... partnerships between police and youth-serving organizations take many forms."[19] Furthermore, the use of school resource officers (SROs), who are sworn police officers assigned to schools and work under the supervision of school administrators, represents a merging of law enforcement with schools. Law enforcement officers can also serve on school safety committees, advisory boards, and planning bodies. Additionally, some schools may rely on law enforcement agency expertise for assessing school security, Drug Abuse Resistance Education (D.A.R.E.) Programs, staff training, and other special projects.

In some schools, law enforcement may be involved in less formal ways, such as speaking to classes or school assemblies, providing assistance with school events, and mentoring students (see Table 3.1 for types of police activities in schools). Like other clients of the police, schools can rely on law enforcement in emergency situations in which crime or violence occurs or is suspected. Some schools may "contract" with the police for special services, such as security at sporting and social events, while other schools choose to avoid contact with law enforcement.

Table 3.1.
Types of Police Activities in Schools

Type of Activity
Law Enforcement Related (e.g., patrol school grounds)
Advising/Mentoring Activities with Staff (e.g., advise staff on law-related issues)
Advising/Mentoring with Groups (e.g., advise parent-teacher organizations)
Advising/Mentoring with Students or Families (e.g., help students with court involvement or intervention)
Presence at School Events (e.g., present at athletic events)
Teaching (e.g., teaching antidrug classes)
Safety Planning (e.g., working with school to develop written plans for crisis situations)

Source: Travis & Coon, 2005.

Law enforcement has been acknowledged as a potentially important partner for schools in the effort to improve school security.[20] In reaction to school shootings during the 1990s, some police departments dramatically changed officer training for handling potential shooters, with the hope that these changes would reduce the number of victims during a crisis situation.[21] Additionally, federal grant money made it possible for many law enforcement agencies to dedicate current officers or hire new personnel as SROs. As of 2005, the U.S. Office of Community Oriented Policing Services had supported the addition of more than 6,500 law enforcement officers in schools.[22] In addition to this federal assistance, there was already a strong interest among school administrators to increase the use of security measures and police officers.[23]

Obstacles to Improving School Safety

Although it is appealing to believe that schools and law enforcement can work together to improve the safety of our schools, interactions between schools and criminal justice agencies are not always smooth. For example, Lawrence examined the connection between the juvenile justice system and schools. He found numerous obstacles to cooperation, including distrust. Lawrence described the conflict as "fear of crime" by the justice officials and "fear of labeling" by school personnel.[24] Similarly, school personnel and law enforcement officials may not always agree about how to handle school problems. The goal of safer schools may be shared, but differing views on how best to achieve this may create barriers for school and law enforcement partnerships.

As noted by Green regarding security technology, school administrators often resist security measures (this presumably applies to law enforcement involvement) because of fear that such efforts will negatively effect the school's social and educational climate. Also, if school personnel believe that police are solely focused on crime control, it is unlikely that law enforcement will be fully included in the operations of the school. As comments during the Strategic Planning Meeting on School Safety suggested, school personnel often view police officers as "muscle" to be relied on for disciplinary matters, but they may not view law enforcement as a preventive or general resource.[25]

WHAT WAS UNKNOWN

Law enforcement can be involved with schools in many ways. Before, little was known about precisely how, and with what frequency, police and schools worked together in school safety efforts. It was established that police officers could be assigned to schools, but the actual role(s) of police in public schools across the country was not yet understood. For example, it was unknown whether police were most likely to be engaged in law enforcement activities (e.g., patrolling the school, investigating crime leads, performing drug sweeps) or had greater involvement in less traditional activities such as mentoring and teaching. Furthermore, we did not know the frequency of police presence in schools. Although law enforcement might be involved in a particular task in schools, we did not know if police engaged in this activity on a daily, weekly, monthly, or yearly basis.

It was largely unclear what the driving forces were for having a presence of law enforcement in schools. For example, we did not know if schools wanted police involvement in their schools because of specific incidents at the school, or if police presence in schools was related to community policing efforts. Although media attention to high-profile violent events in schools might explain some of the initial involvement, other possible reasons for police presence in schools had yet to be fully explored.

The goal of our national survey was to describe the role of law enforcement in schools. We first explain how we conducted the national mail survey of public schools. We then describe principal responses to the survey about how law enforcement works with schools to address school safety.[26] We conclude with a discussion of what we think our results mean and what they do not mean.

SCHOOL SURVEY PROCESS

We developed a nine-page questionnaire that was distributed to schools in our sample. The survey incorporated items from previous surveys, particularly the *School Survey on Crime and Safety* and the *National Assessment of School Resource Officer Programs Survey of School Principals*.[27] The survey included questions about a wide range of possible police activities in schools, the frequency of police presence, the reasons for having SROs, and the use of various security products (e.g., cameras, alarm systems, locks, metal detectors). We obtained information about the school, such as measures of achievement, expenditure per pupil, and characteristics of the student body (e.g., percentage of students eligible for free lunch).

We selected a representative sample of schools from the U.S. Department of Education's Common Core of Data (CCD). The CCD contains detailed information on approximately 90,000 public schools in the United States. The advantage of selecting a representative sample is that the results should more accurately describe the role of law enforcement in schools across the nation.

Surveys were sent to more than 3,000 schools, and we received almost 1,400 completed surveys for a response rate of nearly 45 percent. Compared with the population of public schools in the CCD, our respondents differed in several ways. For example, our respondents were more likely to be rural, Midwestern high schools, with higher proportions of white students, lower proportions of students eligible for free lunch, and a fewer number of grades in the school. There were no significant differences between the sample and the population in terms of other characteristics examined.

Law Enforcement Survey

In addition to the survey of schools, we surveyed the law enforcement agencies that worked with those schools. We received a very good overall response from law enforcement agencies. A total of 1,508 law enforcement surveys were sent, and 1,140 public law enforcement surveys were completed, for a 76 percent response rate.

Site Visits

For the last phase of the study, we conducted site visits at 14 schools. The sample represented all levels of education and types of communities. At the community level, we collected data from four urban schools, four suburban schools, and six rural schools. At the education level, we collected data from five elementary schools, two junior high schools, and seven senior high schools.

Each site visit involved two researchers who interviewed school principals, faculty, staff, SROs, police chiefs, and other law enforcement officers that served the school. Whenever possible, we conducted at least one focus group with students and at least one focus group with parents. In addition, researchers completed a school climate survey (one per researcher) that noted physical and behavioral details of the campus and its environment. Site visits were scheduled for two to three days per campus, depending on the school's availability.

WHAT WE LEARNED

Law Enforcement Reliance

The vast majority of schools (97 percent) indicated that they relied predominantly on public law enforcement rather than private security. We asked schools whether they relied on SROs (defined as officers assigned by a police department or agency to work in collaboration with schools).

Almost half (48 percent) of the principals surveyed reported that their school relied on SROs.

Schools that had an SRO provided a range of reasons for the officer's presence. Approximately 25 percent of schools reported that the use of an SRO was a response to national media attention about school violence. About 18 percent of schools stated that the police presence was a reaction to disorder problems (e.g., rowdiness, vandalism), 6 percent said it was due to parents wanting an officer in the school, and only 4 percent reported that having an SRO was due to the level of violence in the school. Almost half of respondents chose the "other" answer to the question and explained that having an SRO was due to all of the listed factors, or a combination of factors, including crime prevention, available funding through grants, school policy, opportunity to build relationships with students, part of community policing and D.A.R.E. efforts, and safety and security purposes. Principals who reported that their school did not have an SRO most often cited there was no need for an officer in their school or a lack of funding.

Not surprisingly, there were differences in the level and frequency of police activity in schools between those served by an SRO and those without an SRO. More than half of the principals from schools with an SRO reported police engaging in 26 of 42 separate activities listed in one section of the survey, while more than half of the principals in schools with no SRO reported only 8 of the 42 activities. We learned that SROs were significantly more likely to be assigned to schools that were larger, located in urban areas, had higher levels of crime and disorder, located in higher crime neighborhoods (as described by principals), and had students in higher grades. SROs were also significantly more common in schools located in Southern and Western states.

Police Activities

The school survey included a wide range of possible activities in which law enforcement officers may be involved at schools. In addition to questions that had yes or no responses, we asked principals to report how frequently police were involved in various activities (see Table 3.2). We found that the most common (occurring in a majority of schools) and most frequent (e.g., occurring on a daily or weekly basis) police activities tended to be law enforcement related. For example, 70 percent of principals reported that police responded to crime and disorder reports from school staff, patrolled school grounds, and patrolled student travel routes. In terms of frequency of activities, activities occurring on a daily basis for many schools were as follows: police patrolling school grounds (30 percent); patrolling school facilities (26 percent); patrolling drug-free zones beyond school boundaries (23 percent); patrolling student travel routes (23 percent); and performing traffic patrol on or around campus (18 percent). Furthermore, more than 10 percent of principals reported that the police responded to crime and disorder reports from school staff or students, investigated crime and disorder leads provided by staff or students, and wrote police reports at least weekly.

Table 3.2.
Frequency of Police Activities in Schools as Reported by Principals

Type of Activity	Daily	1–4 Times per Week	1–3 Times per Month	1–3 Times per Semester	Once per Year	Never	N
			(Percentage)				
Law Enforcement–Related Activity							
Patrol school facilities	26.2	14.0	11.3	13.4	4.8	30.3	1,262
Patrol school grounds	29.9	17.2	11.0	12.8	5.5	23.5	1,263
Patrol drug-free zones beyond school boundaries	23.0	18.7	12.2	9.9	3.0	33.2	1,193
Patrol student travel routes	23.3	19.7	13.7	11.6	4.2	27.5	1,217
Operate metal detectors	0.9	0.4	1.3	2.9	1.5	92.9	1,271
Conduct safety and security inspections	4.8	4.0	6.9	13.3	19.9	51.1	1,266
Respond to crime/disorder reports from school staff	7.0	9.0	12.3	34.4	17.4	19.9	1,289
Respond to crime/disorder reports from students	6.6	7.4	7.2	17.5	12.2	49.2	1,275
Investigate staff leads about crime/disorder	5.0	6.4	9.2	19.1	20.3	40.0	1,259
Investigate student leads about crime/disorder	5.8	6.7	8.6	15.6	16.2	47.2	1,249
Make arrests	1.6	2.8	6.2	15.6	16.2	57.6	1,266
Issue citations	1.7	5.0	8.7	16.6	13.1	55.0	1,267
Write disciplinary reports	2.0	4.1	5.8	12.9	9.6	65.7	1,267
Write police reports	4.3	6.6	10.6	26.1	20.3	32.2	1,265
Enforce truancy laws or policies	3.3	3.5	8.6	14.9	14.1	55.6	1,274
Solve crime-related problems	4.0	5.1	8.4	16.5	21.7	44.3	1,257
Perform traffic patrol on or around campus	17.5	13.5	10.6	14.6	8.5	35.2	1,277
Perform sweeps for drugs	1.6	1.6	4.7	12.5	12.8	66.8	1,269
Perform sweeps for weapons	1.7	1.4	2.8	7.7	7.8	78.5	1,263
Advising/Mentoring Activities with Staff							
Advise staff on school policy changes	1.7	1.4	4.3	9.4	17.1	66.1	1,266
Advise staff on school procedure changes	1.2	1.3	4.4	9.5	16.2	67.5	1,261

(continued)

Table 3.2. (*continued*)

Type of Activity	Daily	1–4 Times per Week	1–3 Times per Month	1–3 Times per Semester	Once per Year	Never	N
			(Percentage)				
Advise staff on physical environment changes	1.0	1.7	4.2	8.7	14.9	69.6	1,259
Advise staff on problem solving	1.9	2.4	5.3	11.1	14.3	64.9	1,258
Mediate disputes among staff	0.7	0.2	1.2	2.5	4.3	91.2	1,260
Advise staff on avoiding violence/victimization	1.1	1.5	3.0	8.7	18.2	67.4	1,259
Advise staff on student behavior modification	1.2	2.1	3.1	9.1	13.2	71.3	1,260
Advise staff on student rule/sanction enforcement	1.4	2.0	4.2	8.8	11.9	71.8	1,257
Advise staff on law-related issues	2.1	2.1	6.2	13.3	20.2	56.0	1,262
Advising/Mentoring with Groups							
Advise parent–teacher organizations (e.g., PTOs, PTAs)	0.2	0.3	2.1	7.1	27.1	63.2	1,263
Advise police athletic/ activities league (PALs)	0.7	1.3	3.0	4.3	8.3	82.3	1,220
Advise school athletic teams	0.7	1.5	2.9	5.1	8.6	81.3	1,226
Advise community outreach programs	0.4	1.1	4.8	9.8	15.9	68.0	1,219
Advising/Mentoring with Students or Families							
Mentor/provide guidance to individual students	7.4	8.3	12.0	20.9	13.2	38.3	1,246
Help students with court involvement or intervention	2.5	4.7	10.2	15.2	13.6	53.8	1,224
Work with parents to help their children	4.3	7.9	11.2	21.4	14.8	40.5	1,222
Refer students to other sources of help	3.7	7.3	9.5	19.6	11.9	48.0	1,220
Refer parents to other sources of help	3.3	6.1	9.9	21.3	14.1	45.3	1,218

(*continued*)

Table 3.2. (*continued*)

Type of Activity	Daily	1–4 Times per Week	1–3 Times per Month	1–3 Times per Semester	Once per Year	Never	N
	(Percentage)						
Present at athletic events	7.2	18.2	14.6	9.7	4.8	45.6	1,227
Present for school social events (e.g., dances, open houses)	5.2	9.5	12.8	20.1	12.5	39.8	1,258
Present for school perform- ances (e.g., school plays, concerts)	4.0	6.9	9.3	16.7	12.0	51.1	1,252
Chaperone school field trips	1.1	1.5	3.0	5.5	9.1	79.7	1,246
Present at award ceremonies	2.8	2.5	4.1	11.4	22.9	56.3	1,252

Source: Travis & Coon, 2005.

In addition to asking about law enforcement–related activities, the survey included questions about the frequency of advising and mentoring activities and police presence at school events. Advising and mentoring activities were not as common as law enforcement–related activities. When police were involved in advising and mentoring, it tended to be with students and families rather than staff or groups, and it was most likely to occur on a semester or yearly basis. Approximately 25 percent of principals indicated that police were present at school athletic events at least weekly, and more than 10 percent reported a police presence at school social events and school performances at least weekly. Among the least common of all activities were the following: police operating metal detectors; performing sweeps for weapons; mediating disputes among staff; advising athletic or activities leagues; advising school athletic teams; and chaperoning school field trips.

In addition to examining how frequently police were involved in law enforcement–related activities, advising and mentoring, and school events, we also wanted to know whether police had a teaching role in schools. We asked principals to report whether or not police officers taught 13 specific classes (see Table 3.3). Principals reported that police taught a variety of classes for schools with the most common being D.A.R.E. (52 percent); other antidrug classes (34 percent); alcohol awareness/DUI (driving under the influence) prevention (30 percent); crime prevention (24 percent); and other safety education (24 percent). The least commonly taught classes were firearm safety (11 percent) and antihate education (13 percent).

Table 3.3.
Teaching Activities of Police in Schools

Teaching Activity	Yes (%)	No (%)	N
D.A.R.E.	51.6	48.4	1,326
Other antidrug classes	33.9	66.1	1,304
Alcohol awareness or DUI prevention	30.4	69.6	1,295
Antigang classes	20.9	79.1	1,282
Antibullying classes	21.0	79.0	1,293
Antihate classes	12.7	87.3	1,280
Law-related classes	20.3	79.7	1,286
Firearm safety classes	11.1	88.9	1,284
Other safety education classes	24.2	75.8	1,283
Crime awareness or prevention	24.3	75.7	1,286
Career training	19.8	80.2	1,285
Conflict resolution	23.6	76.4	1,290
Problem-solving	21.7	78.3	1,177

Source: Travis & Coon, 2005.

Another area in which police may be involved is school safety planning (see Table 3.4). We asked principals whether or not police participated in numerous safety-related activities: 86 percent said they had an emergency plan agreement with the police, 55 percent reported that law enforcement worked with the school to develop written plans for crisis situations, and 47 percent reported that representatives of law enforcement attended school safety meetings. Other types of safety planning were less common, such as regularly scheduled meetings with public law enforcement to discuss specific incidents (30 percent) and law enforcement working with the school to review school discipline practices and procedures (30 percent).

SCHOOL CHARACTERISTICS RELATED TO POLICE INVOLVEMENT

We were interested in learning more about what types of schools tended to have greater police participation in activities at their schools. We included several school characteristics in our analysis that we believed might be related to the level and frequency of law enforcement involvement in schools. Total level of involvement refers to the number of activities in which police participated, with no reference as to how often police were engaged in these activities. Frequency of a particular activity was measured as either frequent (includes daily, one to four times per week, and one to three times per month) or infrequent/never (includes one to three times per semester, once per year, and never). By using this categorization, we were able to create a measure of the overall frequency of police

Table 3.4.
Police Involvement in School Safety Plans and Meetings

School Plans/Meetings with Public Law Enforcement:	Yes (%)	No (%)	N
Emergency plan agreement with law enforcement	86.3	13.7	1,359
Law enforcement attend school safety meetings	47.4	52.6	1,350
Regularly scheduled meetings with public law enforcement to discuss general school issues	32.3	67.7	1,322
Regularly scheduled meetings with public law enforcement to discuss specific incidents	29.8	70.2	1,305
Law enforcement work with school to develop written plans for crisis situations	54.6	45.4	1,361
Law enforcement work with school to review school discipline practices and procedures	30.3	69.7	1,356
Law enforcement work with school to develop programs to prevent or reduce violence	31.2	68.8	1,354
Law enforcement conduct risk assessment of security of building or grounds	42.2	57.8	1,352
Law enforcement work to develop a plan for increased levels of security	38.8	61.2	1,355

Source: Travis & Coon, 2005.

involvement. We then used regression analysis,[28] which allowed us to assess how each school characteristic was associated with the level and frequency of police involvement.

We found that several school characteristics were associated with the level of law enforcement presence in schools (see Table 3.5). Not surprisingly, we found that schools with more reported school crime and disorder tended to have greater police participation in activities. Also, as might be expected, the presence of an SRO was a significant predictor of higher levels of law enforcement involvement. Additionally, schools with higher grade levels also reported greater police presence in their schools. It was somewhat surprising that urbanism (measured as urban, suburban, rural) was not related to the level of police involvement.

Several school characteristics were also related to the frequency of law enforcement involvement in schools. As we found with total level of police involvement, schools with an SRO, higher level schools, and schools with more reported crime and disorder tended to have more frequent law enforcement presence. Additionally, we found that larger schools were more likely to have frequent police involvement. Furthermore, we found that urbanism was a significant predictor of frequency of police presence, but not in the way we expected. Specifically, rural schools reported more frequent police participation in activities than was reported by suburban and urban schools. It is possible that police officers in urban school

Table 3.5.
Predictors of Level and Frequency of Law Enforcement

School Characteristics	Total Level (Scope) of Police Involvement	Total Frequency of Police Involvement
Expenditure per student per year	0	0
Total number of students	0	+
Region	−	0
Urbanism	0	−
School level	+	+
School crime	+	+
Percent minority students	0	0
Neighborhood crime	0	0
Percent free-lunch students	0	0
Presence of school resource officer	+	+

Notes:
+ indicates positive relationship significant at 0.05 or 0.01 level.
− indicates negative relationship significant at 0.05 or 0.01 level.
0 indicates significant relationship.
Negative relationship (−) for region and total level of police involvement indicates that non-Southern schools were less likely than Southern schools to use law enforcement.
For all other variables, positive sign (+) indicates positive relationship (e.g., + for presence of SRO indicates that schools with an SRO were more likely to have greater level and frequency of law enforcement involvement).
Source: Travis & Coon, 2005.

districts have a greater number of schools for which they are responsible and therefore cannot devote all of their time to a single school.

WHAT OUR RESULTS SUGGEST

Our study indicates that public schools, for the most part, are safe places. Although the majority of schools are not dangerous, enhanced security often is needed. During our site visits, many respondents expressed concern about potential problems with unauthorized access to the school often attributed to the physical structure of the building (e.g., open design, portable outbuildings, pods) or with the location of the main office, which made it difficult to monitor access to all entrances through which people could enter the school. Potentially dangerous traffic patterns during arrival and dismissal and misbehavior on buses were commonly mentioned by administrators, staff, and parents. Despite these concerns, most of the staff and students reported they felt safe on their campuses and in their buildings. Furthermore, the vast majority of principals reported few serious crimes, and violent crime was rare for most schools.

We learned that police may be involved in a wide range of activities in schools, but mostly they engaged in traditional law enforcement–related tasks.

Our survey suggests that principals tend to perceive the current role of law enforcement in public schools to be largely preventive and reactive through patrol, investigating crime leads, and writing reports. From the perspective of many principals, police involvement in schools is a reaction to potential crime and security risks rather than a response to serious crime problems.

We found that opinions regarding the ideal role of police in schools varied widely among school staff, parents, and students. The general trend was that respondents thought police should assist in addressing problems; however, there was a lack of consensus regarding the extent of police involvement and level of authority police should exercise in schools. Respondents stated that they would like to have, in varying combinations, police as educators, legal resources, security, law enforcers, disciplinarians, counselors, role models, and mentors.

SROs tended to see their roles as diverse, with involvement in education, discipline, counseling, and serving as a role model. In some schools, the function of an officer in the school seemed to be limited to performing traditional law enforcement–related activities, teaching D.A.R.E., and providing security for social events. Other schools, however, seemed to view officers as a valuable resource as part of a comprehensive school plan.

It also seems that many police officers want to maintain an official law enforcement position and not be disciplinarians. Schools want order and safety, and therefore may prefer police to assume a more comprehensive role to achieve this. Different perceptions of the appropriate function of law enforcement in schools may lead to conflict. The role of police in schools seems to be something that must be negotiated or defined at the school level.

Police may have various roles in public schools, and based on our site visit data, these roles seem to reflect differences in school-based perceptions of what the problems may be and what the police should do. We found that it is common for the police function to differ by particular school characteristics. For example, the survey results indicate that the type and frequency of police involvement in schools differs by school level, and the results from the site visits indicate that police, school administrators, staff, parents, and students still want this role to continue to vary by school level. Generally, elementary schools have more limited roles for police. Elementary school respondents did not want police in their schools on a daily basis, but they did value police as mentors and wanted them to be available if needed. Respondents at secondary schools generally expressed greater support for broader and more frequent police involvement at their schools. Also, as would be expected, schools that reported higher levels of crime or violence typically had a greater police presence. Not surprisingly, schools with SROs were much more likely to have greater law enforcement involvement in their schools than those schools without a dedicated resource officer.

There were several advantages to law enforcement involvement in schools. Parents and staff believed that officers served several functions, such as deterring student misbehavior and delinquent activity; responding to emergencies; acting as role models; and providing a presence that makes students, staff, and parents feel safer. Participants who believed there were disadvantages to police involvement in schools mentioned that the constant presence of an officer gives the impression that something is wrong at the school or might generate fear; felt that a gun on campus may be undesirable; and thought that, if students became too familiar with officers or became "buddies," they could lose respect for them and their authority.

Overall, students, parents, and staff were supportive of having police in their school. Similarly, law enforcement officials were eager to have dedicated SROs if funds were available and if a police presence was deemed necessary or beneficial for the school. According to some schools, greater presence or involvement of law enforcement was a response to increases in violence or a tragic event.

The site visits also indicated that conflicts sometimes exist between school administrators and police, for example, different expectations about the role of police in schools. We frequently heard from police that they did not want to enforce school rules. Written agreements outlining school and police expectations could clarify the role of police in schools and reduce conflicts and misunderstandings. Additionally, support for police in schools was higher when the administration and staff believed that their SRO did not overstep certain boundaries. It became clear that officers were supervised by their police departments rather than schools. Furthermore, there were a variety of ways officers may be selected or volunteer to become SROs. Efforts to match school needs with officers who are sensitive to school concerns may result in a more appreciated and effective role for police in schools.

In sum, our findings do not suggest that there is a one-size-fits-all solution to school problems. The disagreement about the appropriate role of police in schools, in part, leads to the conclusion that there is no single ideal role for police in schools. The police role should vary by the needs of the school, and often this need is associated with school level, environmental factors, and school climate. The policy of having officers assigned to several schools, however, should be carefully examined. Officers who work at more than one school are often limited to dealing solely with security issues. Although we do not suggest that all schools benefit from full-time law enforcement presence, many schools want to have at least some police involvement. Whether that police presence is full time, part time, or on an as-needed basis, schools tend to value partnerships with law enforcement in working toward the shared goal of safer schools.

NOTES

1. This research was supported by the National Institute of Justice, award number 2001-IJ-CX-0011. Findings and conclusions of the research reported here are those of the authors and do not necessarily reflect the official position or policies of the U.S. Department of Justice.
2. Rubel & Ames, 1986.
3. Gottfredson & Gottfredson, 1985.
4. Zins, Travis, Brown, & Knighton, 1994.
5. Arnette & Walseben, 1998; Catalano, Loeber, & McKinney, 1999.
6. For example, *Safe Schools Study* by the National Institute of Education, 1978.
7. Gottfredson & Gottfredson, 1985.
8. Cantor & Wright, 2001.

9. Lab & Clark, 1996.
10. Metropolitan Life Insurance Co., 1993, 1999.
11. Green, 1999; Johnson, 1999.
12. Ohio Crime Prevention Association, 2000.
13. Lieber & Mawhorr, 1995.
14. Hanke, 1996; U.S. Departments of Justice and Education, hereafter USDJE, 2000.
15. USDJE, 2000.
16. DeVoe, Peter, Noonan, Snyder, & Baum, 2005.
17. USDJE, 2000.
18. U.S Departments of Justice, Education, and Health and Human Services, 2005.
19. Chaiken, 1998, p. xv.
20. Dwyer & Osher, 2000; Dwyer, Osher, & Warger, 1998.
21. Harper, 2000.
22. COPS Office, 2005.
23. Trump, 1998.
24. Lawrence, 1995.
25. Green, 1999, p. 5.
26. For more about the findings from the law enforcement survey and site visits, please see Travis & Coon, 2005.
27. Finn & Hayeslip, 2001; National Center for Education Statistics, 2000.
28. Regression analysis is a form of statistical analysis that allows multiple predictors to be used to determine which variables are most important in predicting an event.

REFERENCES

Arnette, J., & Walseben, M. (1998). *Combating fear and restoring safety in schools.* Washington, D.C.: Office of Juvenile Justice and Delinquency Prevention.

Cantor, D., & Wright, M. M. (2001). *School crime patterns: A national profile of U.S. public high schools using rates of crime reported to the police.* Report on the study of school violence and prevention. Washington, D.C.: U.S. Department of Education, Planning and Service.

Catalano, R., Loeber, R., & McKinney, K. (1999). *School and community interventions to prevent serious and violent offending.* Washington, D.C.: Office of Juvenile Justice and Delinquency Prevention.

Chaiken, M. (1998). *Kids, cops, communities.* Washington, D.C.: National Institute of Justice.

COPS Office. (2005). *COPS in schools: The COPS commitment to school safety.* Retrieved June 19, 2006, from www.cops.usdoj.gov.

DeVoe, J. F., Peter, K., Noonan, M., Snyder, T. D., & Baum, K. (2005). *Indicators of school crime and safety: 2005.* Washington, D.C.: U.S. Departments of Education and Justice and Bureau of Justice Statistics.

Dwyer, K., & Osher, D. (2000). *Safeguarding our children: An action guide.* Washington, D.C.: U.S. Departments of Education and Justice, American Institutes for Research; Dwyer, K., Osher, D., & Warger, C. (1998). *Early warning, timely response: A guide to safe schools.* Washington, D.C.: U.S. Department of Education.

Finn, P., & Hayeslip, D. (2001). *Report on the national survey of SRO programs and affiliated schools.* Cambridge: MA. Abt Associates Inc. (Draft report prepared for the National Institute of Justice).

Gottfredson, G. D., & Gottfredson, D. C. (1985). *Victimization in schools.* New York: Plenum.

Green, M. (1999). *The appropriate and effective use of security technologies in U.S. schools*. Washington, D.C.: National Institute of Justice.

Hanke, P. (1996). Putting school crime into perspective: Self-reported school victimizations of high school seniors. *Journal of Criminal Justice, 24*(3), 207–226.

Harper, T. (2000). Shoot to kill. *The Atlantic Monthly, 286*(4), 28–33.

Johnson, I. (1999). School violence: The effectiveness of a school resource officer program in a southern city. *Journal of Criminal Justice, 27*(2), 173–192.

Lab, S., & Clark, R. (1996). *Final report: Discipline, control and school crime: Identifying effective intervention strategies*. Washington, D.C.: National Institute of Justice.

Lawrence, R. (1995). Controlling school crime: An examination of interorganizational relations of school and juvenile justice professionals. *Juvenile and Family Court Journal, 46*, 3–15.

Lieber, M., & Mawhorr, T. (1995). Evaluating the use of social skills training and employment with delinquent youth. *Journal of Criminal Justice, 23*(2), 127–142.

Metropolitan Life Insurance Co. (1993). *Metropolitan Life survey of the American teacher, 1993*. New York: Metropolitan Life Insurance Co.

Metropolitan Life Insurance Co. (1999). *Metropolitan Life survey of the American teacher, 1999: Violence in America's public schools: Five years later*. New York: Metropolitan Life Insurance Co.

National Center for Education Statistics. 2000. Indicators of school crime and safety: 2000. Washington, D.C: U.S. Dept. of Education.

Ohio Crime Prevention Association. (2000). School safety initiatives. *Ohio Crime Prevention Association Digest*. Dublin, OH: Ohio Crime Prevention Association.

Rubel, R., & Ames, N. (1986). *Reducing school crime and student misbehavior: A problem solving strategy*. Washington, D.C.: U.S. Department of Justice.

Travis, L. F., & Coon, J. K. (2005). *The role of law enforcement in public school safety: A national survey*. Washington, D.C.: National Criminal Justice Reference Service.

Trump, K. S. (1998). *Practical school security: Basic guidelines for safe and secure schools*. Thousand Oaks, CA: Corwin Press.

U.S. Departments of Justice and Education. (2000). *Annual report on school safety 2000*. Washington, D.C.: U.S. Departments of Justice and Education.

U.S. Departments of Justice, Education, and Health and Human Services. (2005). *Safe schools/healthy students*. Retrieved June 19, 2006, from www.ed.gov.

Zins, J., Travis, L., Brown, M., & Knighton, A. (1994). Schools and the prevention of interpersonal violence: Mobilizing and coordinating community resources. *Special Services in the Schools, 8*(2), 1–9.

CHAPTER 4

Juveniles and Reintegrative Shaming

Jennifer L. McGivern

John Braithwaite's theory of reintegrative shaming[1] is a relatively recent theory of crime and that is a part of the larger restorative justice movement. Based on the two main principles, shame and forgiveness, the theory enjoys widespread application in such countries as Australia, New Zealand, England, Wales, the United States, Canada, and Northern Ireland in the form of family conferences within the juvenile justice system.[2] An alternative to the formal criminal justice system, these meetings unify the offender, victim, and support members from both sides in an attempt to reduce future predatory delinquency. Seemingly successful, these programs have been in effect for more than 10 years. Principles of Braithwaite's theory have been examined in the past decade in studies seeking to determine the role that shame and forgiveness play within the problems of school bullying and drunk driving.

This chapter opens with an overview of Braithwaite's reintegrative shaming theory, beginning with a description of the theory's main elements and its key hypotheses. Second, the role that reintegrative shaming plays within the larger context of restorative justice is presented. Third, the reader is familiarized with the research conducted to date on reintegrative shaming theory, as well as its many applications in the legal system. Fourth, modern-day applications of shaming in the United States that do not include reintegration processes are examined, along with the problems that they invite. Closing remarks are made about the future of reintegrative shaming in the United States.

THE THEORY OF REINTEGRATIVE SHAMING

Braithwaite's 1989 theory of reintegrative shaming is the product of the integration of several dominant theories of crime in sociology today, including labeling theory, subculture theory, control theory, opportunity theory, and learning theory. Braithwaite synthesizes core concepts from these theories into an integrated theory that is useful in explaining *predatory crime* (the violation of laws that prohibit a person from preying on another person) and *secondary delinquency* (reoffending). Reintegrative shaming is most often discussed and applied in the case of juvenile offenses. This may be due to the fact that meetings built on reintegrative shaming principles are focused on rebuilding the offender's conscience against committing future crime, which seems most viable when dealing with a youth who may have a more malleable mind than a hardened, older offender. In addition, these meetings provide an appealing alternative to the juvenile justice system, especially for young offenders without any prior criminal history.

Braithwaite acknowledges that reintegrative shaming is useful only in the reduction of predatory crimes, such as robbery, assault, and crimes against property.[3] Shame is only a useful means of *social control* (the process of ensuring members' conformity to the groups' norms) when there is a core consensus that the behavior in question is wrong. In the United States, for example, although it is a criminal behavior, there is no majority opinion on the wrongfulness of smoking marijuana. In essence, there is no guarantee that the offender will be shamed by the ordinary citizen for engaging in this behavior, which is essentially what the theory relies on to work. In the case of nonpredatory offenses such as this, reintegrative shaming will not work and should not be applied.

The key principle of Braithwaite's theory of reintegrative shaming is that the sequential process includes initial disapproval of the offending act (shaming) and subsequent reacceptance of the offender back into the law-abiding society (reintegration). An important agent of social control, Braithwaite argues that the family embodies the main principles of reintegrative shaming because it "teaches us that shaming and punishment are possible while maintaining bonds of respect."[4]

Shaming

Braithwaite argues that "cultural commitments to shaming are the key to controlling all types of crime."[5] Culturally specific, shaming can be expressed through nonverbal, verbal, subtle, and direct gestures, as well as through gossip, the mass media, popular culture, and official pronouncements.[6] Treated within the theory as indistinct from guilt, shame is intended to moralize with the offender about the wrongfulness of their actions through the evocation of their conscience. A uniquely social process, Braithwaite argues that shaming is a positive and integral part of social control that specifically deters the offender from reoffending in the future. It also serves as a warning to observant community members and would-be offenders who are contemplating the commission of a crime. This should not be interpreted to mean that shaming is a painless experience for the offender; indeed, shaming can sometimes be quite harsh and even outright cruel. When the shaming becomes quite punitive and is not followed with any reconciliation between the offender and the community, there runs a very real danger of turning the offender into an outcast and a repeat offender.

Labeling theorists within sociology disagree with Braithwaite, arguing that shaming is not a positive force but instead a counterproductive and stigmatizing force that fosters further delinquency. This argument is best exemplified by the arrest, trial, and conviction sequence. A labeling theorist would argue that when the legal system officially pronounces an individual as an offender (during the arrest) or as a convicted offender (with a guilty verdict), the process changes the individual's *master status* (main identity) of "law-abiding citizen" into that of "delinquent." Because of his new status as delinquent, the offender is subsequently rejected by the law-abiding society, which includes his family and friends. Instead the offender must seek out criminal subcultures that are composed of similarly labeled delinquent peers to find companions. The new group teaches the offender an ideology that is favorable to law violation as well as criminal techniques (e.g., how to break into buildings), and also provides the offender with real opportunities to engage in secondary delinquency. The personal bonds the offenders have formed with these delinquent peers in the criminal subculture not only encourage them to commit delinquent acts, but most important, reduce their remaining attachment to law-abiding parents and peers, ultimately weakening their stake in any type of conformity to the law-abiding community.

The upside to this common situation is that although criminal subcultures may exist in every society, Braithwaite argues that most people do not have the specific taste or opportunity to join them.[7] Consequently, newly labeled deviants may choose to reject an available subculture that they do not find appealing and reintegrate themselves into a law-abiding society. Alternatively, they may decide to act as a lone delinquent, although this does not appear to happen as frequently. According to Braithwaite, the consequence of *stigmatization* (the act of labeling someone as deviant) that results from shaming an individual without providing any form of reintegration into the community depends largely on whether the offender finds or decides to join a criminal subculture.

Reintegration

Braithwaite would agree with labeling theorists that shaming can have negative consequences; however, he provides a viable solution to this problem. To reduce an offender's risk of seeking out a criminal subculture to begin with and committing any subsequent delinquent acts, Braithwaite argues that it is essential to make informal or formal gestures that reintegrate the offender into the law-abiding community after the shaming ceremony. A ceremony that decertifies, or removes, the offender's master status of "delinquent," coupled with gestures from the community that express their genuine forgiveness and reacceptance of the offender, are the key principles of the "reintegration" in reintegrative shaming. At the core of this process is the family model; the ceremony emphasizes the wrongfulness of the action and the goodness of the person's character, while bonds of respect are preserved among all members. Braithwaite argues strongly that internal crime controls are more effective in the long run than external crime controls. Therefore, the most effective way to reduce the risk of secondary delinquency is to rebuild the offender's moral conscience that abhors crime and to sustain the bonds of attachment between offenders and their law-abiding parents through reintegrative shaming.

There are two main hypotheses within Braithwaite's reintegrative shaming theory: (1) reintegrative shaming will decrease an individual's delinquency; and (2) the stigmatization of an individual (shaming an offender without offering any reintegration) in a community in which criminal subcultures are present increases the chances of future delinquency. Braithwaite argues that reintegrative shaming will always be useful, even in communities in which criminal subcultures are absent. The act of reintegration strengthens the individual's moral conscience against committing crime, and maintains the interpersonal bonds that make shaming most effective.

Two additional factors that Braithwaite argues may influence the reintegrative shaming process are interdependency and communitarianism. *Interdependency* refers to the interconnectedness among individuals, or their web of networks, that creates a dependency on others for things they need.[8] Informal sanctioning is most successful when the shame derived from failing to live up to the standards of others is important to the offender. A *communitarian* society is one in which the individual recognizes that his or her duty is foremost to the group, even over personal rights and needs.[9] The stronger the sense of dependency and duty that the individual feels toward the community, the greater the interpersonal cost that he or she will experience when committing delinquent acts. Reintegrative shaming, then, should be most effective in a community in which levels of interdependency and communitarianism are high.

Braithwaite argues that females, young children and mature adults, employed people, married people, and those committed to their long-term goals in education or their occupation will experience lower rates of delinquency, in part because of their strong interdependencies that command a great interpersonal cost following criminal activity.[10] Investment in long-term goals at school or work increases the mutual obligation and trust between student and teacher, or employee and boss, because they rely on each other to maintain their current position and achieve a future goal.[11] Braithwaite also predicts that as the urbanization and residential mobility of a community increase, reintegrative shaming will not be as effective and delinquency rates will increase. This is largely due to the lack of interpersonal bonds and sense of duty established among citizens.

RESTORATIVE JUSTICE

In 1996, Walgrave and Aertsen[12] wrote a reaction to a statement that Braithwaite made during a visit to Belgium and the Netherlands. Braithwaite was observed to have said that he would no longer use the term "reintegrative shaming," but rather adopt the phrase "restorative shaming." In the article, Walgrave and Aertsen consider this statement from a scholarly perspective, and argue that the two terms, reintegrative and restorative, are not interchangeable as Braithwaite posits. Instead, they argue that the real outcome of reintegrative shaming is the rehabilitation of the offender. Restorative shaming, on the other hand, uses shame to promote the making of restoration; this is done on the behalf of the victim (restoring their position as a right-bearing citizen in the community) as well as on the behalf of the community (restoring their value in the norm that was violated by the offender's behavior).

Although it may seem like Walgrave and Aertsen are splitting hairs, the use of the term "restorative" comes with a long history of disagreement. As Mika and Zehr note, there is no singular definition of restorative justice in the field.[13] They, as well as Braithwaite and Strang,[14] argue that there is general agreement among scholars on the main values or processes that underlie restorative justice, which can be characterized by two core concepts. The first concept involves the process of uniting stakeholders who must work together to right a wrong that they have suffered. The second concept characterizes restorative justice principally as a healing process that operates specifically in opposition to the state's punitive justice system. Van Ness and Strong[15] add a third component to the restorative justice process, which calls for the recognition that criminal offenses typically injure more people than is evident by the actual breaking of the criminal law. In a way, Van Ness and Strong's addition explicates the motivation or stimulus behind the other two principles.

As presented by Walgrave and Aertsen, the Leuven Experimental Program provides a useful real-life example from which to examine the connection between the key principles of reintegrative shaming and restorative justice. Beginning in 1993 and continuing for three years in Leuven, Belgium, this program included victim-offender mediations that occurred in conjunction with the offender's formal court hearings. Results of the meetings show a restorative effect experienced by the victim; this typically occurs following an angry confrontation with the offender about the offense, and the offender's expression of shame. This sense of shame on the part of the offender, in turn, may increase the offender's feeling of responsibility and genuine intent to make reparations with all of those injured by his or her behavior. In addition, Walgrave and Aertsen emphasize that the meetings often highlight the fact that the offense affects many more people than just the offender and victim, including children, partners, colleagues, and the larger community, and that these people should be involved in the proceedings as well.

This example showcases the great extent to which reintegrative shaming embodies the three main principles of restorative justice when applied in a real-life criminal justice setting. In their closing, Walgrave and Aertsen suggest that, contrary to Braithwaite's statement, the terms reintegration and restoration are not synonymous and interchangeable. Instead, it seems most appropriate to characterize reintegrative shaming and restorative justice as complementary concepts. The former uses personal relationships to restore harmonious community living, and the latter invokes a formalized response that ends in a constructive manner. It seems evident from the Leuven study example as well as the larger restorative justice literature that this assertion is correct. Restorative justice includes a wide spectrum of programs and ideologies that can vary on multiple dimensions. Although reintegrative shaming does indeed embody the main principles of restorative justice, it is only one small theory within the larger restorative justice concept.

RESEARCH ON REINTEGRATIVE SHAMING THEORY

There are several ways in which scholars can study the effectiveness of reintegrative shaming on the reduction of secondary delinquency. Of the available scientific methods, one of the most favored and rigorous is the empirical study. This method allows the researcher to collect or use previously collected data from both large-scale, national surveys and small-scale data sets, as well as from experiments. To date, the empirical studies researching reintegrative shaming have employed all three of these forms of methodology.

Early Empirical Tests

Contrary to the widespread implementation of the theory's principles, very few empirical studies have tested the veracity of the key hypotheses. They have also produced rather mixed and oftentimes discouraging results.

Makkai and Braithwaite[16] are the first researchers to conduct an empirical test of the hypotheses within Braithwaite's theory of reintegrative shaming. Using data on nursing home compliance with 31 federal standards of care, they test the degree of compliance between two observations in time in relation to the inspector's attitude during the first compliance visit. Makkai and Braithwaite find that, consistent with Braithwaite's hypotheses, the inspectors who stigmatized their clients had a 39 percent increase in noncompliance on the second visit, whereas the inspectors who used reintegrative shaming had a 39 percent reduction in noncompliance at on the second visit.

Two of the early empirical tests focus on the cultural aspect of reintegrative shaming. In one study, Zhang[17] examines whether there are differential applications and outcomes of reintegrative shaming between African American and Asian American cultures. In general, Zhang finds that although Asian American parents use shaming tactics consisting of verbal reprimands more frequently than do African American parents, both groups use disciplinary techniques consisting of nonverbal shaming, communitarian shaming, and reintegration. The second study, conducted by Vagg,[18] explores Hong Kong's Chinese culture to determine whether this Asian culture has a predisposition to interdependency and communitarianism that should work in favor of reintegrative shaming. Although Vagg finds that Hong Kong's culture embraces the two concepts, Chinese culture uses shaming to label and exclude individuals who do not conform to expectations, rather than to disapprove of the offender before reintegrating him or her into society.

Recent Empirical Tests

Three of the most recent empirical studies that test hypotheses within Braithwaite's theory use microlevel, or individual-level, survey data. The first such test, conducted by Hay,[19] finds that, consistent with the theory, interdependency significantly increases the use of both shaming and reintegration. As expected, reintegrative shaming significantly reduces secondary delinquency. Inconsistent with the theory's predictions, however, results indicate that stigmatization significantly reduces delinquency.

A second recent test of reintegrative shaming theory is Zhang and Zhang's[20] analysis of data from the National Youth Survey, a national probability sample of 1,725 adolescents between the ages of 11 and 17. Contrary to expectations, reintegrative shaming as a unit does not significantly reduce secondary offending. Using the same data set as Zhang and Zhang, McGivern[21] finds that reintegrative shaming significantly reduces secondary offending. The difference between the two studies can be explained partially by the fact that McGivern uses a different statistical method to create the reintegrative shaming variable, which appears to have better captured the sequential process.

The lack of consensus on the effectiveness of reintegrative shaming from the above empirical studies should not be completely discouraging. One of the main difficulties facing researchers who analyze reintegrative shaming is the lack of appropriate measures, or questions, within current survey instruments to fully capture the complex concept of reintegrative shaming. The subtle gestures of shame and reintegration are difficult to measure, and the two concepts often are measured separately and must be combined to produce the process of "reintegrative shaming." As the Zhang and Zhang and McGivern studies illustrate, even when using the same data set, a study's results can vary widely depending on how a researcher chooses to create the reintegrative shaming term.

The Canberra Reintegrative Shaming Experiments

One of the best examples of experimental research concerning reintegrative shaming and its effects on recidivism is The Reintegrative Shaming Experiments (RISE) project. The experiments took place in Canberra, Australia, for approximately five years, beginning in 1995, during which time nearly 1,300 offenders were randomly assigned to make a traditional court appearance or to attend a reintegrative shaming conference. Known as the "gold standard" in science, randomized experiments effectively remove the possibility of any factors beyond the "treatment" itself from influencing the results. Offenders charged with four different offense types were included in the experiment: drunk driving, juvenile property offenses, juvenile shoplifting offenses, and youth violent offenses.

Results of the RISE study appear mixed. Sherman, Strang, and Woods[22] report that both victims and offenders found the conferences to be procedurally more fair than traditional court procedures and that victims were more satisfied with conferences than traditional court procedures. Results also indicate that offending rates decreased for all offenders who were charged with a violent offense, regardless of whether they attended a conference or appeared in court. In support of Braithwaite's theory, however, results show that offenders who attended a conference had a 38 percent *lower* offending rate than those who appeared in court for a violent offense.

The study finds that the offenders charged with drunk driving who attended a conference had a small increase in offenses. Harris[23] examined this finding further to determine whether stigmatization may be the motivating factor behind the secondary delinquency of convicted drunk drivers. Findings from interviews with 720 drunk-driving offenders indicate that, although there is no difference in the degree to how stigmatized offenders felt during the two proceedings, offenders who attended the conferences found those involved to show more disapproval and reintegration than did the offenders who attended a traditional court system proceeding. Harris concludes that stigmatization does not appear to be the motivating factor in this case. Instead, he points to emerging literature in sociology and psychology[24] that argues what really matters is not how much shame the offender feels, but rather how the offenders manage their shame (i.e., whether they feel guilt for the action or blame it upon others).

In addition to the discouraging results found with the drunk-driving offenders, the RISE study indicates that offenders charged with property and shoplifting offenses experienced no difference in offending rates after the conference. In sum, the RISE study does not demonstrate an overwhelming success for reintegrative shaming theory. The findings do show, however, that reintegrative shaming conferences generally appear to be a promising alternative to the traditional court appearance, both in the case of victim satisfaction and for the reduction of juvenile violent offenses.

An Empirical Study of Bullying

Bullying is another specific youth predatory offense to which reintegrative shaming theory has been applied and has showed promising results through empirical tests. From the perspective of the theory, the act of bullying becomes a reoccurring problem when the bully is not shamed for his or her behavior and then sequentially is forgiven for his or her action. To reduce school bullying, then, the theory would posit that bullies must be confronted for their behavior, disciplined, and then reintegrated into the school so that they do not become stigmatized by their status of being a "bully." If a youth is treated in this manner and shows *shame acknowledgment* (responsibility and shame) for the behavior, the theory predicts that his or her conscience will be reaffirmed against bullying and future offending will be reduced greatly. If the bully is left alone without invoking any shame acknowledgment for the behavior, however, the theory predicts that the offender will instead blame others for his or her action, and the master status of "bully" will overtake the youth's identity, compelling him or her to continue to bully others.

To empirically test the effects of reintegrative shaming on the reduction of school bullying, Ahmed and Braithwaite[25] surveyed 1,875 males and females in the 7th through 10th grades in the nonwestern country of Bangladesh. They investigated the role of three general aspects of reintegrative shaming theory in the reduction of school bullying: shaming, forgiveness, and shame acknowledgment.

Results from the study show support for the role that reintegrative shaming plays in the reduction of school bullying. Findings indicate that both reintegrative shaming and forgiveness at home reduce children's frequency of self-initiated bullying at school. In addition, children who report using a restorative shame acknowledgment approach (feel shame, accept responsibility, and make amends for committing a hypothetical bullying act) are less likely to report self-initiated bullying. Conversely, a child who reports *shame displacement* (placing blame and anger on others) is more likely to report self-initiated bullying behavior at school.

Ahmed and Braithwaite note that forgiveness seems to play a much greater role in the reduction of school bullying than previously presumed; in fact, it has a greater effect on bullying than either reintegrative shaming or stigmatization. These findings emphasize the powerful role that reintegrative shaming can play in the reduction of bullying, as well as the need for further exploration of the role that forgiveness plays within the reintegrative shaming process.

LEGAL APPLICATIONS OF REINTEGRATIVE SHAMING THEORY

The main principles of reintegrative shaming are common within the formal legal system of several countries in the form of family conferences. The section below highlights specific examples of these programs as they exist today in China, England and Wales, and Singapore. Each case study reflects the main principles of shaming and forgiveness, either through a direct and intentional application of Braithwaite's theory, or as applied through an inadvertent theoretical intersection.

The first family conference model to have originated from Braithwaite's reintegrative shaming theory, and perhaps the prototypical example, is commonly referred to as the Wagga Wagga Model. Developed in

New South Wales, Australia, in 1989,[26] this model of restorative justice conference has been exported not only to other locations in Australia, such as Canberra and Sydney, but also to other countries, including the United States, the United Kingdom, Canada, and Northern Ireland. The Wagga Wagga Model may be considered police-based because the program originally relied on the police to determine whether an offender would be recommended for attendance at a conference. In some cases, such as in New South Wales, this responsibility has been transferred to the Office of Juvenile Justice to develop a greater sense of independence from government authority. In most cases, the proceedings are purposely well scripted to ensure that both shaming and forgiveness processes take place, even when facilitated by untrained mediators.

Bang Jiao in China

Years before the Wagga Wagga Model of family conferencing was developed from Braithwaite's formal theory of reintegrative shaming, the main components of the theory were being practiced as *bang jiao* in China's formal and informal justice systems. This phrase embodies the Chinese practice of preventing crime through the shaming and reintegration of offenders, and has been broken apart and translated by Lu to mean "help" and "education and admonition," respectively.[27] In general, bang jiao refers to the alliance of families, neighbors, communities, and state officials who work to harmoniously reinstate offenders into society. There are six main types of bang jiao, which vary from one another in three different aspects: the degree to which they are run by government or private organizations; their objective; and, their strategies.

The bang jiao process begins with shaming, which can occur through informal gossip networks in the family and neighborhood, as well as through a formal process such as a neighborhood bang jiao conference. Lu describes a young boy in Shanghai who was caught shoplifting and had to attend a bang jiao; his parents, neighbors, a teacher, and a police officer were among those who attended the conference. The communitarian nature of Chinese society places the family in a delicate situation at a bang jiao. Lu argues that although the offender's family must condemn the behavior and side with their community, they, too, are an object of shame because the offender's behavior reflects poorly on them as a family unit. In the case of the boy who shoplifted, this difficult situation was demonstrated by the mother who blamed herself for his behavior and apologized to the community.

After the offender has expressed genuine regret for his or her action at the bang jiao, the reintegration process begins. A contract is produced in the form of a "bang jiao responsibility agreement," which is signed by the offender and the conference leaders and affirms that the bang jiao team will help the offender successfully assimilate back into society. This process can include performing decertification ceremonies that will remove the offender's deviant status, finding the offender a job or enrolling him or her in school, or engaging the offender in community service acts that will increase his or her worth in other citizens' eyes.

Consistent with Braithwaite's theoretical position, Lu argues that juvenile offenders are the group most likely to experience bang jiao, but that the process is not well-suited for habitual offenders or those who have few communal ties. Bang jiao seems to work, at least according to Lu's research on selected neighborhoods in Shanghai, China. In the first of two Shanghai neighborhoods that Lu studied, he found that only two individuals who were on the bang jiao list reoffended (broke a criminal law) in the following three years. In the second of the two neighborhoods, no individuals had reoffended during that same time frame. Although this study is promising, Chinese culture is much more communitarian than most societies in the Western hemisphere. Lu points out that Chinese urban communities like Shanghai are designed to facilitate interaction and ties among residents. In the United States, the closest situation to this may be the simulated village-living developments springing up in many urban areas, which group shops, restaurants, and housing into one condensed subdivision.

Youth Offender Programs in England and Wales

The Youth Offender Panel in England and Wales provides a second example of a successful family conference program based on the principles of reintegrative shaming. Almost a decade ago, the juvenile justice system in England and Wales experienced major reforms following the election of Tony Blair to the position of Prime Minister in 1998. Running on a "get-tough-on-crime" platform, Blair's New Labour government rejected many of the policies that had been in place during the previous decade and a half. Under the preceding Conservative government, the juvenile justice system had been characterized by a cautioning policy that was largely driven at the local level. Rather than arrest juvenile offenders, police officers had issued cautions in an attempt to reduce future offending. The election came on the heels of the publication of a major report entitled *Misspent Youth*, which found that the cautions became less effective over time with repeat offenders, and that the juvenile justice system as a whole was inefficient and expensive. After gaining office, the Labour Party introduced sweeping reforms to the juvenile justice system, as evidenced by the Crime and Disorder Act 1998 and the Youth Justice and Criminal Evidence Act 1999. Together, the new legislation was meant to invoke three main principles of restorative justice: (1) reparation on the part of the offender for their misdeed, (2) reintegration of the offender into the law-abiding community, and (3) creation of a sense of responsibility in the offender and the parent to prevent future offending.[28]

Under the Youth Justice and Criminal Evidence Act 1999, almost all youth offenders who pled guilty were mandated to participate in a Youth Offender Panel (YOP). Designed in part from the experiences of the Scottish Children's Hearings system and victim-offender mediations in

England and Wales, the YOP borrowed heavily from Braithwaite's theory of reintegrative shaming and the family group counseling that it inspired in Australia and New Zealand.[29] In keeping with Braithwaite's emphasis on community participation, the panel includes at least two members from the community, who undergo a minimum of 84 hours of introductory, preservice, and support training, and at least one Youth Offending Team member. If the offender is 15 years of age or younger, at least one parent or guardian is required to attend the meeting, which must be held within 15 days of the court hearing. In addition, the victim or a supporter of the victim, a supporter of the offender, and any significant figure in the offender's life who has a positive influence may also attend the meetings.

The offender's reintegration into the law-abiding community begins formally with the drawing up of a contract that outlines specific reparations that must be made for the offense. In addition, any actions that will be taken to address the root cause of the offender's behavior are included in the contract. Both the offender and a panel member sign the contract; the victim does not.

Crawford[30] outlines several potential difficulties that may be experienced in the implementation of the YOP. For example, every offender referred to a YOP averages between three and four meetings, which results in an increased, and potentially, burdensome caseload for all members involved, as well as increased court costs. There is some concern that offenders may plead guilty to ensure referral to a YOP in the anticipation that it will result in a lesser punishment. Conversely, the potential is just as great that other offenders may not plead guilty to avoid referral to a panel meeting. The victim's lack of signature on the contract greatly reduces their participation in the process, which may potentially undermine their interests. These criticisms aside, however, pilot evaluations of the 2000 YOP released in a 2002 report show that, "the pilots successfully accomplished the implementation of referral orders and youth offender panels."[31] In addition,

> Though initially slightly unsure of what to expect, the vast majority of offenders and their parents say that they feel they are treated with respect at youth offender panels and that the panel members treat them fairly. The panel process and outcomes are viewed as satisfying significant levels of procedural, restorative and substantive justice.[32]

Although there may be some criticisms of the program, it appears to have launched successfully with the application of Braithwaite's reintegrative shaming principles.

Family Conferences in Singapore

The juvenile court in Singapore provides a third and excellent example of the formal application of the principles of reintegrative shaming. Within their legal system, juvenile court is responsible for offenders who are at least 7 years old but no older than 15 years of age.[33] Once the child or young person has been found guilty within this courtroom, they are individually assessed to determine their personal needs and any future risk they may pose to society, as well as their potential for rehabilitation. A final report compiling information from the offender's background, family life, school records, employment history, and psychological evaluations, as well as the severity of the offense, is used by the court to determine the juvenile's sentence. In addition to a variety of possible sentences, a juvenile may also be ordered to attend a Family Conference, which is based on Braithwaite's reintegrative shaming principles.

Established in 1996 in the Singapore juvenile court system, Family Conferences provide an excellent forum for an in-depth analysis of issues that the formal court hearing does not have the time to explore. For example, the Family Conference can provide a forum for the exploration of the juvenile's rehabilitative potential, a proceeding that would cost an overloaded court system too much time and too many resources. Set in a meeting room adjacent to the juvenile court, the Family Conference is facilitated by a trained counselor or psychologist from the Family and Juvenile Justice Center. It is mandatory that the offender and his or her family and friends, as well as any other significant figures in his or her life, attend the Family Conference. Although not required, the victim and the victim's parents often choose to attend the proceedings as well.

In accordance with the main principles of Braithwaite's reintegrative shaming, the facilitator guides the proceedings through a sequence of shame and forgiveness. First, each person in attendance shares their view of the offense and its impact on their life. These types of admissions are meant to create awareness in the offender of the harm he or she has caused his or her victim, friends, family, and community, and to elicit feelings of shame and guilt for the offending behavior. The facilitator may directly reprimand the offender for his or her actions and formally caution him or her not to commit the offense again. This shaming process is meant to lead the offender toward making an honest apology for his or her actions, showing remorse for his or her behavior, and to create the desire for the offender to make true reconciliation with everyone involved, including family and friends. In addition, this process is meant to help transform the offender into a law-abiding citizen by strengthening his or her own conscience against delinquency. To further encourage true reconciliation and positive involvement between the offender and his or her victim and the community, the offender may be sentenced to issue a formal apology to the victim, pay the victim any financial debt incurred by the offense, or perform community service.

At this time, the Family Conference in Singapore appears to be a success. Of the 298 offenders who participated in Family Conferences between July 1994 and December 2002, only 11 individuals (4 percent) have committed another offense.[34] The success of the Family Conference seems to lie in its flexible structure; although each conference follows a similar path of events, the content of the meeting is tailored to each individual case. This format gives the facilitator the leeway to explore comments, topics, and situations that may hold the key to understanding the precipitants of the offender's behavior. Underlying family tensions and broken relationships that may go unnoticed in a formal court proceeding are often revealed and discussed during a Family Conference. Feigned indifference by the offender may be a strong facade built to hide sadness and anger. The facilitator of a Family Conference is in a unique position to delve into these issues and help transform the situations from where the behavior originated, hopefully reducing the likelihood that the juvenile will reoffend.

THE SINGULAR USE OF SHAME

The above sections highlight the degree to which reintegrative shaming has been embraced by the academic community and the legal systems of many countries since its inception in 1989. It is incorrect to assume, however, that every program or law that uses shame is a form of reintegrative shaming. As Braithwaite painstakingly emphasizes, shaming must be followed by forgiveness or reintegration to be a positive and useful form of social control. As labeling theorists have argued, shaming alone often results in stigmatization, humiliation, and further offending. Unfortunately, a multitude of examples from the past several years, particularly in the United States, highlight the use of shame alone.

The most familiar use of shame today in the American legal system is with "johns" who have been arrested or convicted for patronizing or soliciting prostitution. In Oakland, California, "Operation Shame" has launched 10- by 22-foot billboards showing blurred images of convicted offenders with the phrase "How Much Clearer Can We Make It?"[35] The Chicago Police Department posts photos of arrested and convicted johns on their Web site, as do the Metropolitan Nashville Police Department and the City and County of Denver. The city of Lakewood, Washington, is considering the use of billboards along Interstate 5, but it is concerned about the legalities involved with publicly humiliating unconvicted johns.[36]

Shame-driven programs have also developed rapidly around the problem of drunk driving. In 2003, Arizona lawmakers considered a bill that would force convicted DUI (driving under the influence) offenders to purchase an advertisement listing their name and offense in their local newspaper.[37] The same year, convicted drunk drivers in Florida were mandated to paste a bumper sticker on their vehicle that asks, "How is my driving?" followed by a toll-free number and the phrase, "The Judge wants to know!"[38] Beginning on January 1, 2006, first-time convicted DUI offenders in Tennessee face the new penalty of roadside cleanup while wearing orange vests decorated with the phrase, "I am a Drunk Driver."[39]

From the perspective of reintegrative shaming theory, several dangers are associated with the above forms of shaming. Primarily, no allowances are made to reintegrate the offender into society. The shaming ceremonies are obvious and long lasting in most cases, occurring with the placing of the bumper sticker on the back of the offender's car or the offender's photo on a billboard. However, there are no ceremonies to remove the billboard or bumper sticker and renounce the offender's "deviant" status. If his or her penalty is noted by friends, family, colleagues, and neighbors, the risk of stigmatization is quite great. Conversely, if no one recognizes the offender from his blurred photograph or on the roadside wearing an orange vest, the shaming will only be accomplished by the impersonal and anonymous "state." Because the offender does not have a meaningful and personal relationship with the government, he or she most likely will not feel any of the intended shame, making the entire process null and void. Depending on the specific situation, then, these shaming programs risk changing the offender's master status into "deviant" or, at the least, wasting valuable taxpayer dollars.

THE FUTURE OF REINTEGRATIVE SHAMING

The search for meaningful alternatives to the incarceration of juvenile offenders is a growing trend in the United States and around the world. Reintegrative shaming theory provides the basis for a viable alternative that is appealing on many levels. It offers a community the opportunity to exhibit their great displeasure for the offender's behavior through shaming, while the reintegration process reassures the cessation of future criminal activity without imprisonment. Reintegrative shaming does appear to work successfully in some juvenile justice settings as well as in some empirical tests. This optimism, however, must be couched with caution until survey instruments are available that allow researchers to fully capture and measure the complexity of reintegrative shaming, including the important factors of interdependency and communitarianism. In the meantime, it is important to be aware of the danger posed by restorative justice programs that use only shame, and to educate others about the great healing possibility that reintegrative shaming theory offers.

NOTES

1. Braithwaite, 1989.
2. Braithwaite, 1997; Braithwaite & Mugford, 1994; Crawford, 2003; McCarney, 2003.
3. Braithwaite, 1989, p. 38.
4. Braithwaite, 1989, p. 56.
5. Braithwaite, 1989, p. 55.
6. Braithwaite, 1989, p. 58.
7. Braithwaite, 1989, p. 66.
8. Braithwaite, 1989, p. 100.
9. Braithwaite, 1989, p. 85.
10. Braithwaite, 1989, pp. 90–92.
11. Braithwaite, 1989, p. 90.
12. Walgrave & Aertsen, 1996.
13. Mika & Zehr, 2003.
14. Braithwaite & Strang, 2001.

15. Van Ness & Strong, 1997.
16. Makkai & Braithwaite, 1994.
17. Zhang, 1995.
18. Vagg, 1998.
19. Hay, 2001.
20. Zhang & Zhang, 2004.
21. McGivern, 2005
22. Sherman, Strang, & Woods, 2000.
23. Harris, 2006.
24. See Ahmed, 2001; Harris 2003.
25. Ahmed & Braithwaite, 2005.
26. McCarney, 2003.
27. Lu, 1999.
28. Crawford, 2003.
29. Crawford, 2003.
30. Crawford, 2003.
31. Newburn et al., 2002.
32. Newburn et al., 2002.
33. Mesenas & Min, 2003.
34. Ozawa, 2003.
35. Associated Press, June 4, 2005.
36. Voelpel, 2005.
37. Associated Press, October 10, 2003.
38. Associated Press, September 24, 2003.
39. Associated Press, December 31, 2005.

REFERENCES

Ahmed, E. (2001). Part III. Shame management: Regulating bullying. In E. Ahmed, N. Harris, J. Braithwaite, & V. Braithwaite (Eds.), *Shame management through reintegration* (pp. 209–311). Cambridge: Cambridge University Press.

Ahmed, E., & Braithwaite, J. (2005). Forgiveness, shaming, shame and bullying. *The Australian & New Zealand Journal of Criminology, 38*(3), 298–323.

Associated Press. (2003, September 24). *Bumper stickers ordered for drunk drivers.* DUI.com, September 24. Retrieved July 31, 2006, from www.dui.com/drunk_driving_research/dui_bumper_stickers.html.

Associated Press. (2003, October 10). *Arizona bill would publish names of DUI offenders.* Join Together.org, October 10. Retrieved July 31, 2006, from www.jointogether.org/news/headlines/inthenews/2003/ariz-bill-would-publish-names.html.

Associated Press. (2005, June 4). Oakland launches public "shaming campaign." Free Republic.com, June 4. Retrieved July 31, 2006, from www.freerepublic.com/focus/f-news/1416390/posts.

Associated Press. (2005, December 31). Tennessee enlists shame to fight drunken driving. Free New Mexican.com, December 31. Retrieved July 31, 2006, from www.freenewmexican.com/news/37101.html.

Braithwaite, J. (1989). *Crime, shame and reintegration.* New York: Cambridge University Press.

Braithwaite, J. (1997). Conferencing and plurality; reply to Bragg. *British Journal of Criminology, 37*, 502–505.

Braithwaite, J., & Mugford, S. (1994). Conditions of successful reintegration ceremonies: Dealing with juvenile offenders. *British Journal of Criminology, 34,* 139–171.

Braithwaite, J., & Strang, H. (2001). Introduction: Restorative justice and civil society. In H. Strang & J. Braithwaite (Eds.), *Restorative justice and civil society* (pp. 1–13). Cambridge, UK: Cambridge University Press.

Crawford, A. (2003). The prospects for restorative youth justice in England and Wales: A tale of two acts. In K. McEvoy & T. Newburn (Eds.), *Criminology, conflict resolution and restorative justice* (pp. 171–207). New York: Palgrave Macmillan.

Harris, N. (2003). Reassessing the dimensionality of the moral emotions. *British Journal of Psychology, 94*(4), 457–473.

Harris, N. (2006). Reintegrative shaming, shame, and criminal justice. *Journal of Social Issues, 62,* 327–346.

Hay, C. (2001). An exploratory test of Braithwaite's reintegrative shaming theory. *Journal of Research in Crime and Delinquency, 38,* 132–153.

Lu, H. (1999). Bang jiao and reintegrative shaming in China's urban neighborhoods. *International Journal of Comparative and Applied Criminal Justice, 23*(1), 115–125.

Makkai, T., & Braithwaite, J. (1994). Reintegrative shaming and compliance with regulatory standards. *Criminology, 32,* 361–386.

McCarney, W. (2003). Restorative justice: International approaches. In R. Magnus, L. H. Min, M. L. Mesenas, & V. Thean (Eds.), *Rebuilding lives, restoring relationships: Juvenile justice and the community* (pp. 304–348). Singapore: Eastern Universities Press.

McGivern, J. L. (2005). *A test of reintegrative shaming theory and its effects on juvenile delinquency.* M.A. thesis, Department of Sociology, University of Washington, Seattle, WA.

Mesenas, M. L., & Min, L. H. (2003). The juvenile court of Singapore. In R. Magnus, L. H. Min, M. L. Mesenas, & V. Thean (Eds.), *Rebuilding lives, restoring relationships: Juvenile justice and the community* (pp. 3–44). Singapore: Eastern Universities Press.

Mika, H., & Zehr, H. (2003). A restorative framework for community justice practice. In K. McEvoy & T. Newburn (Eds.), *Criminology, conflict resolution and restorative justice* (pp. 135–152). New York: Palgrave Macmillan.

Newburn, T., Crawford, A., Earle, R., Goldie, S., Hale, C., Masters, G., Netten, A., Saunders, R., Sharpe, K., & Uglow, S. (2002). *The introduction of referral orders into the youth justice system.* Home Office Research Study 242. London, UK: Home Office.

Ozawa, J. P. (2003). The family and juvenile justice centre. In R. Magnus, L. H. Min, M. L. Mesenas, & V. Thean (Eds.), *Rebuilding lives, restoring relationships: Juvenile justice and the community* (pp. 45–72). Singapore: Eastern Universities Press.

Sherman, L., Strang, H., & Woods, D. (2000). *Recidivism patterns in the Canberra reintegrative shaming experiments* (RISE). Canberra, AU. Retrieved August 1, 2006, from www.aic.gov.au/rjustice/rise/recidivism/index.html.

Vagg, J. (1998). Delinquency and shaming: Data from Hong Kong. *British Journal of Criminology, 38,* 247–264.

Van Ness, D. W., & Strong, K. H. (1997). *Restoring justice.* Cincinnati, OH: Anderson.

Voelpel, D. (2005, September 11). Dan Voelpel column. *The News Tribune.*

Walgrave, L., & Aertsen, I. (1996). Reintegrative shaming and restorative justice: Interchangeable, complementary or different? *European Journal on Criminal Policy and Research, 4*(4), 67–85.

Zhang, L., & Zhang, S. X. (2004). Reintegrative shaming and predatory delinquency. *Journal of Research in Crime and Delinquency, 41*(4), 433–453.

Zhang, S. X. (1995). Measuring shame in an ethnic context. *British Journal of Criminology, 35*, 248–262.

CHAPTER 5

Making Sense of Community Supervision: Diversion and Probation in Postmodern Juvenile Justice

Gordon Bazemore and Leslie A. Leip

Changes in juvenile justice in the 1990s were by far more comprehensive than all previous reforms in the 100-year history of the juvenile court combined. A trend already being referred to early in that decade as the "new juvenile justice"[1] soon began an undeniable movement toward what were to become two fundamental transformations: (1) a new explicit emphasis on punishment in juvenile justice and (2) a dramatic shift toward a new formality and determinacy in juvenile justice decision making.[2] The former emphasis was apparent in the explicit changes in juvenile justice codes in many states that incorporated punishment as a legitimate goal, in place of or in addition to the focus on the "best interest" of the child. Formalization focused attention on the *offense* rather than the *offender* and was implemented first through determinate sentencing for juveniles in some states and was then followed up by opening court hearings and juvenile records to the public, passage of victim rights statutes in juvenile courts, enhanced security in youth correctional programs, and other related reforms.[3] By the end of the decade, these important changes were almost eclipsed by an even bigger transformation, best characterized by what Torbet and colleagues described as a dramatic loss in the jurisdiction of the juvenile court over more serious offenders.[4]

By making it possible for large categories of young offenders to be more easily transferred to the criminal court and criminal justice system, this loss not only reinforced the punishment and formalization emphasis, but also eroded or erased once-strong boundaries between criminal and juvenile court, which brought even greater challenges to the rationale for a separate juvenile justice system. The new transfer policies, in particular, resulted in an appropriate response of alarm from youth advocates, policy makers, and researchers[5] that appropriately and necessarily focused national policy and research on the plight of youth and the need to preserve the jurisdiction of the court. This public response was motivated by an appropriate concern for youths who were vulnerable to receiving "adult time" in prison at a very young age. Neglected in this important emphasis on more serious offenders being transferred out of the system, however, have been the two primary components of community supervision: probation and diversion. These components seem to be most capable of preventing escalation to eligibility for incarceration in either juvenile or adult secure facilities.

Once viewed as highly informal, second-chance options, probation and diversion may play different roles in the new juvenile justice context of what generally has become a more formal, punishment-oriented system. In this chapter, we summarize selected findings from a recent formative evaluation of a Targeted Community Action Plan in an urban judicial circuit (i.e., Circuit 17 in Broward County, Florida). This plan provides an important case study of community supervision in the new juvenile justice system, which is managed in part by a state Department of Juvenile Justice. Local key decision makers (e.g., prosecutors) make use of formal legalistic criteria not only in the choice of whether to transfer youth to adult court, but also in the choice of diversion or court disposition (most often to probation). Our general concern is on the role and function of the essential community-based components of the juvenile justice system and the relationship between diversion and probation in the context of more formal, determinate, and punitive juvenile justice. Regarding this relationship, our primary focus is on the relative intensity of supervision and services provided by each component in the context of a "continuum" or progressive response to delinquency.

Following a discussion of diversion and probation and the idea of a continuum in juvenile justice, we present descriptive data from a formative study on diversion program failures. We review reasons for these failures, which suggest that this continuum may be out of alignment, and raise concerns about the intensity of diversion relative to probation and the implications of this for escalation of minor offenders in more restrictive placements. Given the ambiguity facing these community supervision functions in the new juvenile justice system nationally, we conclude with a community supervision research agenda focused on assessing the following: (1) the impact of diversion and probation on reoffending for similar low- to moderate-level offenders; (2) the role of intensity of services and supervision and of specific program models and components as key explanations for differences in impact; and (3) the perception of key practitioners and decision makers about the role of both probation and diversion and their adaptations to ambiguity in what continues to function as a "loosely coupled" juvenile justice system.[6]

DIVERSION AND PROBATION IN JUVENILE JUSTICE: COMMUNITY SUPERVISION PAST AND PRESENT

Diversion, as an informal method of response to youth delinquency that does not result in a formal court record, is widely viewed as the most common response to delinquent behavior in the United States. Although there is no systematic method for counting the number of arrested youth actually sent to diversion programs, conservative estimates provided by the National Center for Juvenile Justice suggest that about 42 percent of delinquency referrals to courts in 2002 were not petitioned. About 60 percent of these cases generally are handled informally, or essentially diverted,[7] and this estimate does not include those youth informally cautioned and released by police.

Probation, the most common formal response to youth crime in the country, has in recent years accounted for some 63 percent of all court dispositions for adjudicated cases nationally.[8] To fully understand the policy issues associated with diversion and probation, both need to be examined first in the national context.

Diversion in the National Context: Intervention Assumptions and Policy Issues

Diversion policy emerged in the late 1960s as a response to youth crime and trouble based on a strong critique of the juvenile court.[9] Throughout the 1970s, diversion policy and practice seemed to be informed by a theory that assumed that diversion would "work" not because it provided a new form of intervention that would rehabilitate offenders, but because it reduced the harm of exposure to the *criminogenic influences of the justice process* itself.[10] In contrast to this focus on diversion as a *process* for removing large groups of youth from the court's influence, by the late 1970s, diversion had become defined as a *program* aimed primarily at preventing minor delinquents and status offenders from reoffending.[11] Although many critics argued that failure to complete these programs and subsequent reoffending brought more youth into the system through a "net-widening" process,[12] others appeared to simply change the measure of success in diversion practice. That is, for those who viewed diversion as a kind of prevention or rehabilitation *program*, the new standard was no longer to determine the effectiveness of the process in protecting youth from the negative influence of the court, or reducing penetration into the juvenile justice system, but rather to ensure that programs were effective in identifying and addressing the perceived needs and risks of young people and in reducing rates of reoffending.[13]

Diversion was once welcomed as a new innovation in juvenile justice, then widely evaluated as a process to remove youth from the influence of the juvenile justice system, and finally criticized on the basis of that research for net-widening, stigmatization, and coercion.[14] In recent years, its impact has been evaluated primarily at the program rather than system level,[15] and its role in community supervision as a true alternative to court processing has seldom been examined. The mission of diversion appears to have grown increasingly unclear, but today diversion programs appear to be a permanent, generally unquestioned, part of the urban juvenile justice landscape. As this has occurred, an interventionist, programmatic policy focus[16] has become institutionalized around a practice Potter and Kakar refer to as a "diversion to service"[17] rather than a process to reduce intervention. Although many practitioners seem to retain a real focus on helping youths avoid a formal court record,[18] there appears to be little, if any, of the original concern about possible negative effects of diversion itself. Indeed, proponents of "best practice" models seem generally unconcerned with the practice of displacing the use of courts or probation, as a primary goal, and instead have focused on preventing new offenses. Overall, in the context of more harmful and explicitly punitive developments in the new juvenile justice system (e.g., a dramatic increase in the number of youth transferred to the criminal justice system), an assumption of benevolence regarding the diversion option appears to have shielded it from the critical scrutiny it received in past decades.[19]

Probation in the National Context: Intervention Assumptions and Policy Issues

Now a formal court disposition, probation was originally intended as an informal second-chance alternative to more restrictive and punitive responses.[20] Today, as Torbet and his colleagues note, probation is clearly the "workhorse" of the juvenile justice system and is the most common formal response to delinquent behavior.[21] Nationally, probation is a low-cost disposition, especially when compared with incarceration. Although probation reoffense rates can be high, they are generally better than those observed in postincarceration recidivism studies.[22]

Probation, however, is also one of the most widely criticized components of juvenile justice practice. In the public mind, probation is often viewed as a "slap on the wrist." More realistically, despite innovation in specialized programs and the commitment and creativity of some probation officers in difficult situations,[23] the dominant probation model remains an essentially reactive, rule-driven, offender-monitoring approach that is focused on enforcing court orders and monitoring contact standards. As an intervention often lacking in an outcome focus,[24] probation is perceived by most of the public and many criminal justice professionals as deficient in its focus on accountability and responsibility for one's actions and grounded in passive requirements.[25]

As a result, best practice discussion often seems to completely bypass probation as an intervention. Rather, these discussions have focused on probation officer referrals to programs that might provide specialized treatment intervention and additional supervision at the community level.[26] Despite this focus, and the ongoing concern with institutionalizing risk and need assessments, individual casework and monitoring court-ordered conditions of supervision remain the dominant intervention modalities guiding probation. However, philosophical shifts in the direction of more punitive law enforcement, rather than a social work orientation, have clearly had an impact on case management.[27] Little research has been conducted on the effectiveness of standard juvenile probation, and few if any studies have compared the impact of probation to diversion as a presumably less formal response.

Given these problems and controversies in diversion and probation, how might these community supervision options fit together? Questions remain about the role and function of each of these community supervision components, but conceptual models are available to link these components in a logical way.

A Continuum of Supervision and Services

One of the most influential strategies for reform during the decade of the 1990s emphasized the importance of developing a range of community-based sanctions and services. Notably, the Office of Juvenile Justice and Delinquency Prevention (OJJDP) proposed a "comprehensive strategy" that sought to strengthen the traditional prevention and treatment focus of the court within an overall framework that also addressed concerns with enhancing public safety and accountability.[28] Advocates of this comprehensive strategy proposed to do so largely through a continuum of graduated supervision restrictions coupled with increasing intensity of services.

The continuum featured a primary focus on prevention that targeted all youth for positive support and developmental opportunities,[29] and a second level of prevention focused on at-risk youth. At the next level, "immediate interventions," various juvenile justice system responses to delinquent behavior generally include diversion or informal alternative-to-court programs.[30] This level is followed by a graduated progression to intermediate sanctions, such as probation and day treatment programs, that focus generally on community supervision. Juveniles involved in more serious and chronic offending may then move to a level of more intensive supervision in locked community-based facilities and eventually to training schools followed by aftercare.

Based on the premise that an adjustment is needed in the intensity of services and restrictions or sanctions as the chronicity and seriousness of delinquency increases, the strategy assumes that youth who escalate to the higher level of severity in offense patterns are at a greater risk of committing new or more serious violations and, therefore, should receive more restrictions and services. Such a graduated response is intuitively logical and appears to offer an important guide for administrators and policy makers who wish to ensure that resources are allocated in a rational way at various levels of intensity of intervention. The model also seems to promote fairness and justice objectives by giving logical priority to intervention at the community level and to the "least intrusive" services and sanctions needed in the context of public safety objectives.

Although we know of no direct empirical evidence that achieving the right mix and application of graduated responses will necessarily lead to reductions in offending or reoffending, graduated responses based on risk and need seem preferable—at *least* on grounds of justice and fairness—to the opposite state of affairs in which more serious or chronic offenders receive the least intensive levels of intervention. Moreover, one premise of the model that has been empirically validated is that decision makers should *reduce intervention* for those juveniles at the *lowest risk levels.*[31] Arguments in favor of a continuum of services and supervision or sanctions at the local level can be summarized as follows:

- Services and sanctions should be geared to risk and need.
- Overconsequencing and excessive supervision may lead to reoffending.
- Too little supervision or services may lead to reoffending.
- Fairness and justice values should place limits on restrictions.

Limitations in this conceptualization can be found in its translation to the real world of juvenile justice supervision and assessment in most communities. In this loosely coupled system context, there are multiple decision-making processes and multiple decision makers. These professionals may function autonomously in a highly professional manner, while at the same time working at cross-purposes informed by different professional priorities. For example, the desires to maximize speed in processing cases, to assess risk and need, and to ensure fairness and equity in decision making may compete with each other. By way of illustration, it is entirely possible, as we found in the current study, to have intake staff completing extensive need and risk assessments at a well-funded assessment center, while prosecutors made decisions about whether to file formal charges or recommend diversion—and make referrals to specific diversion programs—without using any of this information.[32] In addition to this lack of coordination and formal professional commitments, specific impediments to developing a useful continuum of services and supervision can be summarized as follows:

- Legal barriers to decision making based primarily on risk and need criteria
- Fairness and equity issues
- Lack of variation in program models and intensity sufficient to accommodate risk-based referral
- Practical referral considerations (e.g., location of diversion programs) and excessive focus on secure programs and deep-end intervention

Levels of Community Supervision

Where do probation and diversion fit into a rational progressive graduated continuum response as prescribed in the comprehensive strategy of supervision and services? Aside from the critical fact that probation requires a formal conviction order and gives the probationer a formal conviction record, outside observers and many within juvenile justice systems may not recognize any fundamental difference in supervision or service intensity between formal probation and "informal" diversion.[33] Although the step from community-based intervention to secure facilities is straightforward, the more nuanced movement from less to more intensive nonresidential, community-based restrictions and services is more difficult to implement or even conceptualize. For purposes of the discussion of the continuum of community-based intervention, an apparent lack of understanding regarding the intensity and content of intervention provided by these two community-based options raises questions about the validity of decision-making criteria for referral to these options and the anticipated results. For example, should decision makers not expect more supervision, services, and punishment or restrictions for probation, and less for diversion? Is the decision to formally file charges on a case, rather than divert, in the hopes of ensuring a more restrictive sanction, misguided if probation is indeed *less* restrictive than diversion? From a risk-focused intervention perspective, the lack of variation in the intensity of services and supervision between diversion and probation similarly calls into question the value and meaning of both the formal and informal responses. From the most practical policy perspective, minor to moderate-level offenders commonly placed on probation could be effectively referred to diversion programs by examining a variety of outcomes for similar offenders receiving each type of response.

It seems likely that uninformed decision making based on a lack of understanding of diversion and probation, as well as the implied inappropriateness or weakness of the response to delinquent youth at these early stages, may create problems later in other parts of the system. For example, as we will illustrate in the following section, disproportionate minority confinement and a general overuse of secure confinement options[34] may be a result of high rates of failure for minority youth inappropriately placed on probation (versus diversion), or it simply may be a result of the decision maker's lack of confidence in either community-based option.

DIVERSION AND PROBATION IN SOUTH FLORIDA: A CASE STUDY

Florida is in many ways a "bell-weather state" for an examination of community supervision and the continuum of supervision and service in the new juvenile justice landscape. With an independent judiciary, a strong decision-making role for prosecutors (state attorneys), and a state-centered Department of Juvenile Justice (DJJ) responsible for operating probation, detention, and secure residential placements at several levels, the state in the past decade has been at the forefront of a national trend toward developing legislative mandates that have increasingly removed discretionary and informal decision-making authority from judges and probation.[35] Consistent with this and the expanded authority granted to prosecution in many states,[36] Florida's state attorneys have discretion over the decision to remove a youth 14 years or older charged with delinquent acts from the juvenile court's jurisdiction to the adult system through direct file procedures. Prosecutors have ultimate responsibility for the decision to divert youth or proceed with a formal court filing that most often results in a probation disposition. The judiciary is the decision maker for determining formal court sanctions for probation dispositions via the court order, while probation supervision is a statewide DJJ responsibility.

Diversion in Florida

Florida has a long tradition of support for diversion practices and was a leader in the diversion movement and diversion programming in the 1980s.[37] Since the 1970s, Florida has been a national leader in implementing the OJJDP Act deinstitutionalizing status offenders and jail removal mandates, and more than many other states, it has resisted pressure to retain jurisdiction of status offenders.[38] Especially since the Florida Juvenile Justice Reform Act of 1990, Florida has been governed by the philosophy of the "least restrictive alternative" approach to juvenile court sanctions and has implemented preadjudicatory detention reform as a pilot project first in Broward County and later through statewide legislation.[39] In this sense, both the state and Circuit 17 have viewed formalization of the court as a way of limiting, rather than expanding, the court's jurisdiction over lower-level offenders.

In the late 1990s, the once well-conceptualized and generally well-funded diversion system in the state underwent several shocks. Most notably, reallocation of much state juvenile justice funding, formerly allocated to prevention and local diversion programs, was designated for an expansion of the state's secure-bed capacity, thus weakening the capacity of most local jurisdictions to support diversion programs. In the past five years, after several years of struggle to replace diversion programs, the Florida State's Attorney Office (SAO) responsible for juvenile cases and other system and community partners, with support from the local Broward Children's Services Council (CSC), was able to develop a variety of diversion programs and intervention models, including drug treatment, family and youth group counseling, restorative justice, and youth development and mentoring. In addition, it developed multiple treatment and service *components* of programs that have become prevalent among many diversion programs, including (1) community service, (2) restitution, (3) family sessions, (4) group sessions, (5) individual counseling, (6) restorative justice conferencing, and (7) academic components. As these findings and our fieldwork in the formative study suggest, although intensity of supervision and number and type of specific intervention components vary by program, diversion intervention as a whole seems highly structured regarding service and supervision requirements.

Diversion requirements do vary by specific program model, but several conditions of diversion supervision are standard across Broward County programs per SAO policy. These include a 45-day minimum period of supervision; standard community service hour requirements; restitution, if applicable; and other individual conditions of supervision and service participation determined by the specific program with SAO approval. The SAO in Circuit 17 establishes and enforces rules of supervision, has oversight over violations of supervision, and approves diversion program completion. Little is known, however, about the extent to which diversion programs vary in intensity of services and supervision.

Probation in Florida

Consistent with national trends,[40] juvenile probation in Florida appears in recent decades to have passed through several reform phases that include a social work model, a law enforcement focus, and a more professional, administrative case management model grounded in a risk and need assessment–based focus. Today, juvenile probation officer (JPO) decision making seems to be more constrained by limited resources than in past years. For example, in the 1990s, the state supported a more comprehensive service–focused case management model as a result of the passage of the Juvenile Justice Reform Act of 1990.[41] The court order determines the specific conditions of probation supervision, and many of these conditions are standard requirements emphasizing rules and restrictions as well as reporting requirements, but DJJ probation intake officers may have substantial input into the case plan, elements of which may be included in the court order.

In recent years, however, the supervision and intake authority of the JPO is increasingly limited to a monitoring and enforcement function defined by caseload contact standards that prescribe three general levels of risk: *minimal* or *demand* (one face-to-face monthly contact), *general* (three face-to-face monthly contacts), and *intensive* (three weekly face-to-face contacts). Despite this limitation, some JPOs still find new ways to exercise creativity and to professionalize their work, often by working "under the radar" and giving less emphasis to the enforcement of what appear to be less sensible supervision rules.[42] Focus groups and informal interviews with JPOs in our formative study, however, suggest a widespread feeling of being trapped by impossible goals and time frames that often are dictated by time spent in court and completing paperwork.[43]

FLORIDA JUDICIAL CIRCUIT 17 FORMATIVE ASSESSMENT: SELECTED FINDINGS

Some youth advocates continue to view probation and diversion responses as viable second-chance options, but critics view diversion and probation as "soft" alternatives that fall short of needed incapacitation and punishment. In a climate in which punishment is now an official component of juvenile justice codes in most states and adult time is increasingly an option, probation increasingly may be understood as a punitive enforcement function. Moreover, with the continuing popularity of community-based informal programs that incorporate punitive and shock components, such as boot camp and Scared Straight,[44] diversion programs clearly are not immune to developing a punitive focus. Although diversion staff in the loosely coupled juvenile justice organizational environment may continue to define their roles as nonpunitive helpers who promote rehabilitation (rather than accelerate punishment), both diversion and probation may play a primary role in moving youth more quickly into secure settings and expanding the reach of juvenile justice on the front end,[45] much as these programs did in the 1970s.[46]

Background and Impetus

Concerns about the nature of diversion and probation and the role of each response in the continuum were primary issues underlying a local initiative in Circuit 17. The authors conducted a critical empirical examination of the referral and intervention process in diversion programs and probation. A primary original impetus for the initiative and formative study grew out of a concern about the very high failure rates in diversion programs for youths involved in low- to moderate-level delinquency, and with the realization that formal probation was being overused relative to informal diversion. In addition, at various points over the past five years, apparent increases in the proportion of minority, relative to nonminority, youths placed on probation, along with declines in the proportion of minority youths diverted in the circuit, have been a source of concern. To address these needs, a working collaborative group of key juvenile justice decision makers developed a Targeted Community Action Plan for Circuit 17 that—along with training, technical assistance, and other services to local programs—supported a formative evaluation of diversion programs and probation in Broward County.

Overall, this formative assessment[47] provided an initial sense of the strengths and gaps in the continuum of services for delinquent youth in Broward County. It documented the range of interventions and program components being provided. Findings raised questions about the following: (1) whether the array of diversion programs offered a graduated range of intensity of service and supervision; (2) whether the intensity of probationary supervision differed from that provided by diversion programs; (3) how decisions were made regarding diversion versus probation orders; and (4) the reasons for these decisions. We focus briefly on the second issue, relative intensity of supervision intensity, in our case study below.

Intensity of Supervision and Services in the Continuum

The national issues in diversion and probation discussed above and our formative assessment of diversion and probation[48] raise a number of questions about community supervision. Despite important strengths of local practice (especially in diversion) and progressive, self-critical leadership among juvenile justice partner agencies responsible for decision making or implementation and monitoring, *weaknesses* in both diversion and probation and in the relationship between these options raise primary questions

about the strength of each community supervision component and the viability of a continuum of supervision and services. First, although a
strength of Broward County's use of diversion is found in its impressive
array of intervention models and components, a weakness is the lack of data
regarding the relative success of programs in achieving basic outcomes. Second, although there are no national standards for gauging program completion in diversion, as a group, diversion programs in the county have what
appear to be high rates of nonparticipation and failure of youths in these
programs to complete requirements. Referred to by the SAO as "kickbacks," these failures to participate in or complete diversion in recent
months have been as high as 40 percent of all referrals. This overall failure
rate includes (1) referred youth who could not be located as well as those
who fail to report to their assigned diversion programs (prewaiver failures);
and (2) failures that occur for various reasons after the agreement to participate has been signed (postwaiver failures).[49] Although we know little about
the relative intensity of diversion supervision and service in Circuit 17, the
appropriateness of this level, or variations within and between programs in
intensity and effectiveness, we do have questions about the meaning of this
failure rate with regard to the relationship between probation *and* diversion,
and the intensity and effectiveness of both.

Does probation represent a "step up" from diversion on the continuum
of intensity of supervision, services, and sanctions from diversion as envi-
sioned in the continuum of community supervision?[50] Is probation more
or less effective than diversion in achieving positive outcomes for similar
youth? Interestingly, findings from the formative study question the premise that probation is more demanding and suggest that diversion actually
may be a more intensive and intrusive form of community supervision.

First, on average, diversion programs in the county typically require
youths to participate at least weekly in one or more intervention activities
and services (three weekly sessions are not uncommon), while the typical
youth on probation may have but one face-to-face contact in a month.
Second, as suggested in the high failure rate for diversion cases, evidence
that intensity of supervision and services is greater on the diversion side is
provided by the fact that 47 percent of the approximately 1,200 diversion
kickbacks who returned to the SAO as program failures between July 1,
2005, and May 15, 2006, occurred during the prewaiver period as a result
of parent and youth failure to agree to participate. Although 18 percent of
the participants in this group were cases for which staff were simply unable
to locate the family, the remainder apparently deliberately *resisted diversion*:
about 13 percent (162 cases) of these cases were the result of parent refusal to allow their child to participate and 5 percent resulted from the
juvenile's resistance. Another 7 percent of respondents reported that they
wished to dispute the charge and reported that they preferred to "take
their chances in court." In all, only 24 percent of prewaiver failures did
not participate for reasons *other than* active or passive resistance (e.g., having moved or not been locatable).

Finally, the relative intensity of diversion is also suggested by the fact
that, during the postwaiver period of actual diversion supervision, about

50 percent of the postwaiver program failures were due to inability or refusal to comply with program requirements or sanctions.[51] These descriptive data are preliminary and do not necessarily lead to the conclusion that diversion programming in Circuit 17 is indeed overly demanding (or that probation is too easy). They do raise concerns, however, about the relative intensity of diversion relative to the probation supervision option. In the worst case, one may consider the seldom-asked question of whether youth would be better off left alone than placed in a diversion program.[52]

Given the implications of the formal court record that accompanies the probation order for the future of young people—including a possible increase in the likelihood of secure confinement for subsequent offenses for supervision rule violations—several important policy questions should be asked about diversion programs and the diversion process. These questions include the following: (1) how effective are diversion programs, in contrast to probation, in addressing what many view as their now primary goal of reducing repeat offending while also achieving other objectives viewed as important to sustained resistance to delinquency and crime (e.g., building life skills, improving school performance); and (2) what accounts for the high rate of failure in these programs? Previous evaluations have addressed the impact of specific programs, but few if any recent efforts have been made to assess the impact of diversion at the system level, and almost no attempt has been made to examine reasons for success or failure.

A RESEARCH AGENDA FOR COMMUNITY SUPERVISION

Broader issues raised in the previous section about the relative effectiveness of diversion and probation for similar offenders, and reasons for differences in effectiveness, are directly related to concerns about how juvenile justice systems invest their resources. Answering these questions will require more rigorous impact analysis, as well as more intensive process evaluation. Both research agendas should attempt to answer questions about *reasons* for differences in effectiveness. It is important to understand how decision makers and practitioners understand and conceptualize the purpose and logic of diversion and probation in the new juvenile justice context. Two practical rationales for an intensive research focus on community supervision are based on (1) the dramatic policy implications of the diversion versus probation choice for the future of youth in trouble, and (2) the lack of understanding of current practitioner views of the logic, theory, and purpose of both responses to youth crime.

Policy Issues in the Choice of Community Supervision Options

Not much is known about the efficacy of placing low- to mid-level risk offenders in diversion programs rather than probation and whether or not such a placement will result in greater or less risk to the community. If diverted youth in fact have the same or lower reoffense rates both during and after supervision, decision makers could spare them from the stigma of a formal court record. If probation is indeed viewed as the "last chance" before a secure placement, these decision makers might, by using the diversion option, add another alternative before using this option and thereby decrease the chance of such a placement. A lower rearrest rate for diverted youth would represent an enhancement in public safety as a result of the diversion choice. Conversely, if youths in the probation sample have lower recidivism rates than similar youths referred to diversion programs, one would then assume that moving to the formal court sanction of probation has crime reduction value, or that depending on the relative effectiveness of both, diversion simply provides a weak alternative for this group of young offenders. In the latter case, it is possible that diversion failure may prove to be a strike against youth in court who might be viewed as less deserving of probation and as posing a greater risk to the community.

Effectiveness and the Need for Intervention Theory

Addressing such policy questions in a meaningful way, however, requires a theory of intervention that has for the most part been missing from probation supervision and often only implicit in many diversion programs. Diversion practitioners may be unclear about the logic of their programs, although some may operate based on various theoretical assumptions about individual program components (e.g., a life skills component). Most important for replication and policy change, however, are answers to the question *why* a probation model or diversion program is more effective. Beyond programs, policy makers need to know whether diversion or probation as intervention systems work best for certain categories of offenders who are deemed appropriate for community supervision.

For researchers, the idea of an "intervention theory" in community supervision suggests that attention be focused on both immediate process results and intermediate outcomes that can link intervention practice with long-term results.[53] More specifically, the intermediate result, or "intervening variable" that some scholars argue may account for key differences between otherwise similar criminological theories,[54] should play a critical role in program evaluation. Although there is often little apparent "theory" in diversion and probation in the sense of scholarly logic that links involvement in crime to social and psychosocial causes or desistance to intervening processes in the case of intervention, it is important to be aware of some subtle theoretical underpinnings of diversion program and treatment or service components that are requirements of both forms of community supervision. In addition, implicit theories are related to the core idea of intensity itself that suggest, as noted earlier in our discussion of the "continuum" idea, that the services and supervision level must be appropriate to level of risk and need.[55] While it is important to assess the impact of specific program components, and completion of these components as intervening variables, it is also important to empirically examine what is often an unwritten assumption in modern diversion—that greater intensity is better. Although we do not know in this case whether enhanced supervision will result in more or less reoffending, there are possible threats of greater consequences for violation of community supervision requirements.

A Systemic Agenda for Multimethod Research

There are many possible research priorities and agendas for community supervision, but our own current focus to expand on our formative study is one focused on diversion and probation in a systemic rather than programmatic way. In conjunction with a rigorous effort to address the impact questions discussed above, it is critical to examine the broader issue of the meaning of diversion and probation for professionals in the new juvenile justice climate. To address the policy decision and theoretical issues concerning program logic, we suggest—based on the formative findings of our previous assessment of the community supervision continuum in Broward County, Circuit 17—a research agenda that would have two components: (1) an exploratory investigation of how juvenile justice practitioners and decision makers "make sense" of the purpose, theory, effectiveness, and role of diversion and probation in the juvenile justice system; and (2) an impact study comparing outcomes for equivalent samples of delinquency cases assigned to probation and diversion, with an emphasis on variation in intensity and type of supervision and services provided by each community supervision option on program completion and impact on reoffending. A brief rationale for both agendas is presented below.

Research Agenda One: Making Sense of Community Supervision in the New Juvenile Justice Context

While new ideas and programs are often held up for critical scrutiny and may be subjected to evaluation, traditional criminal justice functions, such as sentencing, fact finding, and arrest, are seldom questioned in terms of their effectiveness. Because these common functions are seldom critically examined by system insiders, the idea of "effectiveness" may seem as irrelevant as asking whether the practices of arrest or the use of jail and detention are effective. If it is highly unlikely that any evaluation findings would be used to end the practices of arrest and jailing, the same may be true of diversion and probation. It is quite possible, however, that critiques of diversion and probation in the 1970s and 1980s are now viewed as virtually irrelevant in the new juvenile justice context, which seems to have moved in the direction of what has been called "managerial criminal justice."[56] This managerial approach is one no longer concerned with "success," and may eschew outcome measures in favor of a nonutilitarian focus on system and organizational maintenance. Incapacitation strategies in corrections,[57] for example, may have no long-term goal such as offender rehabilitation, reintegration, or even deterrence. They simply maintain order and the status quo, at least temporarily.

Similarly, diversion and probation may be in the process of becoming less about achieving outcomes for youth and more about providing "slots" to hold or incapacitate troublesome and delinquent youth whether or not improvements are made in their behavior and well-being. Like other criminal and juvenile justice functions, there are often very divergent expectations for long-standing practices such as diversion and probation. Different professional groups have a stake in the operation of both probation and diversion, and they may promote positive change or seek to hinder such change. Hope for improvement lies in the fact that, for cost reasons alone, community supervision is unlikely to go away.[58]

The concept of "sense-making" in criminal justice[59] seems to suggest that criminal justice professionals need to create meaning and purpose for various criminal justice functions that fit current system needs and their own needs—regardless of the original intent behind these functions. Because perceptions of what community supervision options should "be" and what they could achieve may differ within and between juvenile justice professionals, it is important to understand similarities and differences between the views of diversion staff, probation officers, judges, prosecutors, and other key system decision makers. If juvenile justice professionals are to develop outcomes that provide standards to measure improvement in community supervision options, it is important to know what professionals wish to accomplish, and how they want to accomplish it during the supervision and postsupervision periods. Answers to these questions may help to determine what "theories-in-use"[60] are being used to structure diversion and probation interventions. Such answers may help to understand competing justice philosophies behind interventions, views about which youths are appropriate for various options, and which interventions are perceived to be most effective. For example, now that it is viewed—for better or worse—more as a program than a process, diversion may be viewed by some as a way to provide treatment, that is, as a prevention program. Conversely, it may be viewed as a punishment or sanction that works because of the threat of harsher punishment and because it holds offenders accountable to their victims and the community.

The primary purpose of this research component would be to assess and compare juvenile justice system professional views about the purposes of diversion and probation, the effectiveness of diversion and probation, and the theory of the community supervision continuum. Research questions would address the following topics:

- How do juvenile justice professionals understand the role and function of diversion and probation?
- How do they view the relationship between the two?
- Which populations of offenders are viewed as appropriate for each approach?
- What is their "theory" of how and why diversion and probation "works" when it does?
- How could both be improved?

Most important, in the loosely coupled juvenile justice context, we may expect to see interesting patterns of professional adaptation within the overall context of formalization and the new emphasis on expanded punishment. Juvenile court judges, probation administrators and managers, probation officers, diversion program administrators and managers, diversion program staff, and prosecutors would be the population of interest for this research. The goals would be to document overall consensus, if any, around both "new" and "old" juvenile justice values regarding community supervision, and to determine differences in attitudes and beliefs within and between categories of juvenile justice professionals.

Many methodological approaches could be used to address these questions, but survey research, supplemented as needed by interviews and focus groups, would allow for comparison among various professional groups in a local or state system using professional role as a key independent variable and the abovementioned questions as dependent variables (e.g., views of purpose of diversion and probation; types of offenders appropriate for each; views of the theory behind diversion and probation). Independent or explanatory variables might include (1) the professional group affiliation (e.g., probation staff, diversion staff); (2) organizational climate and culture measures;[61] and (3) court work group influences and justice philosophy.

Research Agenda Two: A Probation-Diversion Impact Study

The primary purpose of this second component of our community supervision research agenda would be to determine the extent to which either a formal (court-ordered) period of probationary supervision or informal participation in a diversion program is more effective in preventing reoffending for similar offenders who are deemed eligible for community-based supervision. Such a probation-diversion impact study would compare equivalent samples of diversion and probation youths on reoffending and also would examine the impact of intervening processes and outcomes conceptualized as immediate and intermediate variables.

Research questions would first address the extent to which probation is more or less effective than diversion in reducing reoffending and achieving other outcomes for similar offenders. Second, we would wish to know the *reasons* for any difference observed between the two community-based supervision options. A primary expectation, or hypothesis, is that such observed differences might be due to variations in the intensity of service and supervision; variations in completion of obligations, sanctions, and program intervention components; or failure to comply with supervision rules and program requirements.

The preferred research design for this impact evaluation would be a randomized field experimental design (or appropriate quasi-experimental design) that could be used to compare outcomes for similar lower- to middle-range delinquency cases assigned to diversion or probation placement. A pool of moderate-level offenders fitting the profile of youths normally referred to probation could be identified for random assignment by the juvenile justice professional responsible for making the decision to file formal charges or to divert (in Florida, the SAO). Random assignment procedures could then be used to create experimental and control groups to test the hypothesis that youths referred to diversion would have lower rates of reoffending than those assigned to probation.[62]

Because the stated policy objectives of both diversion and probation emphasize public safety and decreased reoffending as primary goals, the dependent variable for the impact evaluation is postsupervision reoffending, which is measured by (1) the number of rearrests during a period of at least one year of time postsupervision; and (2) changes in seriousness of offending as indicated by serious and frequency of pre- versus postsupervision charges, and time between program termination and arrest. The primary independent variable in the experimental study would be group assignment to a probation or diversion placement; however, underlying this group assignment are possible differences in intervention logic, in relative intensity of supervision and services provided in the experimental versus control groups, and rates of successful completion of the supervision alternative. Because intensity is different for those who do not complete the program and those who may participate in specific program components, the research should conceptualize three categories of *intervening variables*,[63] which may provide an underlying explanation for differences observed: (1) intensity of service and supervision; (2) program components and specific services provided for each case; and (3) program failure and individual component completion. Viewing the randomly assigned treatment as the independent variable, it is possible to view the intervention process (and the strength of this process as an intervening variable) by measuring supervision intensity to determine whether significant differences in supervision intensity may account for observed differences in group outcomes.

Several independent variable measures of intensity of youth participation in ancillary service programs that may be related to reoffending and prosocial outcomes will also be available for diversion and probation cases. For diversion cases, service intensity is based in part on referral to specific diversion program components (e.g., anger management, counseling, drug abuse treatment), as well as services provided by other agencies. Probation staff could provide the researchers with logs that do not include personal identifiers.

Although the other two intervening variable categories are focused on the intervention process, this category is outcome based and focused on intermediate results expected to be achieved at the conclusion of the period of supervision. Therefore, these outcomes are included in the concept of successful completion of supervision. On the negative side, outcomes also include reoffending while under the supervision of probation or the diversion program. As a dependent variable, "in-program" reoffending may be viewed as a primary component of an unsuccessful completion of diversion or probation (although a minor offense can occasionally result in a new referral to the same or alternative diversion program). As an independent variable, reoffending could be viewed as a predictor of future reoffending. In-program reoffending will be measured by the number of rearrests during the period of time under supervision measured at program closure. Failure to complete diversion or probation obligations also will be measured at case closure. We will measure school attendance and grade appropriateness as positive, prosocial outcomes. School attendance is a mandatory requirement for youths on either probation or diversion status and is a prerequisite for achieving school-related, prosocial outcomes, which are demonstrated in the research literature of criminology and criminal justice[64] to be negatively related to delinquency and crime. School attendance will be measured by using truancy records (available from the Truancy Program at the county's Juvenile Assessment Center) to calculate an attendance-improvement score to measure pre- and postsupervision change. Grade appropriateness as an outcome will be measured by grade level per age category (e.g., 8th grade) at the time of arrest, which will be obtained from the DJJ fact sheet. We will then compute a grade-appropriateness change score for each case at the termination of supervision—for example, an 8th grader who is 14 has advanced to the 9th grade.

Although the randomization process is expected to create experimental and control samples roughly equal in risk and need profiles, we will also have access to the risk classification score for each case, which will be used as a control variable. Other control variables include demographic indicators such as age, ethnicity, gender, and types of people in the household. As noted, race and ethnicity have been strongly associated with diversion program failure in Circuit 17.[65] Hence, this variable along with other demographic measures listed in Component One will be used in this more-intensive multivariate analysis component. Specifically, we will seek to examine the extent to which disproportionate failure of minority youth as a dependent variable can be predicted by participation in specific programs and program components. In addition, other control variables may be suggested to mediate the impact of various program models and components. Specifically, our measures of intensity of supervision and service will be employed here as factors that may either weaken, or *increase*, the impact of program components. Finally, for some analyses, completion of program components will be viewed as control variables that may mediate the impact of independent variables on reoffending or positive postintervention outcomes. Basic measures of these demographic and family variables, as well as risk scores, which are included on the DJJ face sheets as prior arrest and charging information, are viewed as indicators or risk and prior propensity for delinquent behavior.

CONCLUSION

In the new, more formal and punishment-oriented juvenile justice system, the role of community supervision has received relatively little attention. Yet, despite the importance of loss of juvenile court jurisdiction over more serious offenders who are increasingly transferred to criminal court, the role of diversion and probation as part of a logical continuum of community supervision may be more critical than ever. As the history of diversion and probation suggest, community supervision is not inherently benevolent.[66] Although diversion and probation offer the best opportunities for youth already caught up in the juvenile justice system to receive a second-chance alternative to reduce stigmatization and avoid the life-changing experience of incarceration, this opportunity is not guaranteed. Indeed, some have argued that an emerging "expansionist" juvenile justice system, having lost jurisdiction over more serious offenders, now appears to be taking on more responsibility for lower-level and status offenders in the context of zero tolerance, the proliferation of centralized assessment centers, expanded curfews, truancy intervention, and new specialized courts.[67] In doing so, it appears that juvenile courts are under increasing pressure to criminalize a range of problems once addressed by schools, families, extended families, and neighborhood organizations.

In this context, a strong alternative vision of the role of probation and diversion may be critical to the avoidance of casting community supervision professionals in a case-monitoring and law enforcement role that ultimately may accelerate the processing of young people deeper into the most restrictive components of the juvenile justice system. Whether based on expanding informal support and social control through community-building efforts grounded in restorative justice, positive youth development, or other reform agendas,[68] such a vision might encourage questions about the view that more juvenile justice supervision and services are necessarily better for the generally low- to moderate-level offenders now part of probation and diversion caseloads.

An action research agenda such as the one initiated by system and community leaders in Circuit 17 in South Florida may be helpful in encouraging a critical examination of assumptions about the role and effectiveness of diversion programs and probation—and the viability and value of the continuum of supervision and services at the community level. Generally, such research is needed to document and describe the current state of local juvenile justice systems that have undergone the often-traumatic transformations of the 1990s. Our research agenda to assess how juvenile justice professionals "make sense" of their roles in the new juvenile justice climate, and specifically how they understand the purpose of diversion and probation, seems critical to improving theoretical understanding of the organizational culture of the new juvenile justice landscape. More practical, such research should assist policy makers and juvenile justice administrators in improving their understanding of how staff view their roles and responsibilities. Finally, policy makers need concrete evidence about the cost-effectiveness of diversion versus probation for similar offenders as well as more information about differences in theories associated with various effective practices that can facilitate replication. Criminal justice researchers using rigorous research designs that compare samples of similar cases in diversion programs with those on probation, and examine the relative intensity of supervision and services in both, can contribute to policy-maker decisions, while advancing theory and research on the components of effective intervention in community supervision.

NOTES

1. Forst, 1995.
2. Feld, 1987, 1991; Sanborn & Salerno, 2005.
3. Feld, 1993; Torbet et al., 1996.
4. Torbet et al., 1996.
5. Bishop, Frazier, & Henretta, 1989; Butts & Mears, 2001; Feld, 1999.
6. Weick, 1995.
7. Puzzanchera, Stahl, Finnegan, Tierney, & Snyder, 2003; Whitehead & Lab, 2006.
8. See Puzzanchera et al., 2003.
9. Lemert, 1971; President's Commission on Law Enforcement and the Administration of Justice, 1967.
10. Potter & Kakar, 2002.
11. Binder & Geis, 1984.
12. Polk, 1987; Schur, 1973.
13. Binder & Geis, 1984; Whitehead & Lab, 1996.
14. E.g., Polk, 1987.
15. Whitehead & Lab, 1996.
16. Bazemore, 2001.
17. Potter & Kakar, 2002.
18. Bazemore & Leip, 2005; Minor, Hartmann, & Terry, 1997.
19. E.g., Polk, 1987; Rojek, 1982.
20. Whitehead & Lab, 2006.
21. Torbet et al., 1996.
22. E.g., Lipsey & Wilson, 1998.
23. Jacobs, 1990.
24. Bazemore & Day, 1995; Griffin & Thomas, 2004.
25. Maloney, Bazemore, & Hudson, 2001.
26. Lipsey & Wilson, 1998; Office of Juvenile Justice and Delinquency Prevention, hereafter OJJDP, 1995.
27. Whitehead & Lab, 2006.
28. OJJDP, 1995.
29. Hawkins & Catalano, 1990.
30. OJJDP, 1995.
31. Andrews & Bonta, 1994.
32. Bazemore & Leip, 2005.
33. See Frazier & Cochran, 1986; Potter & Kakar, 2002.
34. Lieber, 2003.
35. Feld, 1988; Sanborn & Salerno, 2005.
36. Torbet et al., 1996; Feld, 1999.
37. At one time several circuits in urban areas could make use of a continuum of intensity of services and supervision *within diversion programming* that included police cautioning and citation at the front end followed by various levels of programmatic intensity.
38. Shiraldi & Soler, 1998.
39. Bazemore, Dicker, & Nyhan, 1994.
40. Whitehead & Lab, 2001; 2004.
41. Bazemore & Day, 1995.
42. Jacobs, 1990.
43. Bazemore & Leip, 2005.
44. Finkenhauer & Gavin, 1999.

45. Bazemore, Stinchcomb, & Leip, 2004; Shiraldi & Soler, 1998.

46. Lemert, 1971; Polk, 1987.

47. Bazemore & Leip, 2005.

48. Bazemore & Leip, 2005.

49. "Waiver" refers to the waiver of speedy trial that must be signed by the offender and his/her parents to participate in diversion. Youths and parents in this category may include those who have moved or cannot be located, as well as those who actively resist diversion or refuse to sign the waiver of speedy trial that signifies a consent to bypass the adjudicatory hearing and be placed on diversion.

50. OJJDP, 1995.

51. Bazemore & Leip, 2005.

52. Schur, 1973.

53. Weiss, 1997.

54. Agnew, 1993; Unnever, Cullen, & Agnew, 2006.

55. Andrews & Bonta, 1994.

56. Feely & Simon, 1992.

57. Feely & Simon, 1992.

58. Although debate is likely to occur about who should be eligible for community supervision, few professionals are likely to oppose the idea of diversion and probation. Hope also lies in a growing commitment to research-based "best practice" models that achieve goals such as reductions in offending (e.g., Elliott, 1997). Although such models could be used in diversion, and could even be applied in probation, program replication in diverse contexts based on adherence to program guidelines alone has often been insufficient. In part because of expense, high expectations for staff, and a variety of practical problems (e.g., Mihalic & Irwin, 2003), implementation has failed due to an absence of understanding of intervention theory and principles and how these can be applied in diverse contexts. Indeed, such application appears to be a key aspect of what has been called the inability to "take programs to scale" in widespread implementation efforts (Schorr, 1988).

59. E.g., Maguire & Katz, 2002; Weick, 1995.

60. Argyris & Schon, 1974.

61. Griffin, 2001; Pritchard & Karasick, 1973.

62. As the "gold standard" for research designs aimed at providing data that allow for valid conclusions about program effectiveness in impact research (Boruch, Snyder, & DeMoya, 2000), random assignment should, in the current study, eliminate selection bias that might result in important differences between samples potentially related to intervention outcomes. Randomized field trials are appropriate in a study like this one because there is no evidence that either probation or diversion is more effective or an easier option (at least in Broward County), and there are not enough diversion program slots to refer all offenders who fit this profile to this option. Under such conditions, random assignment is a fair option for distributing a scarce resource (Boruch et al., 2000; Sherman, 2000).

63. Intervening variables are characteristics, events, situations, or features that come between a set of presumed cause and effect variables. Normally, they affect or mitigate the strength or direction of the causal mechanism.

64. E.g., Elliott, 1994; Hirschi, 1969.

65. Bazemore & Leip, 2005.

66. Cohen, 1985.

67. Bazemore et al., 2004; Stinchcomb, Bazemore, & Riestenberg, 2006.

68. E.g., Bazemore & Schiff, 2004; Brendtro & Long, 1995; Butts & Mears, 2001.

REFERENCES

Agnew, R. (1993). Why do they do it? An examination of the intervening mechanisms between "social control" variables and delinquency. *Journal of Research in Crime and Delinquency, 30,* 245–266.

Andrews, D., & Bonta, J. (1994). *The psychology of criminal conduct.* Cincinnati, OH: Anderson.

Argyris, C., & Schon, D. (1974). *Theory in practice: Increasing professional effectiveness.* San Francisco, CA: Jossey-Bass.

Bazemore, G. (2001). Young people, trouble, and crime: Restorative justice as a normative theory of informal social control and social support. *Youth and Society, 33*(2), 199–226.

Bazemore, G., & Day, S. (1995). The return to family intervention in youth services: A juvenile justice case study in policy implementation. *The Journal of Sociology and Social Welfare, 22*(3), 25–50.

Bazemore, G., & Dicker, T. (1996). Implementing detention intake reform: The judicial response. *The Prison Journal, 76,* 5–21.

Bazemore, G., Dicker, T. J., & Nyhan, R. (1994). Juvenile justice reform and the difference it makes: An exploratory study of the impact of policy change on detention worker attitudes. *Crime and Delinquency, 40,* 37–53.

Bazemore, G., & Leip, L. (2005). *Circuit 17 targeted community action plan report submitted to Broward Sheriff's Office.* Ft. Lauderdale, FL.

Bazemore, G., & Schiff, M. (2004). *Juvenile justice reform and restorative justice: Building theory and policy from practice.* Cullompton, Devon, UK: Willan Publishing.

Bazemore, G., Stinchcomb, J., & Leip, L. (2004) Scared smart or bored straight? Testing a deterrence logic in an evaluation of police-led truancy intervention, *Justice Quarterly, 21*(2), 269–298.

Binder, A., & Geis G. (1984). Ad populum argumentation in criminology: Juvenile diversion as rhetoric. *Crime and Delinquency, 30,* 309–333.

Bishop, D. M., Frazier, C., & Henretta, J. (1989). Prosecutorial waiver: Case study of a questionable reform. *Crime and Delinquency, 35,* 179–201.

Boruch, R., Snyder, B., & DeMoya, D. (2000). The importance of randomized field trials. *Crime and Delinquency, 46,* 156–180.

Brendtro, L. & Long, N. (1995). School reform: What we've learned about breaking the cycle of conflict. ASCD Educational Leadership, 52(5) February, 52–56.

Butts, J., & Mears, D. (2001). Reviving juvenile justice in a get-tough era, *Youth and Society, 33*(2), 169–198.

Cohen, S. (1985). *Visions of social control, crime, punishment and classification.* Oxford, MA: Polity Press.

Elliott, D. (1994). Serious violent offenders: Onset, developmental course, and termination. The American Society of Criminology 1993 Presidential Address. *Criminology, 31,* 1–21.

Elliott, D. (1997). *Blueprints for youth violence prevention* (Vols. 1–11). Boulder, CO: Center for the Study and Prevention of Violence, Institute of Behavioral Science, University of Colorado.

Feely, M., & Simon, J. (1992). The new penology: Notes on the emerging strategy of corrections and its implications. *Criminology, 30*(4), 449–474.

Feld, B. (1988). The juvenile court meets the principle of the offense: Punishment, treatment, and the difference it makes. *Boston University Law Review,* 821–915.

Feld, B. (1991). The transformation of the juvenile court. *Minnesota Law Review, 7*(3), 691–725.

Feld, B. (1993). Juvenile (in)justice and the criminal court alternative. *Crime and Delinquency, 39,* 403–424.

Feld, B. (1999). Rehabilitation, retribution, and restorative justice: Alternative conceptions of juvenile justice. In G. Bazemore & L. Walgrave (Eds.), *Restorative juvenile justice: Repairing the harm of youth crime* (pp. 17–44). Monsey, NY: Criminal Justice Press.

Finkenhauer, J., & Gavin, P. (1999). *Scared straight: The panacea phenomenon revisited.* Prospect Heights, IL: Waveland.

Forst, M. (Ed.). (1995). *The new juvenile justice.* New York: Nelson Hall.

Frazier, C., & Cochran, J. (1986). Official intervention, diversion from the juvenile justice system, and dynamics of human services work: Effects of a reform goal based on labeling theory. *Crime and Delinquency, 82,* 157–176.

Griffin, M. L. (2001). Job satisfaction among detention officers: Assessing the relative contribution of organizational climate variables. *Journal of Criminal Justice, 29,* 219–232.

Griffin, P., & Thomas, D. (2004, January). The good news: Measuring juvenile court outcomes at case closing. *Pennsylvania Progress, 10*(2), 1–9. Harrisburg, PA: Pennsylvania Commission on Crime and Delinquency.

Hawkins, J. D., & Catalano, R. F. (1992). *Communities that care.* San Francisco: Jossey-Bass.

Hirschi, T. (1969). *Causes of delinquency.* Berkeley, CA: University of California Press.

Jacobs, M. D. (1990). *Screwing the system and making it work: Juvenile justice in the no-fault society.* Chicago: University of Chicago Press.

Lemert, E. M. (1971). *Instead of court: Diversion in juvenile justice.* Rockville MD, National Institute of Mental Health.

Lieber, M. (2003). *The contexts of juvenile justice decision-making: When race matters.* Albany, NY: State University of New York Press.

Lipsey, M. W., & Wilson, D. B. (1998). Effective intervention for serious juvenile offenders: A synthesis of research. In Loeber, R. & D. P. Farrington (Eds.), *Serious and violent juvenile offenders: Risk factors and successful interventions* (pp. 313–345). Thousand Oaks, CA: Sage Publications.

Maguire, E., & Katz, C. (2002). Community policing, loose coupling, and sense-making in American police agencies. *Justice Quarterly, 19,* 503–536.

Maloney, D., Bazemore, G., & Hudson, J. (2001, Summer). The end of probation and the beginning of community corrections. *Perspectives,* 23–30.

Mihalic, J., & Irwin, K. (2003). Addressing issues of implementation in blueprint prevention programs. *Youth Violence and Juvenile Justice: An Interdisciplinary Journal, 1*(10), 246–275.

Minor, K., Hartmann, D., & Terry, S. (1997). Predictors of juvenile court actions and recidivism. *Crime and Delinquency, 43,* 328–345.

Office of Juvenile Justice and Delinquency Prevention. (1995). *Guide for implementing the comprehensive strategy for serious, violent, and chronic juvenile offenders.* Washington, D.C.: Office of Juvenile Justice and Delinquency Prevention.

Polk, K. (1987). When less means more: An analysis of destructuring in criminal justice. *Crime and Delinquency, 33,* 358–378.

Potter, R., & Kakar, S. (2002). The diversion decision-making process from the juvenile court practitioner's perspective. *Journal of Contemporary Criminal Justice, 18,* 20–36.

President's Commission on Law Enforcement and the Administration of Justice. (1967). *Task force report: Juvenile delinquency and youth crime*. Washington, D.C.: Government Printing Office.

Pritchard, R. D., & Karasick, B. W. (1973). The effects of organizational climate on managerial job performance and job satisfaction. *Organizational Behavior and Human Performance, 9*, 126–146.

Puzzanchera, C., Stahl, A., Finnegan, T., Tierney, N., & Snyder, H. (2003). *Juvenile court statistics 1999*. Washington, D.C.: Office of Juvenile Justice and Delinquency Prevention.

Rojek, D. (1982). Juvenile diversion: A study of community cooptation. In D. Rojek & G. Jensen (Eds.), *Readings in juvenile delinquency* (pp. 316–322). Lexington, MA: DC Health.

Sanborn, J., & Salerno, A. (2005). *The juvenile justice system: Law and process*. Boston: Roxbury.

Schorr, L. B. (1988). *Within our reach: Breaking the cycle of disadvantage*. New York: Doubleday.

Schur, E. M. (1973). *Radical nonintervention: Rethinking the delinquency problem*. Englewood Cliffs, NJ: Prentice Hall.

Sherman, L. (2000). Reducing incarceration rates: The promise of experimental criminology. *Crime and Delinquency, 46*, 299–314.

Shiraldi, V., & Soler, M. (1998). The will of the people: The public's opinion of the violent and repeat juvenile offender act of 1997. *Crime and Delinquency, 44*, 590–601.

Stinchcomb, J., Bazemore, G., & Riestenberg, N. (2006). Beyond zero tolerance: Restoring justice in secondary schools, *Youth Violence and Juvenile Justice, 4*, 123–147.

Torbet, P., Gable, R., Hurst, H., Montgomery, I., Szymanski, L., & Thomas, D. (1996). *State responses to serious and violent juvenile crime*. Washington, D.C.: Office of Juvenile Justice and Delinquency Prevention.

Unnever, J. D., Cullen, F., & Agnew, R. (2006). Why is "bad" parenting criminogenic? Implications from rival theories. *Youth Violence and Juvenile Justice, 4*, 3–33.

Weick, K. E. (1995). *Sensemaking in organizations*. Thousand Oaks, CA: Sage Publications.

Weiss, C. (1997). How can theory-based evaluation make greater headway? *Evaluation Review, 21*, 501–524.

Whitehead, J., & Lab, S. (1996). *Juvenile justice: An introduction*. Cincinnati, OH: Anderson.

Whitehead, J., & Lab, S. (2001). *Juvenile justice: An introduction* (2nd ed.). Cincinnati, OH: Anderson.

Whitehead, J., & Lab, S. (2004). *Juvenile justice: An introduction* (3rd ed.). Cincinnati, OH: Anderson.

Whitehead, J., & Lab, S. (2006). *Juvenile justice: An introduction* (5th ed.). Cincinnati, OH: Anderson.

CHAPTER 6

Mandatory Mental Health Treatment and Juveniles

Barbara Belbot

Five primary systems provide care to troubled children in the United States: (1) the health care system, (2) the mental health care system, (3) the child welfare system, (4) the juvenile justice system, and (5) the education system. Each of these systems is composed of various professionals, facilities, agencies, and organizations. Unfortunately, there is often little coordination among the five systems. Weithorn reports that troubled youths often are viewed through the different lenses of the mental health, child welfare, juvenile justice, and education systems and may end up in one system or another for reasons not always related to their needs. They may be rejected from one system because of financial considerations or an overburdened system may shift a child to another system. Perhaps authorities did not adequately assess a child's needs. Which system a youth enters determines the services they will receive, because each system is able to offer only a specific set of services. Once a youth enters a particular system, it can be difficult to change direction. It is also common, notes Weithorn, for a troubled youth to be involved in more than one system at any point in time, each with its own mission, service delivery requirements, and nomenclature. The youth's behavior may indicate family problems that need to be addressed by the child welfare system, while school performance and conduct is also affected. He or she may be diagnosed with mental health and emotional problems or involvement with substance abuse.[1]

The juvenile justice system is able to intervene in the lives of youth who violate the criminal law and are labeled delinquents. A wide range of dispositions are available to juvenile court judges who deal with youths adjudicated as delinquents, including probation, suspended sentence, payment of fines and restitution, referral and commitment to a mental health or substance abuse facility, and commitment to a juvenile correctional facility. In certain circumstances, juvenile court judges can transfer juveniles who have been charged with serious crimes to adult criminal courts to be tried as adults. If convicted, these youths are sentenced as adult offenders and can be sentenced to adult correctional facilities. The juvenile court is also able to intervene in the lives of youths who have committed noncriminal status offenses, which include behavior that does not amount to a criminal violation but, when committed by juveniles, can lead to juvenile court intervention. Status offenses include such behavior as truancy, running away from home, or engaging in other types of broadly defined incorrigible, wayward, or stubborn conduct.

According to many researchers, a significant proportion of juvenile offenders and residents in juvenile correctional facilities have mental disorders.[2] A recent study of 1,829 youth in juvenile detention found that, excluding conduct disorders, 60.9 percent of the males and 70 percent of the females met diagnostic criteria for one or more psychiatric disorders. Other disorders that were common included anxiety disorders (21.3 percent of males; 30.8 percent of females); affective mood disorders such as depression (18.7 percent of males; 27.6 percent of females); and attention deficit disorder (16.6 percent of males; 21.4 percent of females). A study conducted by Wasserman that examined youths within several weeks of their admission into a juvenile justice facility found that 67.2 percent of the sample examined met the criteria of at least one mental disorder and 31.7 percent met the criteria of a conduct disorder.[3]

Other research has examined what proportion of youths receiving mental health care are also involved in the juvenile justice system. Vander Stoep and her colleagues conducted research in Seattle, Washington, and found that children receiving public mental health services were almost three times as likely to have had some contact with the juvenile justice system than a comparable group in the general population. The researchers compared youth receiving public mental health services who had contact with the juvenile justice system with those who had no such contact. The dual-system youth were more likely to have been expelled from school (62.1 percent versus 8.4 percent), had below-grade-level performance (51.2 percent versus 31.6 percent), and been identified as seriously behaviorally disturbed (58.1 percent versus 23.3 percent). The dual-system youth also had higher levels of abuse and neglect and foster care placement.[4] Finally, recent research has found that a significant number of all adolescents receiving mental health services in the general population have co-occurring substance abuse disorders.[5]

This chapter examines the mandatory mental health care treatment of adolescents. Youth under the jurisdiction of the juvenile justice system are subject to mandatory treatment in much the same way that some adults involved in the criminal justice system can be legally required to participate in treatment—that is, as part of their court disposition. Not only juveniles who are adjudicated delinquent can be placed into mandatory treatment.

Status offenders under the jurisdiction of the juvenile court also can be required to participate in mental health care treatment programs. In contrast to the adult criminal justice system, the rationale behind the mandatory treatment of juveniles is derived from the doctrine of *parens patriae* and the police power of the state. These same rationales support mandatory treatment of youth who are fortunate enough not to be under the jurisdiction of the juvenile justice system, even though many of them exhibit behavior that could, and might one day, bring them within the ambit of that system.

ADOLESCENTS AND THE LAW

The legal treatment of adolescence has been shaped in large part by the juvenile justice system, *parens patriae*, and jurisprudence that balances the interests of parents, state, and youth.[6] Before the twentieth century, adolescents had no rights and were considered the property of their parents. By the early part of the twentieth century, each state had enacted a version of Illinois's Juvenile Court Act, recognizing that the state may be justified in intervening in the lives of families to protect the health and well-being of children and adolescents. The goal of this paternalism is not to punish but to reform. Termed *parens patriae*, it seeks to promote well-being. The *parens patriae* doctrine had a powerful influence on the enactment of federal and state compulsory education and child labor legislation in the early part of the twentieth century. Courts at the turn of the century also began the difficult job of balancing the tenets of *parens patriae* while also preserving parental authority in the lives of children. The result has been the evolution of piecemeal, often conflicting, policy concerning the role of adolescents in society and their legal status in American law. In 1923, the U.S. Supreme Court in *Prince v. Massachusetts* upheld a Massachusetts child labor law that prohibited parents from authorizing minors to sell newspapers, magazines, or parcels in a public place. A Jehovah Witness, Sarah Prince, allowed her child to sell religious literature on street corners. The Supreme Court denied her claims that the law unconstitutionally restricted her parental authority, finding that *parens patriae* may restrict parental authority in matters affecting a child's welfare. Taking a very different view, in *Wisconsin v. Yoder*, the Supreme Court invalidated a Wisconsin statute that compelled school attendance beyond the 8th grade as it applied to an Amish community, deciding instead that the law interfered with parental religious freedom. In *Yoder*, the Court rejected the *parens patriae* claim.

In *Tinker v. Des Moines*, a group of parents opposed to the Vietnam War encouraged their children to wear black armbands to school in protest. School board officials learned of the plan in advance and announced that the activity was forbidden. The board suspended the students who disobeyed. The Supreme Court struck down the board's edict on the grounds that it violated the students' First Amendment right of free speech.

In *Kent v. United States*, the Supreme Court ruled that the Constitution requires that youths facing juvenile delinquency adjudication have the right to the effective assistance of counsel. The Court noted that the power of *parens patriae* is limited by the rule of law. In *In re Gault*, the Court ruled that a juvenile facing detention must be informed of his or her Fifth Amendment right against self-incrimination, Sixth Amendment right to counsel and confrontation, and Fourteenth Amendment right to notice of the proceeding when facing a charge of juvenile delinquency that entails a loss of liberty. In essence, the Court declared that the Fourteenth Amendment and the Bill of Rights are not for adults alone. In *McKeiver v. Pennsylvania*, however, the Supreme Court held that youths involved in juvenile court proceedings are not constitutionally entitled to trial by jury. In explaining its decision to limit the rights of juveniles, the Court noted the juvenile justice system is different than the adult system and is based on a paternalism, concern, and sympathy that distinguish it from the criminal courts.

To date, the law has failed, either by statute or court decision, to establish a coherent jurisprudence concerning the legal status of adolescents in the United States. Supreme Court decisions recognize the state's authority to intervene in the lives of adolescents under the doctrine of *parens patriae* and its police powers, but it struggles to balance state intervention with the rights of parents to guide their children and decide what is in their best interest. To complicate the issue further, in the 1960s, the Supreme Court recognized that in certain circumstances adolescents enjoy the protections of the U.S. Constitution.

ADOLESCENT DECISIONAL CAPACITY AND MEDICAL CARE DECISIONS

No where else is it more evident that the United States lacks a cohesive and logical policy to define the legal status of adolescents than in matters relating to their right to make decisions about medical care. Decisional capability is the ability to perform a task and understand information, deliberate, and decide. Adults are presumed decisionally capable of making medical and mental health care decisions for themselves. Minors, however, are presumed by the law to be incapable. With respect to adolescents (ages 14 through 17), this legal presumption can be problematic, especially because some of our social norms treat adolescents as if they are decisionally capable.[7] A 16 year old can seek treatment for a sexually transmitted disease but may not decide treatment for a complication related to the STD. A 16 year old who is presumed incapable of deciding about a medical treatment for herself is presumed capable of determining treatment for her infant child and is able to consent to her child's adoption. A 14 year old can be tried in adult court but cannot give consent to basic medical treatment.[8]

Because minors are presumed incapable of medical decision making, the consent of a parent or a legal guardian is required. A doctor treating a child without parental consent can be liable for assault and battery, even if the child consented.[9] Most states reverse this presumption by statute in certain cases and permit adolescent decision making for certain types of medical care, including emergencies in which care is required to save a child's life or well-being, sexually transmitted diseases, drug or alcohol dependency, mental health treatment, contraception, and pregnancy. These exceptions were developed to encourage youths to seek treatment without fear their parents would be contacted and to protect adolescents who might be victims of family abuse. Two other exceptions apply to minors: the emancipated minor and the mature minor doctrine. Emancipated minors are those who no longer live with their parents and are not financially dependent on them, or whose parents have surrendered parental duties. Mature minors are those deemed mature enough to make medical decisions for themselves.[10]

Unfortunately, there is little consensus in case law about what constitutes a mature minor, although court decisions have suggested that health care providers and judges involved in these decisions should consider such factors as the minor's age, experience, education, training, degree of mature judgment, nature of the treatment, risks, probable consequences, and ability to appreciate those risks and consequences. Louisiana's law provides that adolescent consent to treatment shall be binding and valid as if the minor had achieved the age of majority. Rhode Island recognizes the medical decision-making ability of 16-year-old adolescents for routine care, assigning physicians the task of distinguishing between routine and non-routine care. Both Louisiana and Rhode Island recognize adolescent medical decision making to choose treatment but not to refuse it, which is common among mature minor statutes in other states.[11] Many states have not enacted mature minor statutes for adolescent medical decision making. Several state courts have rendered decisions concerning adolescent medical autonomy and have created mature minor doctrines that vary from state to state. These decisions emphasize that their rulings are not a general license to treat minors without parental consent and that the application of the mature minor doctrine depends on the facts of each case.[12] Importantly, these statutes and court decisions give mature minors the right to consent to treatment rather than the right to refuse it. Few state court cases have recognized the right of adolescents to refuse medical treatment.[13] Reported case law addressing adolescent medical decision making is sparse, and most of the relatively few reported cases have focused largely on end-of-life care.

ADOLESCENT AUTONOMY AND MENTAL HEALTH CARE DECISIONS

The exceptions that allow adolescents to seek mental health care without parental notification have evolved for several reasons. Escalating rates of adolescent suicide caused some state legislatures to improve access to mental health treatment through laws that allow adolescents of a certain age to consent to treatment without parent contact or consent. For example, California law permits minors 12 years of age or older to consent to mental health treatment, but it requires health care providers to determine whether the minor is mature enough to participate intelligently, would endanger themselves or others, or is the alleged victim of incest or child abuse. Pennsylvania recognizes the consent of any person 14 years or older, requiring the health care provider to judge whether the adolescent believes he or she is in need of treatment and substantially understands the nature of voluntary treatment and to determine whether the adolescent is voluntarily deciding to submit to treatment. Virginia and Connecticut do not impose age restrictions for adolescent consent to mental health treatment. Connecticut, however, requires physicians to determine whether parental consent or notification would cause the minor not to obtain care, treatment is clinically indicated, failing to provide it would harm the adolescent, and the adolescent voluntarily seeks treatment and is mature enough to participate in treatment productively.[14]

State mental health legislation has been moving in the direction of restricting the time period for which an adolescent may consent to outpatient treatment without parental notification with limits that vary considerably from state to state. Michigan allows 12 sessions or four months of treatment before the clinician must end treatment or require parental notification and consent. Ohio permits an adolescent to consent to six sessions or one month, and Florida permits a mere one-week period or two sessions. At the point at which the legislation requires parental involvement to continue treatment, it directs providers to assess and document whether such notification and consent by parents would be detrimental to the minor and whether that treatment is necessary for the minor's best interest. Should the provider determine that continued treatment is necessary and authorized by the adolescent, these statutes eliminate parent or guardian liability for the costs of treatment.[15]

Interestingly, research suggests that adolescents are thoughtful and thorough in making health care decisions. Scherer found that the ability of older adolescents to make sound and reasonable medical decisions appears to be comparable to the abilities of young adults.[16] Studies have also found that allowing youth to determine their health care is therapeutic and improves their response to and active participation in treatment.[17]

MENTAL HEALTH COMMITMENT AND ADOLESCENTS

The difficulties associated with decisional autonomy and adolescents are magnified when dealing with mental health issues—whether the decision involves in- or outpatient treatment, or voluntary and involuntary civil commitment. Special considerations arise when the juvenile's liberty has been curtailed because of state action, whether incarceration or institutionalization. As with adults, commitment to a mental health facility should not render an adolescent incompetent who is otherwise decisionally capable. However, state statutes that establish civil commitment procedures do not always address or provide specific guidance for the commitment of adolescents.

The U.S. Supreme Court has addressed the situation. In *Parham v. J.R.*, a Georgia statute allowed an adolescent to be involuntarily civilly committed to a mental health institution with the consent of one parent along with an evaluation of a mental health professional at the commit-ment facility. Given the gravity of the social stigma and loss of liberty resulting from institutionalization, the case went to the U.S. Supreme Court as a class action due process challenge. The Court upheld the Georgia statute as constitutional under the Fourteenth Amendment. The Court ruled that additional safeguards such as a hearing before an administrative judge with the evidentiary standards, which must be afforded adults in the identical situation, are not constitutionally required. The Court accepted the assumption that parents generally are motivated by a desire to protect the best interests of their children and that the public mental health sys-tem is efficient, competent, and deserving of the Court's deference. The Court did not consider empirical evidence about adolescent decisional ability.

In *Parham*, the Supreme Court concluded that the involuntary com-mitment of juveniles to state hospitals must facilitate parents' ability to obtain care for their mentally ill children, which is in keeping with the *parens patriae* tradition. Parental interest dominated the child's interests. Admission procedures were kept to a minimum, so parents would not be discouraged from seeking treatment by processes that were burdensome or contentious. The Court required evaluation by a neutral party, usually the admitting physician, to protect the child from risks of error without violat-ing parental authority. The evaluation was not required to be a formal or quasi-formal hearing. The Court required periodic evaluation of the child's condition but provided no time period for reevaluation.

The *Parham* decision has been the subject of intense criticism by legal and mental health professionals. Many state legislatures, perhaps in response to that criticism, enacted additional protections for adolescents facing involuntary commitment in their jurisdictions. By 1985, fewer than half of the states authorized the voluntary commitment of minors solely on the application of a parent or guardian and the approval of the hospi-tal.[18] *Parham* addressed admissions to state hospitals, but not admission to private institutions. This has allowed states to create additional admis-sion criteria for private facilitates, and many have done so. Fourteen states have extended *Parham* procedures for admission to private faculties, and one of those states requires additional procedures in some cases. Fifteen other states have laws that cover both public and private psychiatric hospi-tals, requiring the minimal *Parham* procedures for commitment of younger children and providing older children with additional safeguards, such as consent requirements and evaluations before and after admission. Six states require the consent of older children, and two states require judicial review if a child of any age objects to commitment. One state prohibits parental commitment of children over 14 years old and requires consent of children under the age of 14. Four states prohibit parental commitment of children over 16. Three states prohibit third-party com-mitment of juveniles, instead requiring involuntary civil commitment pro-ceedings like those required for adults. Postadmission review procedures have been enacted by 21 of the states that allow parental commitment, including allowing a minor to file an objection to treatment or a request for discharge, automatic court hearings after admission, 3- to 15-day limits on inpatient treatment without judicial review, and independent clinical reviews. Most states have specific age requirements for triggering procedures.[19] Minors are appointed counsel in four states.[20]

The U.S. Supreme Court has held that the due process clause applies to the right of an individual to refuse unwanted medical treatment. Courts and legislatures recognize the right to refuse medication even if that decision may lead to harm. Competent people have a liberty interest under the due process clause to refuse unwanted medical treatment. The U.S. Constitution protects a person's right to privacy and self-determination, including the right to refuse lifesaving treatment. This protection extends to the mentally ill, even when the state thinks such measures are in their best interests. However, in disagreements over the medical treatment of a minor, only the minor's parents and the state have standing to go to court. Courts defer to parental choice in medical treatment cases out of respect for parental authority, however, judges may not always view the best interests of the child in the same way that parents do. The question then becomes whether the state has the child's best interest at heart. Most of the reported court decisions involving a state overriding parental authority entail allegations of parental neglect to consent for a minor's medical care on religious grounds and claims that a child was harmed following a surgical procedure to which a physician permitted the minor to consent.

State legislation affords a measure of decision-making autonomy to adolescents for medical treatment, but the legislation is piecemeal and there is no cohesive policy. Redding has canvassed state law and proposed a standard statutory scheme for civil commitment, outpatient psychopharmacological treatment, and outpatient psychotherapy that allows mature adolescents to exercise their decisional autonomy.[21] He proposed that maturity should be determined by an independent clinician as opposed to a judge. Melton and colleagues have proposed a Model Act for the Mental Health Treatment of Minors that acknowledges that most older minors are sufficiently competent to make informed decisions to seek or refuse mental health treatment and that people under the age of majority have a fundamental right to make those decisions.[22]

As discussed, despite the numerous rights accorded adolescents to seek treatment, the right to refuse treatment has not been granted. For example, adolescents can obtain psychiatric treatment without their parents' consent, but they cannot refuse treatment—even if adolescents sought the treatment themselves, including inpatient treatment that deprives them of civil liberties without the benefit of constitutionally mandated procedural safeguards afforded adults. During the 1980s, psychiatric inpatient treatment of adolescents more than quadrupled. Weithorn found that most of these admissions were for nonpsychotic, nonacute conditions—two-thirds were for conduct disorder, oppositional defiant disorder, personality disorders, adjustment disorders, mild depression, and nondependent drug and alcohol abuse. By comparison, approximately one-half to two-thirds of adults who receive inpatient care are admitted for psychosis, severe depression, or organic disorder. Weithorn suggests that, in many cases, adolescents are admitted for behaviors typical of the age group rather than for genuine psychopathology and that these behaviors are developmentally limited to adolescents.[23]

PSYCHOTROPIC DRUGS AND ADOLESCENTS

Drugs used in managing psychiatric disorders are usually referred to as psychotropic drugs that act on the mind. Psychotropics are considered effective treatment for acute and chronic psychoses, particularly schizophrenia. There are three major categories: mood stabilizers (including antidepressants), antianxiety sedatives, and antipsychotics.

Antipsychotics have become the mainstay of treatment for inpatients and primarily are used to treat thought disorders. Unfortunately, antipsychotics have many unpleasant and sometimes dangerous side effects. They alter the chemical balance in the brain and change cognitive processes, sometimes deadening a patient's ability to think. Some side effects are temporary; others can be permanent. Side effects include muscle spasms, especially in the eyes, neck, face, and arms; irregular flexing, writhing, or grimacing movements; protrusion of the tongue and a mask-like face; drooling; muscle rigidity; shuffling gait; and tremors. Tardive dyskinesia is one of the most serious side effects caused by long-term use of these drugs and can produce a neurological disorder characterized by involuntary muscular movements.[24]

Antipsychotics can be administered voluntarily or involuntarily. The legal basis for forced administration of psychotropic drugs is rooted in both the police and *parens patriae* powers of the state. *Parens patriae* authority recognizes that there are circumstances in which the state has an interest in protecting the welfare of the mentally ill person. Police power authority relates to the state's responsibility to protect others from the potentially violent acts of a mentally ill person. Under both theories, forced administration of psychotropic drugs can be justified. In *Mills v. Rogers*, the U.S. Supreme Court ruled that an involuntarily committed mental patient had a constitutional right to refuse antipsychotic drugs, except where the state's police or *parens patriae* powers outweigh the patient's rights. Although committed patients have a liberty interest in refusing drugs, this interest can be superseded when outweighed by the state's interest. The Court held that the judicial determination of substituted judgment was required before the administration of drugs, but it did not clearly address how to determine the competence of a mental patient to make treatment decisions.[25]

The level of incompetence required for involuntary psychiatric hospitalization is based on the dangerousness of the patient to himself, herself, or others. This level of incompetence, however, is not the same as what is required for forced administration of psychotropic medications. A person can be considered incompetent to refuse psychiatric hospitalization but sufficiently competent to refuse psychotropic medications. Courts have recognized that mental illness often strikes only limited areas of functioning and leaves other areas untouched. A person's mental illness and involuntary commitment raises questions about his or her ability to make informed treatment decisions, but they cannot justify the forced administration of psychotropic medications.[26]

If a mentally ill person is determined to be incompetent, informed consent laws require the individual who has authority to make treatment decisions for the incompetent person to assess the choices and the risks. Informed consent is a patient's choice about a medical treatment, which is made after a health care provider discloses all the information that a reasonably prudent provider would give a patient about the risks involved in the proposed treatment. It is generally required for all medical treatment. Under the best interest standard, treatment decisions on behalf of an incompetent person should advance their best interests, as opposed to the independent interests of parents or others. Under the substituted judgment standard, the decision maker must determine the incompetent person's interests and preferences and make the decision the incompetent person would have made if they were competent. The substituted judgment standard has never been applied to children because children, including adolescents (except in limited circumstances), are not considered competent under the law. Their parents' judgment is substituted instead.[27]

Although there are court cases addressing forced medication and a patient's competence, none directly address the issue of whether a child has a liberty interest that allows him or her to refuse psychotropic medication. Because the law considers the interests of the parents and children to be the same, courts presume parents will make medical decisions in their child's best interests. In certain limited circumstances, a state may use its *parens patriae* power to override a parental decision, and act *in loco parentis*, deciding that the parents are not acting in the best interests of the child.[28]

STATUS OFFENDERS AND THE ROAD TO MANDATORY TREATMENT

When the juvenile justice system was originally created in the first half of the twentieth century, no distinction was made between children who violated the criminal code and children who were incorrigible, wayward, or out of control. The juvenile court had jurisdiction over any child that it determined was in need of state intervention. The court's job was to determine the child's needs and supervise them in whatever way was deemed appropriate. There were no restrictions on what type of child could be sent to a secure juvenile facility. According to Costello, from the beginning, this broad jurisdiction over status offenders has proved problematic. Runaway children are often involved in difficult, sometimes abusive, family relationships. Some truants have learning disabilities. Other status offenders have serious mental health disorders that contribute to their incorrigible conduct. Conversely, status offender jurisdiction brings some children to the attention of juvenile authorities who really do not need formal state intervention.[29]

By the mid-twentieth century, Costello maintains that the juvenile justice system was bogged down with status offenders. For example, a status offender defies a judge's order to comply with his or her parents' demands, returns to court and is placed in a juvenile detention center for a short time, returns to court again and is given additional orders, defies those orders, returns to court yet again, and eventually ends up in a secure or semisecure juvenile facility. At that time, the juvenile court was not required to provide the same due process protections to juveniles that criminal courts were constitutionally required to extend to adults in the criminal justice system.

Beginning in the 1960s, the Supreme Court issued a series of decisions that gave juveniles who were charged with delinquent offenses or facing institutionalization many of the due process rights available in the adult criminal justice system. Attempts to deinstitutionalize status offenders began in the 1970s. In 1974, the federal government enacted the Juvenile Justice and Delinquency Prevention Act (JJDPA), requiring states that wanted federal funds to prohibit the confinement of status offenders in secure facilities and to submit annual reports to the federal government detailing the progress they made to comply with the law. Although juvenile authorities agreed that status offenders should be separated from juvenile delinquents and be placed in secure facilities only as a last resort, federal funding for alternate dispositions was insufficient, and by the late 1970s and early 1980s, public sentiment had shifted toward a more punitive approach to juveniles. Many states responded to the conflicting mandates by amending their laws to prohibit secure detention of status offenders. At the same time, they developed ways to sidestep the JJDPA by referring or committing increasing numbers of status offenders to mental health facilities, alleging juvenile delinquency jurisdiction instead of status offender jurisdiction, developing semisecure facilities that complied with the JJDPA, or using the juvenile court's contempt powers to bootstrap a status offender to a juvenile delinquent. Depending on state law, a status offender who, for example, is found to be truant and defies court orders to attend school regularly can be found in contempt of court and reclassified as a delinquent, giving the juvenile judge authority to place him or her in a secure facility, all of which is permitted under the 1980 amendments to the JJDPA.

The state of Washington provides an interesting example of the major changes taking place with status offenders in the juvenile justice system. Washington deinstitutionalized status offenders in 1977 with legislation emphasizing that state services should be available to these offenders on a voluntary basis as opposed to a mandatory basis. In 1995, however, Washington enacted the Becca Bill, named after a juvenile runaway girl, Rebecca Hedman, who was raped and murdered while she was living on the streets. Rebecca had a history of running away and had been placed in a group home. She ran from the home, and was later placed in foster care and eventually into a drug treatment center. She was murdered after she ran away from the treatment center. The Washington legislation that bears her name is aimed at giving police and parents greater control over runaway children. Because running away from home was not a crime in Washington, Becca's parents had little authority to stop her. State law frustrated efforts of local police and the juvenile court to detain her for any length of time. The Becca Bill altered the rights of status offenders in Washington. It now authorizes police to take runaway youth to a secure facility for up to five days, revises court procedures to compel minors to receive needed services, and gives parents additional power to consent to treatment for their minor children. The bill also created multidisciplinary teams composed of parents, case workers, mental or substance abuse counselors, and other appropriate people with authority to evaluate a juvenile and his or her family to develop and assist in the implementation of a service plan. Most important, juvenile courts have the authority under the bill to approve a residential placement outside of the home when the court feels such a placement is appropriate. Juvenile judges are required to review all petitions filed by parents asserting that their child is at risk and in need of services. The bill gives parents the authority to place their children in chemical dependency or mental health treatment programs without the juvenile's consent.[30]

The "reinstitutionalization" of status offenders has particular importance in the controversy surrounding mandatory mental health treatment for juveniles. Legislation like that in Washington extends the *parens patriae* authority of the juvenile court, as does the practice of boot-strapping these offenders into delinquency status, and gives the court more power to order a status offender into mandatory treatment.

IS MANDATORY TREATMENT EFFECTIVE?

For many reasons, it is difficult to assess the effectiveness of mandatory treatment for adolescents with mental health disorders. In 2000, Cocozza and Skowyra reported that concern about the mental health care needs of youths in the juvenile justice system received more attention at the federal government level in 1998 and 1999, than in the previous three decades combined. This concern is in stark contrast to past neglect. Cocozza and Skowyra note that the neglect was not restricted to youths in the system; the mental health care needs of children in general had not been adequately addressed in policy, practice, or research. A significant amount of research remains to be done about the nature and extent of mental health disorders among America's youth. Enormous confusion still exists across the primary systems that serve youths in this country on both the policy and practice levels about who is responsible for serving youths with problems. Youth screening and assessment are inadequate. Training, staffing, and program development is lagging. Not surprisingly, funds are inadequate, too. Obvious attention must be paid to creating better and stronger cross-collaboration among the systems that currently serve troubled youth. More troubled youth should be diverted out of the juvenile justice system, more effective community-based alternative treatment programs should be created and used as often as possible to keep youth at home, and youth in juvenile correctional facilities should receive better mental health care.[31] Many youth with mental health problems have co-occurring substance abuse disorders, making treatment even more challenging.[32] More research needs to be done to identify the overlap of mental health disorders with problem behaviors, including drug use, academic failure, truancy, running away from home, and delinquent conduct.

According to Kamradt, it is difficult to find effective treatment models for youths in the juvenile justice system who have serious mental health and emotional problems.[33] The traditional models are residential and day treatment centers, and they tend to follow a one-size-fits-all approach. Progress, however, is being made. New, innovative programs are coming online across the country, and research evaluating these programs is ongoing. An example of a successful community-based program is the Wraparound Milwaukee Program, which provides more individualized treatment and engages the youth's family when appropriate. Clear goals are established for the youth and his or her family that are measured and evaluated regularly. Since its inception, the use of residential treatment has decreased 60 percent, inpatient hospitalization for youth has dropped by 80 percent, clinical outcomes for the youth have improved significantly, and the recidivism rates of the participants have dropped for a variety of offenses.[34] Jainchill, Hawke, and Messina describe a successful residential therapeutic program in New York for delinquent youth with multiple behavior and mental disorders.[35]

This program, Recovery House, uses positive peer role models and educational interventions that focus on reducing antisocial activity. The principles of balanced and restorative justice, including the participation of victims and community members to stress accountability, are also employed. A five-year follow-up indicated decreases in conduct disorders and appeared to be even more effective with females than males.

CONCLUSION

Mandatory treatment of youth with mental health disorders is a complex legal issue, and the rights of youths, their parents, and the state vary considerably depending on the jurisdiction where the youth resides. Mental health professionals treating adolescents with mental disorders should be aware of the legal restrictions they face. In some states, depending on the age of the adolescent, treatment can be provided at the youth's request, without parental notification or permission. In other jurisdictions, at some point, parents must be notified and involved. Some states have mature minor statutes or case laws that allow older adolescents to seek treatment; many states do not. Inpatient hospitalization opens up entirely new issues for adolescents, health care professionals, and parents, as does the use of psychotropic medications, which are commonly prescribed to institutionalized patients. *Parens patriae* theory and the police power of the state remain the foundation for the development of the law as it relates to adolescents, even in the wake of growing empirical evidence that older adolescents are capable of making sound, reasoned, thoughtful medical and mental health care decisions.

Because youths are subject to the power of the juvenile court, those who are involved in the juvenile justice system have even fewer legal protections than troubled youth not in the system. Despite the movement toward a more punitive juvenile justice system and the granting of greater constitutional protections to youth involved in it, *parens patriae* gives the juvenile judge extensive authority to mandate a youth's treatment. As states like Washington enact legislation to strengthen the ability of juvenile judges to address certain status offenders, *parens patriae* will make it even more likely that some of these youth will be subjected to mandatory mental health treatment, even residential treatment. Juvenile judges in other states may rely on their contempt powers to bootstrap status offenders to delinquency status, giving the court authority to intervene more extensively in the juvenile's life.

Is mandatory treatment in the best interest of an adolescent with mental health disorders, regardless of his or her involvement or lack thereof in the juvenile justice system? There is no definitive answer. Without adequate treatment options, however, we may never know. Mandatory treatment in a community-based or residential program that is not suited to provide good care may be an expensive exercise in futility. Unfortunately, we know that not enough good treatment programs are available and that mental health treatment in juvenile correctional facilities is inadequate. There is little dispute that a court's or parents' power to initiate mandatory treatment should result in the provision of appropriate and adequate care. The other issue related to mandatory treatment is whether we are widening the net and bringing into treatment youth who do not suffer from mental health disorders, especially as we extend juvenile courts' power to address status offenders. As mentioned earlier, there's already evidence that this may be happening. Without adequate screening and assessment, the likelihood of those types of "mistakes" occurring is high. Although courts and legislatures are beginning to recognize that older adolescents possess the ability and right (although often restricted) under certain circumstances to request medical and mental health treatment, the right to refuse treatment has not been extended. What's not in doubt is that this is a controversial area of law and one that is continuing to evolve. Hopefully, the recent attention focused on youth with mental health disorders will trigger policy and program development, accompanied by research that creates an effective, cohesive, and comprehensive approach while protecting the autonomy rights of older adolescents.

NOTES

1. Weithorn, 2005.
2. Teplin et al., 2006; Robertson, Dill, Husain, & Undesser, 2004.
3. Wasserman, as cited in Weithorn, 2005, p. 14.
4. Vander Stoep, as cited in Weithorn, 2005, p. 14.
5. Cocozza & Skowyra, 2000.
6. Hartman, 2000.
7. Hartman, 2000.

8. Hartman, 2000.
9. Lexcen & Reppucci, 1998.
10. Hartman, 2001.
11. Hartman, 2001.
12. Talmadge, 2006.
13. Talmadge, 2006.
14. Hartman, 2001.
15. Hartman, 2002.
16. Scherer, 1991, as cited in Hartman, 2000, p. 56.
17. Hartman, 2000; Talmadge, 2006.
18. Reeves, 2004.
19. Lexcen & Reppucci, 1998.
20. Reeves, 2004.
21. Redding. 2000.
22. Melton, et al., 1998.
23. Weithorn, 2005.
24. Talmadge, 2006.
25. Talmadge, 2006.
26. Talmadge, 2006.
27. Lexcen & Reppucci, 1998; Talmadge, 2006.
28. Lexcen & Reppucci, 1998.
29. Costello, 2003.
30. Eggers, 1998.
31. Cocozza & Skowyra, 2000.
32. Teplin et al., 2006.
33. Kamradt, 2000.
34. Kamradt, 2000.
35. Jainchill, Hawke, & Messina, 2005.

REFERENCES

Cocozza, J. J., & Skowyra, K. (2000). Youth with mental health disorders: Issues and emerging responses. *Juvenile Justice, VII*(1), 3–13.

Costello, J. (2003). "Wayward and noncompliant" people with mental disabilities: What advocates of involuntary outpatient commitment can learn from the juvenile court experience with status offender jurisdiction. *Psychology, Public Policy and Law, 9*, 233–257.

Eggers, T. Z. (1998). The "Becca Bill" would not have saved Becca: Washington state's treatment of young female offenders. *Law and Inequality, 16*, 219–257.

Hartman, R. G. (2000). Adolescent autonomy: Clarifying an ageless conundrum. *Hastings Law Journal, 51*, 1265–1362.

Hartman, R. G. (2001). Adolescent decisional autonomy for medical care: Physician perceptions and practices. *University of Chicago Law School Roundtable, 8*, 87–134.

Hartman, R. G. (2002). Coming of age: Devising legislation for adolescent medical decision-making. *American Journal of Law and Medicine, 28*, 409–453.

Jainchill, N., Hawke, J, & Messina, M. (2005). Post-treatment outcomes among adjudicated adolescent males and females in modified therapeutic community treatment. *Substance Abuse & Misuse, 40*, 975–996.

Kamradt, B. (2000). Wraparound Milwaukee: Aiding youth with mental health needs. *Juvenile Justice, VII*(1), 14–23.

Lexcen, F. J., & Reppucci, N. D. (1998). Effects of psychopathology on adolescent medical decision-making. *University of Chicago Law School Roundtable, 5,* 63–106.

Melton, G. B., Lyons, P., & Spaulding, W. J. (1998). *No place to go: The civil commitment of minors.* Lincoln: The University of Nebraska Press.

Redding, R. E. (2000). Barriers to meeting the mental health needs of offenders in the juvenile justice system. *Juvenile Justice Fact Sheet.* Charlottesville, VA: Institute of Law, Psychiatry, and Public Policy, University of Virginia.

Reeves, R. (2004). Voluntary hospitalization and adolescents. *Adolescent Psychiatry, 28,* 47–58.

Robertson, A. A., Dill, P. L., Husain, J., & Undesser, C. (2004). Prevalence of mental illness and substance abuse disorders among incarcerated juvenile offenders in Mississippi. *Child Psychiatry and Human Development, 35*(10), 55–74.

Talmadge, S. A. (2006). Who should determine what is best for children in state custody who object to psychotropic medication? *Loyola University Chicago Institute for Health Law Annals of Health, 15,* 183–211.

Teplin, L. A., Abram, K. M., McClelland, G. M., Mericle, A. A., Dulcan, M. K., & Washburn, J. J. (2006). Psychiatric disorders of youth in detention. *Juvenile Justice Bulletin.* Washington, D.C.: Office of Juvenile Justice and Delinquency Prevention.

Weithorn, L. (2005). Envisioning second-order change to America's responses to troubled and troublesome youth. *Hofstra Law Review, 33,* 1305–1506.

CASES CITED

In re Gault, 387 U.S. 1 (1967).

Kent v. United States, 383 U.S. 541 (1966).

McKeiver v. Pennsylvania, 403 U.S. 528 (1971).

Mills v. Rogers, 457 U.S. 291 (1982).

Parham v. J.R., 442 U.S. 584 (1979).

Prince v. Massachusetts, 321 U.S. 158 (1923).

Tinker v. Des Moines, 393 U.S. 503 (1969).

Wisconsin v. Yoder, 406 U.S. 205 (1972).

CHAPTER 7

Faith-based Juvenile Justice Initiatives

Edward J. Schauer, Elizabeth M. Wheaton,
and Ila J. Schauer

INTRODUCTION AND DEFINITIONS

Faith-based initiatives are based on "charitable choice." Sider defines charitable choice as follows:

> The fundamental purpose of the Charitable Choice section of the Personal Responsibility and Work Opportunity Act of 1996 was to remove illegitimate restrictions of faith-based organizations so that when state and local governments using federal welfare block grant funds from the 1996 Welfare Bill chose to contract with non-governmental social service providers, all types of faith-based providers including very religious ones would experience a level playing field and enjoy full opportunity to compete with all other non-governmental providers on an equal basis.[1]

The concept of charitable choice has been broadened since 1996 to include most state and government grant funding.

Definitions of faith-based programs are critical to scientific understanding of the issues surrounding these programs. The literature is rife with information based on extremely broad definitions of the term "faith based." These definitions may include any programming relating in any way to any religious belief regardless of the centrality of the religious belief to the programming, and may be applied without regard to whether the programming is receiving state or federal funding or whether an application has been made for state or federal funding. This is to say, in a nutshell, that the definition of faith-based programming is extremely nebulous, unclear, and imprecise, as presented in the literature. This imprecision makes scientific quantification and evaluation of faith-based programs almost impossible.

Conversely, for the purposes of this chapter, a narrow definition has been chosen. Faith-based initiatives are herein defined as juvenile justice programs or interventions sponsored or supervised by religious organizations that are funded totally or in part with state or federal government monies provided for their operation.

ARGUMENTS FOR AND AGAINST

Several arguments favor charitable choice and government funding of faith-based organizations. First, no governmental funds may be used for "sectarian worship, instruction or proselytization."[2] Second, charitable choice does not focus on the degree of an organization's religion or secularization, but only on the quality of services provided. Third, agencies have for many years received government funding—for example, religious foster care agencies, colleges, and hospitals have received government funding for decades. Those funded in times past, however, have tended to be more inclined toward service—service more or less as an end in itself—without the added goal of making religious converts.[3]

Fourth, proponents argue that often in inner-city environments, religious institutions are among the few functioning organizations that remain; and they appear to be succeeding when other institutions are failing.[4] Fifth, religious discrimination is reduced. Sider asks the rhetorical question, "Is it not blatant religious discrimination for government to fund only naturalistic and deistic providers and refuse to fund theistic programs?"[5] Thus, with a focus on outcomes, charitable choice offers equal funding opportunity to all providers, for all are to be judged on the basis of their effectiveness. Last, charitable choice is said to protect the religious integrity of providers, as well as the religious liberty of those served. Clients are free to demand secular providers and to opt out of religious activities.[6]

Four chief arguments are provided by those who oppose charitable choice. First, that charitable choice violates the establishment clause of the First Amendment of the U.S. Constitution in that it advances religion. Second, religious organizations use government monies to discriminate in hiring practices. Third, charitable choice endangers the religious freedom and choice of clients. And, fourth, through charitable choice, the vitality and autonomy of religious organizations is endangered.[7]

HISTORY OF FAITH-BASED INITIATIVES

Large faith-based organizations (FBOs) in the United States, such as Lutheran Services of America, Catholic Charities, United Jewish Communities, and the Salvation Army, have partnered with governments for more than 100 years in providing social welfare programming. These programs have received federal, state, and local government funding through their nonprofit subsidiaries.[8] These early FBOs were allowed to receive government funding for programs carried out in secular settings; and these early funding arrangements allowed their parent organizations to maintain their religious identities without government interference.[9]

The passage of the Welfare Reform Act of 1996 allowed federal, state, and local governments to fund a larger range of religious organizations with relaxed restrictions governing religious practice and the settings of social service delivery. FBOs could contract with states on the same basis as other service providers, could offer social services in religious settings, would not have to organize as nonprofit providers, and were free to use religious criteria in hiring practices. Beneficiaries would not be forced to receive services in religious settings or from religious service providers, but they would be provided with secular alternatives, if desired. Government funds, however, could not be used to fund sectarian worship, sectarian instruction, or proselytization.[10]

The charitable choice provisions from the Welfare Reform Act of 1996 were incorporated into subsequent social welfare programs. Included were the Department of Labor's Welfare to Work Initiative in 1997, the Community Services Block Grant in 1998, and the Substance Abuse and Mental Health Services Administration in 2000.[11]

Since 2000, President George W. Bush has been the major promoter of government collaboration with FBOs in the provision of social welfare services, including criminal and juvenile justice initiatives. During the presidential race, George Bush declared, "In every instance where my administration sees a responsibility to help people, we will look first to faith-based organizations, charities and community groups that have shown their ability to save and change lives."[12]

President Bush brought with him to the White House his experiences of implementing charitable choice programming while governor of Texas. Under then-Governor George W. Bush, the Texas Governor's Office successfully overcame difficult funding regulations to direct more government monies directly to faith-based programs for the poor and encouraged legislation that resulted in greater government funding for faith-based programming for prison ministries, day care, and drug-treatment centers.[13]

While in Texas, Governor Bush was successful in encouraging legislation in support of faith-based initiatives; however, although U.S. senators and representatives showed much interest in faith-based initiatives, Congressional legislation was not passed in support of the President's commitment to meet America's social needs through faith-based funding. Thus, President Bush formulated, promoted, and implemented faith-based initiatives by issuing executive orders to that end.

Centers for faith-based initiatives were created in five cabinet departments by Executive Order (EO 13198), which President Bush issued in 2001.[14] These centers were to coordinate departmental efforts to eliminate programmatic obstacles that face FBOs in seeking federal social service monies.

Private charitable giving to FBOs was promoted by a second Executive Order issued by President Bush in 2001 (EO 13199).[15] EO 13199 established the White House Office of Faith-Based and Community Initiatives (OFBCI). The OFBCI was created to integrate presidential policy across federal government agenda—to ensure rapid development, expansion, and implementation of faith-based initiatives.

A third Executive Order (EO 13279) was issued by President Bush in December of 2002, in part to clarify the components of faith-based initiatives, and in part to speak to First Amendment concerns.[16] EO 13279 prohibits religious discrimination on the part of federal agencies when awarding social service monies; eliminates the need for FBOs to establish a nonprofit status; and requires FBOs to separate social services from religious activities. It also states that the involvement of social service beneficiaries in religious activities must be voluntary.

Thus, although legislation is lacking in the formulation and parameters of faith-based initiatives and programming, President Bush has crafted policy guidelines through the use of Executive Orders. Included in the concept of faith-based initiatives, therefore, is the urging of federal, state, and local governmental agencies by President Bush to, first, welcome grant applications from FBOs and, second, encourage FBOs to collaborate with the government in providing social welfare and juvenile justice interventions and services. Newlin concludes, "(T)he Bush administration propelled faith-based initiatives into the policy implementation phase by issuing an executive order (EO), thereby empowering faith-based initiatives with the force of law."[17]

RESEARCH ON THE MERITS OF FAITH-BASED SERVICES

At this time, it is extremely difficult to show empirical merit for faith-based juvenile justice or social welfare interventions. Walton, special editor for the *Research in Social Work Practice* journal, summarized the present state of evaluation research in the following words:

> I share your bewilderment with regard to the definition of "faith-based programs." When Bruce Thyer and I decided to do a special issue for RSWP, we were thinking more along the lines of government-funded programs. We wanted to capitalize on the Charitable Choice initiative. However, I'm afraid we were a bit premature. Most of those government-funded programs have not been running long enough to be evaluated.[18]

Studies do exist that purport to show effectiveness with faith-based programming. Many of these are invalid, however, in the sense that they show the results of involvement in communities of faith or in religious programming, but they do not consider the results of government-funded, faith-based juvenile justice and social welfare interventions.[19] In a very real sense, therefore, these studies are measuring the effects of religiosity or religious activity on the subjects' mental, emotional, or physical health or on the subjects' behaviors. But they are not measuring the effects of government-funded, faith-based interventions on juvenile (or adult) behaviors or health.

A third research consideration would be to measure the effectiveness of faith-based interventions against that of pervasively secular interventions or against that of government agency interventions. The preceding statement will elicit smiles from juvenile justice practitioners and academics, because they know that successes in interventions are measured by extremely small percentages, and sometimes these successes are not discernable.

If indeed the recently government-funded faith-based organizations have not been running long enough to be evaluated, as Walton believes, how well have the large traditional faith-based agencies done in effectiveness of interventions? Newlin states that before 2001, "[l]ong-time recipients of federal funding—such as Catholic Charities, United Jewish Communities, and Lutheran Services of America—had not measured the effectiveness of their work."[20] Thus, in supporting the concept of faith-based initiatives, yet lacking outcome data, the Republican majority in the U.S. House of Representatives instead used the existing research that showed the *successful implementation* of faith-based programs as well as research that indicated *public support* for faith-based and government collaborations.[21]

Although it is difficult to show success in significant proportions of social welfare or juvenile justice interventions, the authors have many years of experience in observing the faith-based community. Based on these two points, the authors posit that the programs of the traditional faith-based agencies were driven and directed more by the need to do what they believed to be *right*, than by the need to base program particulars on the small, incremental differences discovered through vigorous empirical testing. This concept was stated, in a nutshell, by Mother Teresa when she said, "It's not success that we're called to, it's faithfulness."[22] Thus, a philosophical goal differential exists between FBOs and government researchers. Additionally, many taxpayers simply support the more austere and low budget operating base of the FBOs, particularly in terms of overhead and staffing. The monies received by these FBOs appear to be largely spent directly on programs for, and service to, their beneficiaries.

EXAMPLES OF FAITH-BASED PROGRAMS

We review five programs below as examples of different approaches to faith-based initiatives in juvenile justice. Interested readers might want to compare their features for similarities and differences. It becomes clear that there is no one approach being embraced.

Ten-Point Coalitions

Ten-Point Coalitions are ecumenical groups of clergy and laity that focus on issues affecting black and Latino youth. This movement was born in 1992 as a direct reaction to escalating youth gang violence in Boston, which could no longer be ignored after a shooting that disrupted a funeral service at the Morning Star Baptist Church. The Coalition's ten points are as follows: adopting youth gangs, sending mediators/mentors into juvenile facilities, placing youth workers on the streets, creating concrete and specific economic alternatives to the drug economy, linking churches to inner-city ministries, establishing neighborhood watches, partnering church and health care facilities, promoting brotherhood as a rational alternative to violence, supporting rape crisis and battered women centers, developing curriculum to increase literacy, and enhancing young people's relationship with their creator. Several cities have established Ten-Point Coalitions and are receiving government grants to support their programs, such as partnerships between the community and police, courts, and detention personnel.[23]

Straight Ahead

Straight Ahead is a Boston program oriented toward juvenile offenders. Straight Ahead ministries have as their goal to share faith in God with youth in jails and juvenile facilities. Volunteers work with these juveniles as mentors, tutors, and counselors. One program example is their Aftercare Home Ministry, a halfway house for youths coming out of detention. These youth are expected to go to school and work part time. They live in a home with a family atmosphere, and they participate in service projects and have the opportunity to attend a summer wilderness trip. Straight Ahead attempts to be a connection between facilities and the faith community. Funded by private donations and federal grants, Straight Ahead has clearly defined goals, philosophies, and training guidelines.[24]

Youth and Congregations in Partnership

Youth and Congregations in Partnership (YCP) is a prosecutor-created program in Brooklyn, New York. "Too often a youth gets into trouble just because he or she has no one to show them how to succeed," says Charles J. Hynes, Kings County District Attorney.[25] It was this thought that prompted the district attorney's office to reach out to the faith community for help. Youths who have become involved with the courts are offered the opportunity to work closely with a trained mentor on a weekly basis. This one-on-one life training offers the young person such help as tutoring, teamwork, anger management, and conflict resolution. A contract is drawn up, and it is by meeting the stipulations of the contract that the partners measure success. Jointly funded by federal grants and the Pinkerton Foundation, this program has been actively changing young people's lives since 1997.

Amachi

Amachi, which began in Philadelphia, seeks to link volunteers with children who have an incarcerated parent. There are approximately seven million children in America with a parent in prison and as many as 70 percent of them are at risk of going to prison themselves. A unique partnership between the faith community and human services providers, Amachi seeks to connect these children to a local congregation in or near their neighborhood, build a strong relationship between them and their mentors, and provide professional case managers for support. Amachi is funded by federal grants and the Pew Charitable Trusts. The Amachi model has been adopted by more than 100 cities in 38 states. It calls for community impact directors to oversee two church volunteer coordinators, who in turn coordinate the efforts of their volunteers. In many cities, the Amachi program is operated under the auspices of Big Brothers Big Sisters.[26]

Faith and Action

Using a holistic approach to solving their social problems, the United Way of Massachusetts Bay (UWMB) took a close look at the offers to help that come from faith-based groups. Instead of viewing spirituality as a problem, they embraced it along with mentoring, tutoring, job training, and counseling as acceptable and desirable parts of a healthy youth program. They focused on three basic criteria: (1) a strong commitment to youth, (2) faith-based efforts to reach youth beyond the congregations, and (3) spirituality. Both the United Way board and donors saw the wisdom of this approach and accepted the policy. The United Way decided that they would not fund any religious services or permit proselytizing, but they would accept help with their troubled youth. With the support of the Annie E. Casey Foundation and President Bush's Faith Based Initiative, the volunteer programs of Massachusetts Bay have grown and flourished.[27]

PROGRAM TYPES

The Office of Juvenile Justice and Delinquency Prevention's (OJJDP) *Model Programs Guide* (MPG) lists the different program types involved in the various stages of juvenile justice stages.[28] These programs can be divided into four categories: voluntary prevention, intervention, diversion, and aftercare. Many faith-based programs that are receiving funding from the U.S. government through the Compassion Capital Fund are involved in these different categories.

Some aspects of programming span several of these program types with different emphasis. For instance, academic skills enhancement projects occur in voluntary prevention, diversion, and aftercare; conflict resolution and interpersonal skills projects are found in voluntary prevention, intervention, and diversion; and drug/alcohol therapy and education projects occur in voluntary prevention, intervention, and aftercare. Mentoring is a big part of all of the subcategories of delinquency prevention programs. These programs pair an older, caring adult with a young person who needs support and guidance.

The following information is organized by the program types and is based on the definitions listed in the MPG. Examples of faith-based programs involved in each subcategory are provided.

Voluntary Prevention

Programs in voluntary prevention focus on steering youth toward healthy life choices. Voluntary prevention programs include academic skills enhancement, after-school recreation, conflict resolution/interpersonal skills, drug/alcohol therapy and education, gang membership prevention, leadership and development, mentoring, and truancy prevention.

The Leon de Juda congregation's Higher Education Resource Center in Boston, Massachusetts, predominantly serves Hispanic inner-city high school students to help them prepare for college. The church matches urban teens with Christian college student mentors. In addition, the program helps students with their college applications and the financial aid process.

Gang membership prevention programs seek to deter youth from joining gangs and gang-related activities. Open Door Youth Gang Alternatives Program of Denver, Colorado, offers counseling and support groups to youth who are being pressured to join gangs and to youth who wish to leave a gang.

Leadership and youth development programs promote activities that challenge youth to build new skills and develop their own strengths. Petersburg Urban Ministries' YouthBuild in Petersburg, Virginia, works with youth who are unemployed, low-income, and possibly homeless. Among the benefits to youth in this program are learning leadership and life skills, getting job training, and receiving mentoring.

Voluntary prevention programs like Coopersville Reformed Church's Kids Hope program in Coopersville, Michigan, pairs adults with at-risk public elementary students for tutoring and mentoring. Youth learn the value of schoolwork as well as life lessons.

Regular school attendance is the goal of truancy prevention programs. Many faith-based programs that provide academic skills enhancement, youth development programs, and mentoring indirectly provide truancy prevention services. Catholic Charities' Teen Community Awareness Program (T-CAP) provides services to teens who are at risk of becoming high school dropouts and teens who have truancy problems. The program also serves runaways.

Intervention

Intervention programs are designed to lead youths away from delinquency. These programs include alternative schools, school/classroom environment, drug/alcohol therapy and education, conflict resolution and interpersonal skills, drug court, family therapy, gang intervention, gun court, mentoring, teen and youth courts, and wraparound programs.

Conflict resolution/interpersonal skills projects are again found in intervention. The Juvenile Interventional and Faith Based Follow-up (JIFF) program in Memphis, Tennessee, provides tutoring, mentoring, and Bible study to youths who have been incarcerated. Programs related to gang prevention also take the form of gang intervention. At this stage, programs work with gang members to ease conflict situations. Hope Now for Youth of Fresno, California, serves youth who have been or currently are gang members. Among the program's services to gang members are job and life skills training, substance abuse treatment, and medical and legal services. Mentoring is a large part of gang intervention and other intervention programs.

Diversion

During diversion, nontraditional methods are used as alternatives to detention. Acceptance in these programs usually requires the agreement of the court, counselors, and parents. Programs in diversion include classroom curricula, cognitive behavioral treatment, day treatment, correctional facilities, group homes, home confinement, mentoring, residential treatment centers, and wilderness camps and challenge programs.

Mentoring plays a large role in diversion. Friends in Transition in Colorado pairs volunteers with youth who are in their last year of secure custody. The volunteers mentor the youth for several months as they transition back into the community.

Wilderness camps and challenge programs may be used for residential placement of juvenile offenders. These programs physically and mentally challenge youth toward personal growth. Love Demonstrated Ministries' Christian Boot Camp in San Antonio, Texas, challenges juvenile offenders with physical training and community service projects.

Aftercare

Aftercare may be defined in different ways depending on whether the practitioner considers aftercare to begin after an offender's release from detention or after sentencing. Here, aftercare is defined as programs that work with juveniles, who have spent time in out-of-home placement, to reintegrate them into the community. Programs within aftercare include academic skills enhancement, drug/alcohol therapy and education, classroom curricula, family therapy, mentoring, probation services, restorative justice, and vocational/job training.

Similar to voluntary prevention and diversion, aftercare includes academic skills enhancement, drug/alcohol therapy and education, classroom curricula, and family care. Catholic Charities' Teen Community Awareness Program provides substance abuse education, tutoring, mentoring, and cultural activities to youth.

Similar to intervention, family therapy and mentoring are a large part of aftercare. The absence of a parent from a family because of incarceration places the children at risk. Urban Ventures' Center of Fathering in Minneapolis, Minnesota, seeks to support and educate fathers and to mentor their sons and other boys with no active fathers. Amachi in Philadelphia, Pennsylvania, serves the children of prisoners by providing them with adult mentors.

Restorative justice programs seek to repair harm caused by juvenile delinquency through acts such as mediation, restitution, and community service. Catholic Charities' Restorative Justice Programs work with juvenile offenders to teach them about the impact of their actions, how to become accountable, and how to make amends for past actions.

NOTES

1. Sider, 2002, p. 2.
2. Carlson-Thies, 2000, pp. 38–39.
3. Sider, 2002, p. 3.
4. DiIulio, 2002, p. 21.
5. DiIulio, 2002, p. 6.
6. Sider, 2002, p. 6.
7. Matsui & Chuman, 2001, pp. 31–33; Sider, 2002, p. 7.
8. Newlin, 2003, p. 2; Monsma, 1996.
9. Small, 2002.
10. Newlin, 2003, p. 3; Small, 2001.
11. Newlin, 2003, p. 4.
12. Bush, 1999.
13. Newlin, 2003, p. 7; Safire, 1999.
14. Executive Order No. 13198, 2001.
15. Executive Order No. 13199, 2001.
16. Executive Order No. 13279, 2001.
17. Newlin, 2003, p. 2.
18. Walton, 2006.
19. For example, Johnson, Tompkins, & Webb, 2002; Koenig, McCullough, & Larson, 2001.
20. Newlin, 2003, p. 10.
21. Newlin, 2003, p. 10; H. R. Report No. 107–138, 2001.
22. Austensen & Poag, 2002, p. 10.
23. National TenPoint Leadership Foundation Web site, 2006.
24. Straight Ahead Ministries Web site, 2007.
25. Kings County District Attorney's Office Web site, 2007
26. Amachi Mentoring Web site, 2007; Goode & Smith, 2005.
27. Anne E. Casey Foundation, n.d.
28. Office of Juvenile Justice and Delinquency Prevention, n.d.

REFERENCES

Amachi Mentoring Web site. (2007). Retrieved January 17, 2007 from www.amachimentoring.org.

Anne E. Casey Foundation. (n.d.). *Faith and action: Improving the lives of at-risk youth.* Baltimore: The Anne E. Casey Foundation.

Austensen, B., & Poag, D. (2002). *Site visit to cornerstone assistance network: A faith-based intermediary organization.* Takoma Park, MD: Welfare Peer Technical Assistance Network.

Bush, G. W. (1999). *The duty of hope*. Retrieved May 15, 2006, from www.vote-smart.org.

Carlson-Thies, S. W. (2000). *Charitable choice for welfare community services*. Washington, D.C.: Center for Public Justice.

DiIulio, J. J. (2002, May 4). *Faith-based programs can enjoy success where secular programs have failed*. Speech to the National Institute of Justice, Washington, D.C.

Executive Order No. 13198. (2001). Retrieved April 17, 2006, from www.white house.gov.

Executive Order No. 13199. (2001). Retrieved April 17, 2006 from www.white house.gov.

Executive Order No. 13279. (2002). Retrieved April 17, 2006 from www.white house.gov.

Goode, W. W., Sr., & Smith, T. J. (2005). *Building from the ground up: Creating effective programs to mentor children of prisoners*. Philadelphia, PA: Public/Private Ventures.

House of Representatives, June 7, 2001. Report 107–138. Washington, D.C.: 107th Congress, First Session.

Johnson, B. R., Tompkins, R. B., & Webb, D. (2002). *Objective hope, assessing the effectiveness of faith-based organizations: A review of the literature*. Unpublished manuscript. Philadelphia, PA: Center for Research on Religion and Urban Civil Society, University of Pennsylvania.

Kings County District Attorney's Office Web site. (2007). Retrieved January 17, 2007 from www.brooklynda.org/ycp/ycppage.htm.

Koenig, H. G., McCullough, M. E., & Larson, D. B. (2001). *Handbook of religion and health*. New York: Oxford University.

Matsui, E., & Chuman, J. (2001). The case against charitable choice. *The Humanist, 61*(1), 31–33.

Monsma, S. V. (1996). *Religious non-profit organizations and public money: When sacred and secular mix*. Lanham, MD: Rowman and Littlefield.

National TenPoint Leadership Foundation Web site. (2006). Retrieved January 17, 2007 from www.ntlf.org.

Newlin, K. (2003, October 23). *Social welfare policy on the national agenda: Bush administration advances faith-based initiatives*. New Haven, CT: Yale University School of Nursing.

Office of Juvenile Justice and Delinquency Prevention. (n.d.). *Model programs guide*. Retrieved July 30, 2006, from www.dsgonline.com.

Safire, W. (1999, June 27). The way we live now: 6-27-99: On language; faith-based. *New York Times Magazine*, Section 6, p. 16.

Sherman, A. (2002). *Collaborations catalogue: A report on charitable choice implementation in 15 states*. New York: Hudson Institute.

Sider, R. J. (2002, October 15). *Evaluating the faith-based initiative: Is charitable choice good public policy?* The Sorensen Lecture. New Haven, CT: Yale Divinity School.

Small, M. A. (2001). Public service and outreach to faith-based organizations. *Journal of Higher Education Outreach and Engagement, 6*(1), 57–65.

Small, M. A. (2002). Comment: Achieving community justice through faith-based initiatives. *Behavioral Sciences and the Law, 20*(4), 411–421.

Straight Ahead Ministries Web site. (2007). Retrieved January 20, 2007 from www.straightahead.org.

Walton, E. (2006, May 10). Personal e-mail message from the special editor for the *Research in Social Work Practice* journal.

CHAPTER 8

Resurrecting Radical Nonintervention: Stop the War on Kids

Randall G. Shelden

It has been 30 years since noted sociologist Schur published a book called *Radical Non-Intervention: Rethinking the Delinquency Problem.*[1] His approach, which was part of the "labeling" tradition in criminology and the sociology of deviance, seemed quite novel back then as he challenged a number of assumptions taken toward the problem of delinquency. Ironically, I believe that his approach has more relevance to what is happening today with the various "get-tough" approaches to delinquency, especially "zero-tolerance" policies.

GETTING TOUGH, ZERO TOLERANCE, AND NET WIDENING

In recent years "law and order" politicians have stoked the fears of the public with their rhetoric about the new "menace" of teen "superpredators."[2] Despite the fact that serious crime among juveniles has dropped in recent years, many politicians continue the "get-tough" talk. "Zero tolerance" is one of the new mantras. Variations of the "zero-tolerance" mentality within schools and elsewhere in the community have taken us back more than 100 years as far as juvenile justice policy is concerned. More important, it has "widened the net" of social control—increasingly, minor offenses (or no offenses at all) are now being processed formally by the police and the juvenile court.

Examples abound, including the following: (1) a five-year prison sentence is handed out to a 17-year-old Texas high school basketball player who "threw an elbow" to the head of an opposing player in a basketball game; (2) two six-year-old children were suspended for three days for playing "cops and robbers" with their fingers (pretending their fingers were guns and going "bang, bang" toward other children); (3) a girl who gave a friend a Nuprin was suspended for "dealing drugs"; (4) some high school baseball players were suspended for possessing "dangerous weapons" on school grounds—a teacher who suspected them of having drugs searched for but found none, instead finding baseball bats in their cars; (5) a 14-year-old boy was charged by school police with a felony for throwing a deadly missile (which turned out to be a Halloween "trick or treat" of throwing an egg)—he was taken away in handcuffs and put in juvenile detention; (6) in Florida, a six-year-old was charged with trespassing when he took a shortcut through the schoolyard on his way home (how many of us did that as a kid?); (7) in Indianola, Mississippi, elementary school children have been arrested for talking during assemblies; (8) in Spokane, Washington, three boys were suspended for bringing two-inch-long "action figure toy guns" to school; (9) a 13-year-old girl in Massachusetts was expelled for having an empty lipstick tube in her purse—this was considered a "potential weapon"; and (10) in Texas, a "model student" was expelled when officials found a blunt-tipped bread knife in the back of his pickup, left there by his grandmother.[3]

One of the most recent incidents comes from Toledo, Ohio, where school officials have engaged in perhaps the most absurd forms of zero tolerance. According to a *New York Times* story,[4] on October 17, a 14-year-old girl was handcuffed by the police and hauled off to the local juvenile court. Her "crime" was the clothes she was wearing: a "low-cut midriff top under an unbuttoned sweater," which was a "clear violation of the dress code." The school offered to have her wear a bowling shirt, but she refused. Her mother came in and gave her an oversize T-shirt, which the girl also refused to wear, saying that it "was real ugly." According to the story, the girl is one of the more than two dozen arrested in school this past October for such "crimes" as being "loud and disruptive," "cursing at school officials," "shouting at classmates," and, of course, violating the dress code. Such "crimes" are violations of the city's "safe school ordinance." The juvenile court judge in this case remarked that this girl "didn't come across as a major problem at all. She just wanted to show off a certain image at school. Probably she just copped an attitude. I expect that from a lot of girls."[5] A new offense should be added to the ever-growing list of "zero-tolerance" offenses: "copping an attitude."

In schools all over the country, there has been a swelling of arrests by school police, mostly on minor charges, typically appearing within the "miscellaneous" category, which appear after serious assaults, property crimes, and drug offenses have been totaled in annual reports. One study found that between 1999 and 2001, there was a 300 percent increase in student arrests in the Miami-Dade public school system.[6] Where I live, in Las Vegas, Nevada, the school district police have reported increasing arrests for "crimes" placed in this miscellaneous category, going from about 80 percent of the total to more than 90 percent in the past 10 years. Such draconian measures have been put in place despite the facts that schools are the safest places for children and that serious crime on school grounds began declining long before such policies went into effect.[7]

Schools have been described as "day prisons," because they often have had that drab look of a prison and have been surrounded by plenty of fences. These days, it has become even worse, as a growing number of reports have noted. One recent report noted that many high school students are complaining that we are "making schools like prisons." This perceptive account further notes that:

> Most U.S. high school students will have to walk by numerous hidden cameras, outdoors and indoors, and go through an institutional-size metal detector manned by guards just to get into school each morning. Once there, students are subject to random searches of their bodies and belongings. Lockers can be searched without warning with or without the student present, and in many places police will use drug-sniffing dogs during raids where they search lockers and even students' parked cars.[8]

A lawsuit filed in June 2001 by the American Civil Liberties Union (ACLU) addressed some of these concerns at Locke High School in Los Angeles. Among the complaints were unreasonable searches, in which students were frisked and had their personal belongings examined in front of their peers. One of the plaintiffs in the case said, "The searches are embarrassing. They're treating us like we're criminals. It's turning school into a prison." A former student told a reporter that "There are 27 cameras on the second floor alone and they are going to put up more cameras to supposedly make it a safer place, when really you feel more like a criminal."[9] At Oswego High School in upstate New York, one such search was done without warning when several police squads with their drug-sniffing dogs searched students' lockers upon the request of the principal. They found a small amount of pot and a marijuana pipe in one student's pocket.[10]

Perhaps the most infamous case occurred in a small town called Goose Creek, South Carolina. Videotape from surveillance cameras shows dozens of students, some of them handcuffed, sitting on a hallway floor against the wall as they are watched by police officers with guns drawn and as police dogs sniff the backpacks and bags strewn across the hall. A report in the *Los Angeles Times* noted that parents were outraged over the incident, saying that the police went overboard.[11] No drugs were found. The author saw portions of the videotape and it looked like the Gestapo with about 10 or 12 armed police roaming the halls yelling and making the students lie down on the floor.

Hundreds more such examples could be presented, which brings us to my point. In recent years, the juvenile justice system has been accused of being too lenient (actually adults often get treated more lightly for comparable crimes) and so a get-tough movement has taken over. One result is that minor indiscretions that once were handled informally or even ignored are now being formally processed, thus clogging the system so much that it barely has time to deal with the serious crimes and truly problematic youth. Upon the passage of various get-tough laws, officials now look in vain to find the superpredators and, finding few, end up targeting minor offenders. I call this the "trickle-down" effect.

Contrary to the media and most politicians, the most serious juvenile offenders—the so-called chronic violent predator or superpredator—are rare. All across the nation, we search in vain for these kinds of youths and discover that they usually constitute less than 3 percent of all juvenile offenders (but they dominate the headlines, making us think they are the norm; after all, "if it bleeds, it leads"). Sometimes we are told that a certain percentage of youths referred to juvenile court are charged with "crimes against the person" or "violent crimes," when in fact the majority of these crimes are rather minor in nature—a fist fight between teenagers, a fight between children and their parents or between siblings, a mere threat, and so on. In short, the kinds of personal confrontations that people of my generation were involved in all the time when we were young, but no police showed up and no referrals were made to court. What happened? The community handled it on its own—the schools, neighbors, community groups, and even the kids themselves. Even the police—like those where I grew up—handled these infractions through a stern lecture and a warning (chances are they knew you or your parents).

But now we are driven by media images of the young predator, the rare killers on school campuses, or the so-called gang-bangers, and we are reacting as if this represents the typical youthful offender. I call these reactions "exception-based policies." Conservatives, and to a large extent liberals, have responded to worst-case scenarios by instituting policies as if the exceptional cases are the norm. The rare case in which a youth brings a gun on school grounds, the rare serious violent crime on school grounds, and other such incidents determine public policies.

We are obsessed with the need to identify the next superpredator, preferably at the earliest age possible. This means we crack down on minor offenses, or no offenses at all, as in cases in which we target so-called high-risk children. There is an assumption that minor offenses will inevitably lead to bigger crimes later in life and that there is an easy way to identify future criminals, both of which are not true.

Part of the problem is that America really loves its wars, as we always seem to want to solve a problem by declaring a "war" on it. As soon as we have declared a war, this immediately creates an "us versus them" situation and a siege mentality—as in the erroneous, but ever-popular belief that criminals, gangs, and drug dealers are taking over. In this case, we have launched, in effect, a "war on children." And as in any other war, the attitude tends to be that we may have innocent casualties or, continuing the war metaphor, that there will be "collateral damage," meaning that losses must be anticipated for the greater good of winning the war (suggesting that it is too bad that some innocent children are victimized or that minor offenses are criminalized). It is time we made some drastic changes in the way we handle crime and delinquency in this society. We don't need to "get tough" with these kids; we just need to "get smart" by changing our attitude toward minor juvenile transgressions. More important, however, we adults need to look in the mirror and realize that we are part of the problem; guess what age group commits the most crime and the most horrible of crimes? And guess what age group uses the most drugs, drinks the most alcohol, and abuses (and even kills) the most kids? It's the adults. But we avoid our own problems by making juveniles our scapegoats.[12]

We need another approach to this problem, and we don't have to look very far to find a model to guide us, for it appeared 30 years ago in Schur's excellent book. The aim in this chapter is to first provide a brief summary of Schur's book and next outline a policy that can take advantage of his insights from some 30 years ago.

THE LABELING PERSPECTIVE: AN OVERVIEW

Schur's work was one of many during the 1960s and 1970s that endorsed the "labeling" perspective. The labeling perspective does not address in any direct way the causes of criminal or deviant behavior but rather focuses on three interrelated processes: (1) how and why certain behaviors are defined as criminal or deviant, (2) the response to crime or deviance on the part of authorities (e.g., the official processing of cases from arrest through sentencing), and (3) the effects of such definitions and official reactions on the person or people so labeled (e.g., how official responses to groups of youths may cause them to come closer together and begin to call themselves a gang).[13] The key to this perspective is reflected in a statement by Becker more than 40 years ago, who wrote, "Social groups create deviance by making the rules whose infraction constitutes deviance, and by applying those rules to particular people and labeling them as outsiders."[14]

One key aspect of the labeling perspective is that the juvenile and criminal justice system (including the legislation that creates laws and hence defines crime and criminals) helps to perpetuate crime and deviance. Definitions of "delinquency" and "crime" stem from differences in power and status in the larger society, and those without power are the most likely to have their behaviors labeled as "delinquency." Delinquency may be generated, and especially perpetuated, through negative labeling by significant others and by the judicial system; one may associate with others who are similarly labeled, such as gangs. One of the most significant perspectives on crime and criminal behavior to emerge from the labeling tradition was Quinney's theory of the "social reality of crime." Among other things, Quinney argued that "criminal definitions describe behaviors that conflict with the interests of the segments of society that have the power to shape public policy" and that such definitions "are applied by the segments of society that have the power to shape the enforcement and administration of criminal law." Moreover, he explained, "behavior patterns are structured in segmentally organized society in relation to criminal definitions, and within this context, persons engage in actions that have relative probabilities of being defined as criminal."[15]

One of the key concepts for Quinney is *power*, which is an elementary force in our society. Power, says Quinney, "is the ability of persons and groups to determine the conduct of other persons and groups. It is utilized not for its own sake, but is the vehicle for the enforcement of scarce values in society, whether the values are material, moral, or otherwise." Power is important if we are to understand public policy. Public policy, including crime-control policy, is shaped by groups with special interests. In a class society, some groups have more power than others and therefore are able to have their interests represented in policy decisions, often at the expense of less powerful groups. Thus, for example, white upper-class males have more power and their interests are more likely to be represented than those of working- or lower-class minorities and women. Another way of putting it would be to say that *the imposition of a deviant (or delinquent) label is an exercise in power*. Thus, those with the most power and resources at their disposal are able to resist being so labeled.

Two types of offenses perhaps best illustrate this problem: status offenses and drugs. In each case, the laws are directed against powerless groups: juveniles and lower-class racial minorities. Historical studies have documented the biases built into the very definitions of both of these types of offenses.[16] For juveniles, however, the very existence of "status offenses" demonstrates the power that the adult world has over kids. Offenses like behavior that is labeled "incorrigible," "unmanageable," and "beyond control" are so vague as to defy precise definitions. Similarly, running away from home is often responded to differently depending on gender. For instance, girls, who are about as equally as likely as boys to run away, are far more likely to be arrested, sent to juvenile court, detained, and even institutionalized.[17]

In *Radical Non-Intervention*, Schur takes a key feature of the labeling perspective, namely that it allows us to question traditional responses to delinquency and proceeds to outline a totally different, radical approach. The radical nonintervention approach begins with the premise that we should "leave kids alone wherever possible."[18] Schur's book is divided into three major sections, each corresponding to three typologies used to address the problem: (1) treating the individual, (2) reforming society, and (3) radical nonintervention. Each of these typologies will be briefly reviewed.

TREATING THE INDIVIDUAL

One of the most popular explanations of delinquency is that it is a "symptom" of some "underlying problem" within the individual delinquent. Although the "child-savers" who helped create the first juvenile court in Chicago in 1899 could be described as "social reformers," the basic approach has always been to focus on the individual delinquent, with perhaps some lip service given to the social causes of crime and delinquency. As Schur notes, there is an "assumption of basic differentness" in that delinquent behavior is "attributed primarily to the special characteristics of individual delinquents." Therefore, the appropriate treatment response is to determine that "we have delinquency because we have delinquents; we must do something *to* or *for* them if we are to rid ourselves of the problem."[19] The favored method of treatment is the clinical model, which seeks to first identify youths who are "predelinquent" (or the modern equivalent, "at risk") and subject them to some form of intervention. At the same time, this model seeks to intervene clinically after these individuals have been formally defined as "delinquents" by the juvenile justice system. One of the main criticisms of this approach is that such predictions always tend to *overpredict* and therefore creates a lot of "false positives" (in which a juvenile is predicted to become a delinquent and they do not). Schur cites the famous Glueck studies that spawned the Cambridge-Sommerville Youth Study in which less than one-third of those identified as predelinquent actually got into trouble and most of these youths, then and now, only commit minor offenses and do not continue into a life of serious crime.

Some of the techniques used by those adhering to this approach have had extremely negative results, such as various "behavior modification" procedures, especially those that endorse the use of drugs. Such techniques have had a sinister history, beginning with the "eugenics" movement during the late-nineteenth and early twentieth centuries. This movement occurred in the context of widespread fear and nativism. The aim of this movement was to eliminate, or at least physically remove, so-called bad seeds from an otherwise healthy American soil. This movement was based on the theory of eugenics, which holds that certain problem behaviors are inherited and can be reduced and perhaps eliminated altogether by preventing the carriers of these bad seeds from reproducing. This theory was based in part on the idea that there are certain groups—especially racial groups—that are inherently "defective" (it was during this same period of time that the term "defective delinquent" was popular), somewhat less than human, and naturally inferior.[20]

Although Schur was warning us about the possible negative effects of behavior modification, mentioning specifically the use of drugs, he never could have predicted what would transpire within the next 30 years. One of the most recent ventures into this subject area can be found in the work of Dr. Gail Wasserman, a professor of Child Psychiatry at Columbia University, who is in charge of one of the most recent in a long line of attempts to get to the so-called root causes of violent crime. What are these root causes? They supposedly are found in the genes of certain kinds of children. What kinds of children? Let Dr. Wasserman tell you: "It is proper to focus on blacks and other minorities as they are over represented in the courts and not well studied." So she and her colleagues decided to "study" these "predisposed to violence" youth—all males, all minorities, all ages 6 to 10—by giving them doses of a dangerous drug called fenfluramine (the main ingredient in the diet drug "fen phen"). These children, who had no criminal record but were considered to be at "high risk" (code word for poor urban minorities) for future violence, were given a dose of this drug to examine the effects of "environmental stressors" on their levels of serotonin. Fenfluramine, by the way, was withdrawn just a few months after this research was completed (late 1997) because, among other things, it causes potentially fatal heart valve impairments in many patients, as well as brain cell death in others.[21]

In 1989, the Department of Health and Human Services and the Public Health Service issued a report calling for strategies of intervention in "minority homicide and violence." The report cited as causes of violence factors like poverty, unemployment, homelessness, the availability of guns, and the glorification of violence within American culture. Yet its recommendation for prevention focused on identifying *individuals* and *modifying* their behavior—mostly, as it turned out, with medication. The report flatly stated that "[t]argeting individuals with a predisposition to, but no history of, violence would be considered primary as in programs to screen for violent behavior." This would require "tools to facilitate screening out high-risk individuals for early intervention." Such screening would target hospital emergency rooms, health centers, jails, and schools "at the lowest levels" where "acting out" behavior can be identified and dealt with. Perhaps more important, the program would conduct research "on the biomedical, molecular, and genetic underpinnings of interpersonal violence, suicidal behavior, and related mental and behavioral disorders."[22]

More alarming is the fact that infants would be a central focus, with many studies starting at birth. After all, so the logic goes, biological factors must be present at that age, which would predict future violent behavior. It does not take much of an imagination to deduce which children would be the target of such interventions. In fact, subsequent developments of these various violence initiatives specifically stated that the children of the poor and racial minorities would be the target, as suggested by Wasserman's quote. Consider the findings of a paper delivered at a 1989 conference of the American Association for the Advancement of Science, which claimed that research shows that whites and Asians are superior to African Americans who, the paper claimed, are "smaller brained, slower to mature, less sexually restrained and more aggressive." This is not occurring the nineteenth century, nor even the 1930s and 1940s, when such racist beliefs were generally accepted. It's occurring in the twenty-first century when we are supposedly more enlightened.

The Department of Justice soon got into the action with its "Program on Human Development and Criminal Behavior." Illustrating the "scientific" basis of this program and the role of academics in legitimating such movements, it should be noted that both the director and codirector of this project were, respectively, Felton Earls, professor of Child Psychiatry at Harvard Medical School, and Albert J. Reiss, professor of Sociology at Yale's Institute for Social and Police Studies. (The search for the "genetic" source of criminal behavior has always been led by noted academics. The early eugenics movement was at least indirectly supported by academic criminologists, sociologists, and anthropologists from Harvard University, among others. Such support is crucial for the continuation of such programs.) This program would screen and identify children as "potential offenders" who are "in need of preventive treatment or control." Specifically, the research would target nine age groups starting in infancy and continuing at ages 3, 6, 9, 12, 15, 18, 21, and 24. The key question to be answered would be, according to the directors of the research, "What biological, biomedical, and psychological characteristics, some of them present from the beginning of life, put children at risk for delinquency and criminal behavior?"

Led by psychiatrists and funded by some of the largest pharmaceutical companies (such as Lilly, the maker of Prozac, Pfizer, Upjohn, Hoffman-La Roche, Abbott Laboratories, and many more), a program of "research" called the Violence Initiative Project is now under way and has received additional funding from the National Institute of Mental Health. The "crime-control industry" has expanded to include what may be called the "drug-control industry" because all sorts of alleged "problem behaviors" exhibited by children are viewed as biological in nature and in some cases genetic. As Breggin and Breggin write,

> Children's disorders and disruptive or violent behavior in particular remain growth markets. Powerful vested interests, including giant pharmaceutical firms, stand to profit mightily from proposed applications of biological research. Biomedical researchers and their labs and institutes will not readily fold or refrain and retool for wholly different kinds of research.[23]

I am certain Schur would agree that these approaches to delinquency should be rejected outright, because they violate some of the most elementary principles of social justice and individual liberty. But the approaches persist mainly because it is the adults who are in charge who have the most power over children.

Schur continues his analysis of individual approaches by focusing on such techniques as counseling, probation services, and various kinds of community treatment. His review of the literature on these approaches found little to be enthusiastic about 30 years ago; more recent updates continue to find few success stories. For the most part, typical probation and parole approaches continue to use individualized techniques and, in fact, often accomplish little more than surveillance. This approach is symbolized perfectly by a sign Jerome Miller, juvenile justice reformer and former head of the Massachusetts Department of Youth Services, saw on the office wall of a California probation officer, which read "trail 'em, surveil 'em, nail 'em and jail 'em."[24]

Institutional treatment has come under constant criticism for many of the same reasons, namely that the method continues to focus on the individual delinquent. Schur's analysis 30 years ago noted this inevitable conflict between treatment and custody, with the latter almost invariably winning. More recent reviews of institutional treatment are no more promising.[25]

REFORMING SOCIETY

Traditional sociological theories stress the importance of the surrounding social structure and culture as the most important causes of crime and delinquency. These theories shift the focus away from the *individual* characteristics and toward the *social* characteristics that cause people to become delinquents. As Schur pointed out, however, with these theories, delinquents are still to be distinguished from nondelinquents. The only change is that under sociological theories it is the *social conditions* that differentiate them rather than *personal attributes*. Therefore, the goal should be to change the surrounding social conditions rather than changing individuals.

Although he reviews most of the standard sociological theories (e.g., strain, cultural deviance), Schur challenges the assumption that delinquency is strictly a lower-class phenomenon, noting that self-report studies demonstrate that virtually every juvenile commits some form of delinquent act. Over the years, many have taken these research findings and concluded that class and race don't matter when it comes to causes of delinquency. So, for instance, we see that Hirschi's control theory stipulates that it is the lack of bonding that causes delinquency, regardless of race or class.[26] A great body of research now demonstrates that social inequality and racism are indeed major causes of crime and delinquency. As Schur and many others have pointed out, however, these are causes of certain kinds of criminal behavior, but certainly not all criminal behavior. When we consider the fact that white-collar and corporate crime costs society between $500 billion and $1 trillion per year, the relatively petty crimes of the lower class pale in comparison.[27] Nevertheless, the criminal and juvenile justice system focus almost exclusively on the behaviors of the lower and working classes.[28]

Efforts to reform society have hardly been pursued, for few programs have been established that challenge the basic foundations of our class society. Most of the efforts that can be described as having addressed the social causes of crime have consistently tried to change either individuals or groups. Schur cites the "detached worker" programs that have attempted to reduce gang activities.[29] These and similar programs have not been very successful. Indeed, after 30 or more years of "street work" with gangs, we have more gangs than ever before (although official estimates are usually exaggerated) and the major sources of gangs (especially social inequality) have worsened.[30]

One of the few attempts to seriously address social inequality was the "war on poverty," which began in the 1960s. One part of this program was the Mobilization for Youth program in New York City. These initiatives did not last long, however, because money that would have gone toward them was quickly siphoned off to continue the Vietnam War. It is ironic that within an often-cited publication on crime and justice, the President's Commission on Law Enforcement and Administration of Justice, we find these lines:

> The underlying problems are ones that the criminal justice system can do little about ... Unless society does take concerted action to change the general conditions and attitudes that are associated with crime, no improvement in law enforcement and administration of justice, the subjects this Commission was specifically asked to study, will be of much avail.[31]

Most of the people who read this and other reports from the Commission apparently ignored this simple truism and instead focused on making the existing system of justice more efficient or, more correctly, more efficient at processing mostly lower-class and minority offenders.[32]

More than 30 years have passed since the President's Commission wrote those words. Since that time, the crime rate is not much different, but expenditures on the criminal justice system have soared by more than 1,500 percent, the overall incarceration rate has increased by about 500 percent, and the overall "clearance rate" of "crimes known to the police" has remained virtually unchanged.[33] As an old saying goes, it is time to "think out of the box." And this "box" is our present criminal and juvenile justice system. It is also time to reconsider what Schur said 30 years ago about pursuing "radical nonintervention" as a unique approach.

THINKING OUTSIDE THE BOX: RECONSIDERING RADICAL NONINTERVENTION

Schur noted the general disenchantment with delinquency policies because they had generally failed (with some notable exceptions) to reduce delinquency. In a statement that is just as relevant today as ever, he observed that "[a] traditional response to this situation has been to assume that the system merely needs improvement. Hence the calls for more and better facilities, increasingly experimental studies and elaborate 'cost-benefit' and 'systems' analyses."[34] Whether or not the system has been noticeably "improved," it is certainly much larger and it is making more arrests than ever before, mostly stemming from the "war on drugs." On any given day, more than six million people are somewhere within the criminal justice system, with perhaps another million or so youths somewhere within the juvenile justice system. At the same time, the fear of crime among American citizens appears to be higher than ever.[35] Something different is needed and part of this something may be found in Schur's proposal.

In the final chapter of his book, Schur outlined in broad form, five general proposals. These proposals are as follows:[36]

- Proposal 1: "There is a need for a thorough reassessment of the dominant ways of thinking about youth 'problems'." Schur maintained that many, if not most, behaviors youth engage in (including many labeled as delinquent) are "part and parcel of our social and cultural system" and that "misconduct" among youth is inevitable within any form of social order. We pay a huge price, he charged, for criminalizing much of this behavior.
- Proposal 2: "Some of the most valuable policies for dealing with delinquency are not necessarily those designated as delinquency policies." Schur quotes a passage from the report of the American Friends Service Committee that "the construction of a just system of criminal justice in an unjust society is a contradiction in terms." Checking my own copy of this report (which we would all do well to read again), the first part of this

sentence says, "To the extent, then, that equal justice is correlated with equality of status, influence, and economic power...."[37] Clearly this committee (John Irwin was one of the members) saw the need to go beyond the usual focus on isolation and punishment of individual offenders and seriously challenge the inequality of the larger society.

- Proposal 3: "We must take young people more seriously if we are to eradicate injustice to juveniles." Schur notes that so many young people lack a sound attachment to conventional society, to borrow one of Hirschi's "social bonds." Thus, while we address some of the inequalities noted in the second point above, it would behoove us to try and make the existing system more just in the sense that it respects young people. The lack of respect that Schur noted seems to be even greater today, as we continue the conflicting feelings of fear and admiration toward young people. Indeed, today we see the Bush proposal to "leave no child behind," while at the same time increasing the punishments for relatively minor offenses under zero-tolerance policies. We often embrace "diversity," yet at the same time punish differences, such as the heavy penalties levied for mere possession of marijuana and the continued targeting of racial minorities in the "war on drugs."

- Proposal 4: "The juvenile justice system should concern itself less with the problems of so-called 'delinquents', and more with dispensing justice." Schur was talking specifically about narrowing the jurisdiction of the juvenile court, specifically over "status offenses." Little did Schur realize the extent to which "net-widening" would occur in the intervening years. Although technically some "status offenders" have been "diverted" from the juvenile justice, many are returned under new "delinquency" charges stemming from "bootstrapping," whereby a second status offense is labeled a "violation of a court order" (e.g., probation violation) or even "contempt of court." This has been especially the case for girls.[38]

- Proposal 5: "As juvenile justice moves in new directions, a variety of approaches will continue to be useful." Schur specifically suggests such approaches as prevention programs that have a "collective or community focus," plus programs that are voluntary and noninstitutional in nature and programs that use "indigenous personnel," to name just a few. One of those new approaches has been the Detention Diversion Advocacy Project (DDAP), which began in San Francisco in the late 1980s and has spread to other parts of the country. The first evaluation found positive results from the program (see the discussion below).[39]

AN ASSESSMENT OF SCHUR'S IDEAS

As already indicated, much of what Schur articulated 30 years ago remains relevant in today's society, as does the labeling approach itself. Although people may disagree on some of his points, the central thrust remains true as ever, namely that the juvenile justice system extends far too broadly into the lives of children and adolescents. Males has made this point perhaps more forcefully that most others when he accuses criminologists and public policy makers of blaming kids for most ills of society while ignoring the damage done by adults.[40] In a more recent study, Males compared the rhetoric of law enforcement officials and criminologists such as James Q. Wilson. He points out that in Los Angeles during the 1990s (and likewise in Oakland) two-thirds of the murder suspects were under 25, but in 2002 less than half were. He chastises both James Q. Wilson and James Alan Fox for erroneously claiming that more young people equal more crime. As Males correctly points out, in the years and in the states where there were a higher percentage of young males in the population, there were fewer violent crimes. Both James Alan Fox and John DiIulio predicted in 1995 that we were headed for a rise in the teenage population, which would result in a spike in the number of "adolescent superpredators." Contrary to such dire predictions, there were 60,000 fewer juvenile arrests for violent index crimes in 2001 than in 1994.[41] Perhaps we would be more correct to stress the importance of greater intervention by the adult courts into the lives of "adult superpredators" instead of extending the reach of the juvenile court.

The overreach of the juvenile justice system is perhaps best demonstrated in referral statistics published by OJJDP. The most recent Juvenile Court Statistics note that between 1989 and 1998 the two offense categories that showed the largest percentage gains were drug law violations (up 148 percent) and simple assaults (up 128 percent), with obstruction of justice rising by 102 percent and disorderly conduct increasing by 100 percent.[42] Black youths consistently have higher rates of referrals to court for drug offenses, a pattern that reflects trends in the adult system.[43] The proportion of referrals to the juvenile court for relatively petty acts is staggering. Why criminalize what could be considered normal adolescent behavior like disturbing the peace and minor fighting? (One may reasonably ask, "Whose peace is being disturbed?")

As noted, one of the questions the labeling perspective poses is why certain acts are labeled "criminal" or "delinquent" and others are not. Another pertinent question this approach asks is how we account for differential rates of arrest, referral to court, detention, adjudication, and commitment based on race and class. These are not merely academic questions, for the lives of real people are being affected by recent get-tough policies. We continue to criminalize normal adolescent behavior or behavior that should be dealt with informally, outside of the formal juvenile justice system. Status offenses immediately come to mind, such as truancy and incorrigibility. Criminalizing truancy has always puzzled me. Why take formal police action because a child is not going to school? Certainly, kids should stay in school, for an education is a prerequisite for a decent life. But why use the immense power of the state to make these children stay in school? Likewise, children should obey the reasonable demands of their parents, but they also should be left alone to figure things out for themselves. There is no need to involve the state in private family matters, unless some direct physical or other obvious harms are being committed. How many times have we heard stories or read research reports about runaways who have experienced incredible abuse or discovered that many children referred to juvenile court as "incorrigible" have been abused?[44]

A MODEL PROGRAM: DETENTION DIVERSION ADVOCACY PROJECT

Consistent with the ideas discussed here is a program with a great deal of promise. The DDAP was started in 1993 by the Center on Juvenile and Criminal Justice (CJCJ) in San Francisco, California. The program's major goal is to reduce the number of youth in court-ordered detention and provide them with culturally relevant community-based services and supervision. Youths selected are those who are likely to be detained pending their adjudication. DDAP provides an intensive level of community-based monitoring and advocacy that is not presently available. It is based in part on the concept of "disposition case advocacy."

Disposition case advocacy has been defined as "the efforts of lay persons or nonlegal experts acting on behalf of youthful offenders at disposition hearings."[45] It is based in part on the more general concept of "case management," which has been defined as a "client-level strategy for promoting the coordination of human services, opportunities, or benefits." Case management seeks to achieve two major outcomes: (1) "the integration of services across a cluster of organizations and (2) continuity of care."[46] The main focus of case management is to develop a network of human services that integrates the development of client skills and the involvement of different social networks and multiple service providers.[47]

Among the goals the program is designed to accomplish are the following: (1) to provide multilevel interventions to divert youth from secure detention facilities, (2) to demonstrate that community-based interventions are an effective alternative to secure custody and that the needs of both the youths and the community can be met at a cost savings to the public, and (3) to reduce disproportionate minority incarceration.[48]

The DDAP program involves two primary components:

- *Detention Advocacy.* This component involves identifying youth who are likely to be detained pending their adjudication. Once a potential client is identified, DDAP case managers present a release plan to the judge. The plan includes a list of appropriate community services that will be accessed on the youth's behalf. Additionally, the plan includes specified objectives as a means to evaluate the youth's progress while in the program. Emphasis is placed on maintaining the youth at home, and if the home is not a viable option, the project staff will identify and secure a suitable alternative. If the plan is deemed acceptable by a judge, the youth is released to DDAP's supervision.
- *Case Management.* The case management model provides frequent and consistent support and supervision to youth and their families. The purpose of case management is to link youths to community-based services and closely monitor their progress. Case management services are "field

oriented," requiring the case manager to have daily contact with the youth, his or her family, and significant others. Contact includes a minimum of three in-person meetings a week. Additional services are provided to the youth's family members, particularly parents and guardians, in areas such as securing employment, day care, drug treatment services, and income support.

Clients are identified primarily through referrals from the public defender's office, the probation department, community agencies, and parents. Admission to DDAP is restricted to youths currently held, or likely to be held, in secure detention. The youths selected are those theoretically deemed to be "high risk" in terms of their chance of engaging in subsequent criminal activity. The selection is based on a risk assessment instrument developed by the National Council on Crime and Delinquency. The target population consists of those whose risk assessment scores indicate that they ordinarily would be detained. This is what Miller has termed the "deep-end" approach.[49] This is quite important; by focusing on detained youth, the project ensures that it remains a true diversion alternative rather than a "net-widening" activity. Youths are screened by DDAP staff to determine whether they are likely to be detained and whether they present an acceptable risk to the community.

Client screening involves gathering background information from probation reports, psychological evaluations, police reports, school reports, and other pertinent documents. Interviews are conducted with youths, family members, and adult professionals to determine the types of services required. Once a potential client is evaluated, DDAP staff present a comprehensive community service plan at the detention hearing and request that the judge release the youth to DDAP custody.

Because the project deals only with youths who are awaiting adjudication or final disposition, their appropriateness for the project is based on whether they can reside in the community under supervision without unreasonable risk and on their likelihood of attending their court hearings. This is similar in principle to what often occurs in the adult system when someone is released on bail pending their court hearings (e.g., arraignments, trial).

The primary goal of the project is to design and implement individualized community service plans that address a wide range of personal and social needs. Services that address specific linguistic or medical needs are located by case managers. Along with the youth's participation, the quality and level of services are monitored by DDAP staff. The purpose of multiple collaboratives is to ensure that the project is able to represent and address the needs of the various communities within San Francisco in the most culturally appropriate manner. Because youth services in San Francisco historically have been fragmented by ethnicity, race, and community, a more unified approach is being tried with DDAP. It has become a neutral site within the city and is staffed by representatives from CJCJ and several other community-based service agencies (e.g., Horizon's Unlimited, Potrero Hill Neighborhood House, and Vietnamese Youth Development Center).

More specific goals include the following: (1) ensuring that a high proportion of the program clients are not rearrested while participating in the
program, (2) achieving a high court reappearance rate, (3) reducing the
population of the Youth Guidance Center, and (4) reducing the proportion of minority youths in detention. Currently, the Youth Guidance Center is the only place of detention in the city. It has a capacity of 137, but
the daily population typically ranges between 140 and 150 youths. The
average length of stay is around 11 to 12 days.

The evaluation compared a group of youths referred to DDAP with a
similarly matched control group of youths who remained within the juvenile justice system.[50] The results showed that after a three-year follow-up,
the recidivism rate for the DDAP group was 34 percent, compared with a
60 percent rate for the control group. Detailed comparisons holding several variables constant (e.g., prior record, race, age, gender) and examining
several different measures of recidivism (e.g., subsequent commitments,
referrals for violent offenses) showed that the DDAP youths still had a significantly lower recidivism rate.

DDAP has been expanded to additional sites, such Washington, D.C.,
and Philadelphia. Preliminary reports suggest continuing success, as
measured by lower recidivism rates.[51] Presently, the concept has been further expanded to include a focus on juvenile offenders who have been
committed to institutional settings in California. In other words, these are
youths who are headed for such institutions as the California Youth
Authority (CYA). The program, called New Options, operates on the same
principle as DDAP, namely, going into the "deep end" of the juvenile justice system. This program has been in operation for about one year, yet
some preliminary figures suggest that it will have the same kind of success
as DDAP.[52] One example illustrates this program. A 16-year-old male had
a long history of involvement in the juvenile justice system, including five
failed out-of-home placements within the past four years. Instead of being
sent to the CYA, he was placed in a private school called the Challenge to
Learn Academy. Here, in addition to receiving an excellent education, he
receives individual therapy, substance abuse treatment, and anger management counseling. The cost totals about $2,300 a month (paid for by
grants from several local foundations). As of January, 2004, more than 50
youths have been placed in such alternatives during the past year.[53]

This is just one of many similar programs that owe their intellectual
debt not only to Schur's work, but also to the labeling perspective. Such
programs are derived by challenging taken-for-granted notions about those
youth who are found in the "deep end" of the juvenile justice system and
giving them a chance to succeed in friendlier environments.

CONCLUSION

Giroux,[54] a leading sociologist, recently observed the growing support
in this country for the abandonment of young people, especially minorities, "to the dictates of a repressive penal state that increasingly addresses

social problems through the police, courts, and prison system." This has been accomplished while the state has been increasingly reduced to providing police functions, at the expense of serving as the "guardian of public interests." The policies of social investment, continues Giroux, "have given way to an emphasis on repression, surveillance, and control." One result is what he calls the "criminalization of social policy" or, perhaps more correctly, "domestic warfare."

A specific instance of this can be seen in New York City where, says Giroux, Rudy Giuliani essentially assigned the role of discipline within the schools to the police department. In effect, the school principal has assumed the role of "warden," while many schools have taken on a new function of serving as a "feeder system for the penal system."[55]

The war on terror and the war on Iraq, along with the expansion of American military might all over the globe, which is little more than another form of empire building and imperialism,[56] is being matched by a growing crime-control industry on the home front. Zero-tolerance policies can be seen, therefore, as part of something much larger. Given the current political climate, instituting anything remotely like radical nonintervention will be an uphill battle. Such a hands-off policy toward youth does not fit in well to today's climate, particularly given the almost paranoid need to identify troublemakers, superpredators, and potential terrorists.

NOTES

1. Schur, 1973; see also his other noteworthy work on the labeling perspective (Schur, 1971).
2. An excellent treatment of the subject of "superpredators" is provided in Elikann, 1999. A good illustration of this conservative view is provided in Bennett, DiIulio, & Walters, 1996.
3. Juvenile Law Center, 2004; Shelden, 2000a; "Zero tolerance," 2003, May 7.
4. Rimer, 2004.
5. Rimer, 2004.
6. Browne, 2003.
7. Shelden, 1998.
8. Lyderson, 2003.
9. Lyderson, 2003.
10. Lyderson, 2003.
11. "Drug sweep," 2003, November 9.
12. Males, 1996.
13. This is outlined in more detail in Schur, 1971.
14. Becker, 1963, pp. 8–9.
15. Quinney, 1970, pp. 15–25.
16. Documentation that race and class bias exist with regard to drug laws and status offenders is provided in my book (Shelden, 2001); for juvenile court laws and their bias, see Platt, 1969; for the race bias in drug laws, see Helmer, 1975.
17. Chesney-Lind & Shelden, 2004.
18. Schur, 1973, p. 155.
19. Schur, 1973, p. 29.

20. The information about the eugenics movement and subsequent discussions is based in part on Shelden, 2000b. Another good source for this topic is Rafter, 1988.

21. Breggin & Breggin, 1998; Cohen, 2000.

22. Breggin & Breggin, 1998, p. 16.

23. Breggin & Breggin, 1998, p. 40.

24. Miller, 1996, p. 131.

25. Bortner & Williams, 1997; Dryfoos, 1990.

26. Hirschi, 1969.

27. Costs of white-collar and corporate crime are provided in Shelden and Brown (2003, chap. 2).

28. Shelden & Brown, 2003, chap. 2; this is also documented in studies too numerous to cite here. See, e.g., Chambliss, 1999, and especially Reiman, 2004.

29. Klein, 1995; Shelden, Tracy, & Brown, 2004.

30. For documentation of recent increases in inequality see Shelden et al. (2004, chap. 7) and Phillips (2002).

31. President's Commission on Law Enforcement and the Administration of Justice, 1967, p. 1, as quoted in Schur, 1973, p. 105.

32. A good critique of the Crime Commission and of criminal justice policy in general is found in Quinney (2002).

33. Shelden & Brown, 2003, chaps. 1–2.

34. Schur, 1973, p. 117.

35. Shelden & Brown, 2003.

36. Schur, 1973, pp. 166–170.

37. American Friends Service Committee, 1971, p. 16.

38. Chesney-Lind & Shelden, 2004.

39. Shelden, 1998.

40. Males, 1996, 1999.

41. Males, 2002.

42. Office of Juvenile Justice and Delinquency Prevention, 2003, p. 7.

43. Office of Juvenile Justice and Delinquency Prevention, 2003, p. 7. Numerous studies have documented the racist nature of the drug war. See Tonry, 1995, and Miller, 1996.

44. Chesney-Lind & Shelden, 2004.

45. Macallair, 1994, p. 84.

46. Moxley, 1989, p. 11.

47. Moxley, 1989, p. 21.

48. The ability of case advocacy and case management to promote detention alternatives was demonstrated by the National Center on Institutions and Alternatives (NCIA). Under contract with New York City's Spofford Detention Center, NCIA significantly augmented the efforts of that city's Department of Juvenile Justice to reduce the number of youth in detention and expand the range of alternative options (Krisberg & Austin, 1993, pp. 178–181). A similar case management system has been in use in Florida through the Associated Marine Institutes (Krisberg & Austin, 1993, pp. 178–181). The Key Program, Inc., also uses the case management approach, but in this instance the youth are closely supervised, meaning that they are monitored on a 24-hour basis and must conform to some strict rules concerning work, school, counseling, victim restitution, and so on (Krisberg & Austin, 1993, pp. 178–181). Additional evidence in support of the use of case advocacy comes from a study by the Rand Corporation (Greenwood & Turner, 1991). This study compared two groups of randomly selected youths, a control group that was recommended by their probation officers for incarceration, and an

experimental group that received disposition reports by case advocates. Of those who received case advocacy disposition reports, 72 percent were diverted from institutional care, compared with 49 percent of the control group. The Rand study found tremendous resistance from juvenile justice officials, especially probation officers, to alternative dispositions, especially those coming from case advocates. It appeared that the probation staff resented the intrusion into what had heretofore been considered their own "turf" (Greenwood & Turner, 1991, p. 92).

49. Miller, 1998.

50. For a complete overview of the evaluation, see Shelden, 1999.

51. Feldman & Kubrin, 2002.

52. Center on Juvenile and Criminal Justice, 2003.

53. Based on the author's interview with the director of New Options. A detailed evaluation, using control groups, is being proposed. For further details, see the Web site for the Center on Juvenile and Criminal Justice at www.cjcj.org.

54. Giroux, 2001.

55. Giroux, 2003, quoting Jesse Jackson.

56. Johnson, 2004.

REFERENCES

American Friends Service Committee. (1971). *Struggle for justice*. New York: Hill and Wang.

Becker, H. S. (1963). *Outsiders: Studies in the sociology of deviance*. New York: The Free Press.

Bennett, W., DiIulio, J., & Walters, J. P. (1996). *Body count: Moral poverty and how to win America's war against crime and drugs*. New York: Simon and Schuster.

Bortner, M. A., & Williams, L. M. (1997). *Youth in prison*. New York: Routledge.

Breggin, G., & Breggin, P. (1998). *The war against children of color*. Monroe, ME: Common Courage Press.

Browne, J. (2003, September 15). Schoolhouse to jailhouse. *The Progressive Populist*, 9, 16, pp. 45–46.

Center on Juvenile and Criminal Justice. (2003). *An overview of the new options initiative*. Retrieved August 1, 2006, from www.cjcj.org. San Francisco: Center on Juvenile and Criminal Justice.

Chambliss, W. J. (1999). *Power, politics and crime*. Boulder, CO: Westview.

Chesney-Lind, M., & Shelden, R. G. (2004). *Girls, delinquency and juvenile justice* (3rd ed.). Belmont, CA: Wadsworth.

Cohen, M. (2000, April). Beware the violence initiative project—Coming soon to an inner city near you. *Z Magazine*. Retrieved August 1, 2006, from www.zmag.org/zmag/articles/cohenapril2000.htm.

Drug sweep at South Carolina high school sparks investigation. (2003, November 9). *Los Angeles Times*, p. A34.

Dryfoos, J. (1990). *Adolescents at risk: Prevalence and prevention*. New York: Oxford University Press.

Elikann, P. (1999). *Superpredators: The demonization of our children by the law*. Reading, MA: Perseus.

Feldman, L. B., & Kubrin, C. E. (2002). Evaluation findings: The detention diversion advocacy program in Philadelphia, Pennsylvania. Washington, D.C.: George Washington University, Center for Excellence in Municipal Management.

Giroux, H. A. (2001, January). Zero tolerance: Youth and the politics of domestic militarization. *Z Magazine* Retrieved August 1, 2006, from www.zmag.org/ZMag/articles/jan01giroux.htm.

Greenwood, P. W., & Turner, S. (1991). *Implementing and managing innovative correctional programs: Lessons from OJJDP's private sector initiative.* Santa Monica, CA: Rand Corporation.

Helmer, J. (1975). *Drugs and minority oppression.* New York: Seabury Press.

Hirschi, T. (1969). *Causes of delinquency.* Berkeley, CA: University of California Press.

Johnson, C. (2004). *The sorrows of empire: Militarism, secrecy, and the end of the republic.* New York: Metropolitan Books.

Juvenile Law Center. (2004). *End zero tolerance.* Retrieved August 1, 2006, from www.jlc.org/EZT.

Klein, M. (1995). *The American street gang.* New York: Oxford University Press.

Krisberg, B., & Austin, J. (1993). *Reinventing juvenile justice.* Newbury Park, CA: Sage Publications.

Lydersen, K. (2003, July 1). *Zero tolerance for teens.* Retrieved August 1, 2006, from www.alternet.org/story/16305/.

Macallair, D. (1994). Disposition case advocacy in San Francisco's juvenile justice system: A new approach to deinstitutionalization. *Crime and Delinquency, 40,* 84–95.

Males, M. (1996). *The scapegoat generation: America's war on adolescents.* Monroe, ME: Common Courage Press.

Males, M. (1999). *Framing youth: Ten myths about the coming generation.* Monroe, ME: Common Courage Press.

Males, M. (2002, December 15). Forget the "youth menace": Crime, it turns out, is a grown-up business. *Los Angeles Times,* p. M1.

Miller, J. (1996). *Search and destroy: African-American males in the criminal justice system.* Cambridge, MA: Cambridge University Press.

Miller, J. (1998). *Last one over the wall: The Massachusetts experiment in closing reform schools* (2nd ed.). Columbus, OH: Ohio State University Press.

Moxley, R. (1989). *Case management.* Beverly Hills, CA: Sage Publications.

Office of Juvenile Justice and Delinquency Prevention. (2003). *Juvenile court statistics 1998.* Washington, D.C.: U.S. Department of Justice.

Phillips, K. (2002). *Wealth and democracy.* New York: Broadway Books.

Platt, A. (1969). *The child savers.* Chicago: University of Chicago Press.

President's Commission on Law Enforcement and the Administration of Justice. (1967). *The challenge of crime in a free society.* Washington, D.C.: U. S. Government Printing Office.

Quinney, R. (1970). *The social reality of crime.* Boston: Little, Brown.

Quinney, R. (2002). *Critique of legal order.* New Brunswick, NJ: Transaction Books (reprinted from 1974).

Rafter, N. H. (Ed.). (1988). *White trash: The eugenic family studies, 1899–1919.* Boston: Northeastern University Press.

Reiman, J. (2004). *The rich get richer and the poor get prison* (7th ed.). Boston: Allyn and Bacon.

Rimer, S. (2004, January 4). Unruly students facing arrest, not detention. *New York Times,* section 1, p. 1.

Schur, E. (1971). *Labeling deviant behavior.* New York: Harper and Row.

Schur, E. (1973). *Radical non-intervention: Rethinking the delinquency problem.* Englewood Cliffs, NJ: Prentice Hall.

Shelden, R. G. (1998, August 16). Campus crime? School's the safest place for kids. *Las Vegas Review-Journal*, p. 10.

Shelden, R. G. (1999). *An evaluation of the detention diversion advocacy program.* Washington, D.C.: Office of Juvenile Justice and Delinquency Prevention.

Shelden, R. G. (2000a, May 11). Stop the war on kids, *Las Vegas City Life*, p. 6(A).

Shelden, R. G. (2000b). Gene warfare. *Social Justice, 27* (2), 162–167.

Shelden, R. G. (2001). *Controlling the dangerous classes: A critical introduction to the history of criminal justice.* Boston: Allyn and Bacon.

Shelden, R. G., & Brown, W. B. (2003). *Criminal justice in America: A critical view.* Boston: Allyn and Bacon.

Shelden, R. G., Tracy, S. K., & Brown, W. B. (2004). *Youth gangs in American society* (3rd ed.). Belmont, CA: Wadsworth.

Tonry, M. (1995). *Malign neglect: Race, crime, and punishment in America.* New York: Oxford University Press.

Zero tolerance, zero sense (editorial). (2003, May 7). *Los Angeles Times*, p. B12.

CHAPTER 9

Private versus Public Operation of Juvenile Correctional Facilities

Chad R. Trulson and Craig Hemmens

Although the government has traditionally been the owner and operator of correctional facilities, the private sector has always played a role in corrections. One of the earliest forms of corrections was transportation and this type of eighteenth-century punishment was largely privatized.[1] Transportation entailed shipping or transporting criminals to foreign lands to serve their sentences. Private merchants sometimes served as the transporters. They could pay the sheriff a price per convict, and then sell the convict as an indentured servant.[2] Another early form of privatization in corrections was the convict lease system, which was prevalent primarily in southern United States in the late 1800s and early 1900s, and involved the state leasing out convicts to private contractors.[3] These examples show that "penology for profit"[4] has its roots in the earliest correctional enterprises—it is certainly not a new concept.

Although privatization in corrections has occurred for hundreds of years, it is only in the last quarter century that private entities have made significant inroads into corrections. Private corporations concerned exclusively with correctional services have emerged. These private corporations have contracted out specific services such as meals and health care to state, county, and local correctional jurisdictions. At the most extreme, private correctional agencies have been charged with the wholesale design, construction, ownership, and operation of correctional institutions for both adults and juveniles.

The trend toward privatization in corrections is best evidenced by the growth in the number of private institutions and in the number of inmates held at these private institutions. In the 1990s alone, the capacity of private adult correctional facilities increased almost 900 percent.[5] According to the Bureau of Justice Statistics, there was nearly a sixfold increase of the number of privately held adult prisoners from 1995 to 2000. At last official count, private correctional facilities held 7 percent of the adult incarcerated population and public facilities held roughly 93 percent of the adult incarcerated population.[6] Although private correctional facilities for adults make up only 15 percent of the total number of adult correctional facilities in the United States, and public facilities hold the vast majority of adult inmates, the dramatic increase in private correctional capacity and privately held prisoners in the 1990s suggests that privatization continues to spread among the adult correctional population.[7]

Unlike in the adult system, the number of private juvenile correctional facilities in the 1990s increased only slightly (9 percent). This does not mean, however, that privatization is less prevalent in the juvenile correctional system than in the adult correctional system. In reality, privatization in juvenile corrections began before the 1990s.[8]

Private facilities for juveniles account for roughly 60 percent of all custodial correctional facilities for juveniles, compared with 15 percent of all correctional facilities for adults. Moreover, private juvenile correctional facilities hold almost 30 percent of all incarcerated juveniles—well above the proportion of adults held in private correctional facilities.[9] Despite the fact that the actual number of incarcerated juveniles has declined by some 10,000 juveniles over the last several years, from 1997 to 2003, the proportion of incarcerated juveniles held in private facilities has increased.[10] The bottom line is that an increasing number of states are relying on the private sector to deal with the incarcerated population of juveniles—and have been doing so for several years.[11]

In this chapter, we compare the operation of public and private juvenile correctional facilities. To better inform the reader with the information necessary to determine whether one type is better than the other, we examine the characteristics, history and evolution, types, and legal issues associated with these juvenile correctional facilities.

DEFINING PUBLIC AND PRIVATE JUVENILE CORRECTIONAL FACILITIES

What Is a Public Juvenile Correctional Facility?

A public juvenile correctional facility is one that is owned, funded, and operated by the government. The ownership and operation of public juvenile facilities exist at the state, county, and local levels, and these facilities are primarily supported by tax revenues. Because they are owned and operated by the government, employees are considered public employees.

Public juvenile correctional agencies may be considered hybrids to some degree. The distinction lies within the concepts of ownership and operating authority.[12] In addition to being owned and operated by the government, public institutions for juveniles may be owned by the government and operated by private authorities or may be operated by public authorities and owned by private agencies. Where a public juvenile correctional institution falls on this continuum of operation and ownership is determined primarily by state laws and contractual arrangements with private agencies. What this discussion suggests, however, is that whether a juvenile correctional facility is "public" or "private" depends on certain factors. In other words, one person's public facility may be another's private facility.

What Is a Private Juvenile Correctional Facility?

In general, private juvenile correctional facilities are those that are owned and operated by a private sector entity, are not directly supported by tax revenues, and have employees who are not considered public employees. Like the definition of public institutions, however, there are various forms of privatization involving juvenile institutional corrections. Using the ownership and operation continuum, private facilities may be owned and operated by a private agency, may be owned by a private agency and operated by the government, or may be owned by the government and operated by a private agency. Thus, like the definition of a public juvenile correctional facility, there is much variation regarding what is and is not a private facility. Whether an institution is considered public or private relates to the different ideas of ownership and operation. Perhaps the bottom line is that both public and private juvenile correctional institutions can be considered hybrids, for often the boundaries are blurred.

HOW PRIVATIZATION WORKS IN CORRECTIONS

Characteristics of Privatization in Corrections

Privatization in juvenile corrections comes in many different forms. One of the most common forms of privatization is the contracting out of services by the government to a private agency. Numerous states engage the services of private organizations, such as medical and mental health care, drug treatment, education, and various forms of counseling.[13] These services are contracted out to private agencies for a variety of reasons; one being that the expertise and experience with these types of issues may lie outside of the government agency. Another commonly cited reason is that these services may be provided at a lower cost or performed more efficiently than what could be offered by a governmental agency. McDonald and Patten outline the different ways that governments have contracted with private agencies for correctional needs based on these and other reasons:[14]

- Narrow contracts for select services such as food service, cafeteria operation, and various forms of health care (e.g., medical, dental)
- Contracts for beds in facilities operated by the private firms and owned by the private firm or by other private agencies that partner with the

private firm (in these circumstances, the "beds" may be available to a number of agencies, not exclusively a particular correctional system or governmental agency)

• Government contracts with a private firm to finance, construct, and operate a correctional facility for the exclusive use of one governmental agency (e.g., state juvenile correctional system) during a particular contract period

• Government-created private corporations that exist to serve the needs of the government. In this circumstance, the private corporation is responsible for financing and constructing a correctional facility; however, it is controlled by public officials via a board of directors, and is considered legally independent of the government (therefore, the facility can then be leased to the government)

The way in which private corporations exist in correctional arenas around the country varies considerably. For example, in the absence of a preconstruction contract, private agencies may actually design, finance, and construct a private facility and "shop it around" to correctional agencies within and outside the state. Although this is rare, it has occurred. The list above is not exhaustive but shows the typical forms of privatization in corrections.

Administration and Oversight of Public and Private Agencies

In a pure example, public facilities are owned and operated by the government, and private facilities are owned and operated by private entities. There are many more subtle and not so subtle differences between these two broad categories, and such differences undoubtedly affect how they are operated in juvenile correctional environments. Key differences are examined below to shed some light on how public and private juvenile correctional facilities are similar and different concerning their administration and oversight.

In broad terms, public agencies are created by laws and are justified by need—some government action must create them and a reason must explain their existence. Thus, those who govern public agencies must constantly justify their existence and demonstrate the "need" for their institution.[15] In reality, however, some public agencies are so ingrained in the fabric of public life that it is hard to believe that their existence must be constantly justified. Many juvenile correctional institutions are public agencies, but it is unlikely that these public institutions will simply be closed by state legislatures. It could happen that some juvenile institutions are transferred to the operation of the adult system or, perhaps more likely, modified for another correctional purpose when a certain level of "need" is not met. Thus, it is not a matter of institutions being needed or not, but rather the "degree" of need involving public juvenile correctional facilities.

Conversely, private agencies and their institutions are created by market demands and primarily are driven by profit—when market demands wane and profits fall, private agencies are in jeopardy.[16] Therefore, administrators of both public and private facilities must justify their existence and need to some degree.

Public agencies receive oversight by the state legislature or some other governing body depending on the level of government. Juvenile correctional systems, for example, must answer to legislators, juvenile correctional system board members, public interest groups, legal organizations, and society at large. Private agencies must answer to a board of directors, but private agency administrators are also scrutinized by stockholders, employees, public interest groups, and regulatory agencies. On the latter point, many government-private contractual arrangements require that private correctional institutions meet all government standards (legal or otherwise) when it comes to operating a private correctional facility. Although the facility may be owned and operated by a private corrections corporation, state laws or contractual agreements with the government may still require the private facility to meet minimum operating standards as determined by the legislature or other public governing bodies. This can be a rigorous process for private juvenile correctional agencies that may be scrutinized by any number of agencies from the contracting government agency, to the Office of Inspector General, to the state's department of child protective services. Therefore, in many cases, even private agencies have to answer to the government. It simply is not the case today that private agencies can "run wild" without any constraints or regulations in corrections.[17]

There are other differences between public and private juvenile correctional facilities, but in terms of their administration and oversight, public and private juvenile correctional facilities have many similarities.

THE EVOLUTION OF JUVENILE CORRECTIONAL FACILITIES

Public Juvenile Correctional Facilities

Before the 1800s, separate institutions for juveniles did not exist. There simply was no organized juvenile justice system in operation and no institutions to deal with juvenile lawbreakers. When children were wayward or delinquent, it was the responsibility of the family to deal with the situation. When parents were absent or neglected their duties, the responsibility to deal with delinquents was left to the larger community of neighbors, townspeople, and the church.[18]

Life in colonial America was relatively simple and orderly before the 1800s. The population in the American colonies was approximately 1.5 million individuals. By the early to mid-1800s, however, the population of early America soared to nearly 25 million. Not surprisingly, the simpler rural life in the former colonies became more diverse and complex. Methods of informal social control were challenged, and social disorder emerged as a massive social problem. It was in the face of these massive social changes that institutions were adopted to supplement, and in some instances supplant, informal social control systems. Institutions such as prisons and asylums, it was believed, could be fashioned to mimic the ideal puritan life of earlier times and stabilize an unstable society.[19]

The earliest institutions for juveniles actually were privately operated. Opened in the early 1800s, these institutions are best characterized as almshouses (e.g., poorhouses) or orphanages. Although not technically what might be considered a juvenile correctional institution today, these facilities functioned to some degree as centers for youth who had taken a wayward path. More important, they were the seeds to growth in juvenile institutionalization around the country. But they were not only for delinquents—these institutions held all youth who were in need of supervision or protection.

The first recognized institution designed primarily for juvenile lawbreakers was the House of Refuge. As with almshouses and orphanages, houses of refuge were private facilities. In 1825, the Society for the Prevention of Pauperism, a private society, established the first House of Refuge in New York City.[20] By 1828, two more cities followed New York's lead, and by the 1850s, houses of refuge were situated in every major city in the United States.[21] Although many houses of refuge around the country were privately managed, it was not unusual for these institutions to receive some resources from the state in which they were located. Thus, to some degree, the earliest juvenile institutions in America can be considered hybrid facilities that relied on public and private authorities.

Over time, houses of refuge deteriorated and came to resemble the disordered society that they were meant to replace. They became overcrowded and filthy, almost unmanageable in size, and the founding ideas of discipline, order, and care digressed into chaos, disorder, and recidivism.[22] Critics noted that they were akin to "schools of crime," for they admitted a range of youths from the abandoned to the delinquent.[23] Eventually, the promise of the houses of refuge waned in America and so did the stranglehold that these early forms of privately managed juvenile correctional institutions had on the not-yet-formalized juvenile court and justice system.

By the mid- to late-1800s, what were once houses of refuge became referred to as reformatories, reform schools, training schools, and industrial schools. This distinction was more semantics than substance, but one significant difference emerged—that is, these reform schools became primarily state-managed facilities as opposed to privately operated institutions. The first reform school in the United States was established in Westboro, Massachusetts, in 1847. Originally called the Massachusetts State Reform School in Westboro, the facility's name was changed in the 1860s to the Lyman School for Boys. Massachusetts opened the Massachusetts School for the "idiotic and feebleminded" in 1848 and the State Industrial School for Girls in 1856. In 1849, New York completed construction on an industrial school, and by the 1870s, several states such as Ohio, New Jersey, and Maryland had opened training schools for delinquents. By 1890, nearly every state operated a facility for delinquent youth.[24]

This brief history shows that private societies were the first entities to establish institutions for juveniles. Although many of these early private societies were nonprofit and thus different than many for-profit efforts in private juvenile institutional corrections today, private societies made their initial entrance into juvenile corrections more than 100 years ago. Privatization in juvenile corrections, however, was replaced in the mid- to late-1800s primarily by state-operated facilities. Variations exist, but for the most part, correctional institutions for juveniles, particularly those holding adjudicated delinquents, became a state function. Although this trend continues today, private programs, services, and institutions still play an important role in juvenile corrections.

The Emergence of Private Juvenile Correctional Facilities

The first juvenile institutions in America were privately operated. However, little is known about the evolution and emergence of privatization in juvenile corrections in more modern times. The best evidence suggests that private sector emergence in corrections began in the late 1970s and early 1980s with the federal government and focused exclusively on adult prisoners. According to McDonald, Fournier, Russell-Einhourn, and Crawford, the Immigration and Naturalization Service (INS) began contracting with private firms to house illegal immigrants either awaiting deportation hearings or finishing sentences in state or federal prisons. This action set the stage for specific private correctional corporations to emerge: Corrections Corporation of America (CCA); Wackenhut, which modified its private security service to corrections; and Correctional Services Corporation (CSC), currently the leader in institutional corrections for juveniles. In 1983, CCA opened its first detention center in Houston, Texas. Soon after, other private correctional corporations were contracted to design, construct, and operate facilities for the INS.[25]

Eventually, the private correctional industry became a major growth market, extending contracts to state-operated institutions for adults. Some attribute the emergence of privatization in juvenile justice to the success experienced in adult correctional enterprises.[26] Although most of the popularity in juvenile corrections has occurred in the last 30 years, it is inaccurate to say that private agencies simply emerged for juvenile delinquents in the 1980s as they did in the adult arena. Throughout its history, the juvenile justice system has engaged numerous private programs and services at every stage from before arrest to after release from a correctional institution. In many ways, the variety of private programs, services, and institutions employed in the juvenile justice system are almost foreign to the adult system.

Even if privatization in juvenile justice was limited only to secure institutionalization, private institutions for juveniles are not new, and they are much more prevalent than in the adult correctional system.[27] In the United States, there are approximately 260 privately operated facilities for adults, nearly 1,800 privately operated institutions for juveniles, and a number of other privately operated programs and services for delinquent youth. These high numbers suggest that private facilities have had a significant place in juvenile corrections and will continue to in the future.

Types of Public and Private Juvenile Correctional Institutions

One of the main reasons that privatization is prevalent in juvenile corrections relates to the versatility required in the juvenile correctional system. The need for versatility in the juvenile justice system relates to the three distinct types of youths it serves, all of whom may be institutionalized for protection, rehabilitation, supervision, or punishment. Different than the adult system, the juvenile justice system deals with (1) delinquents; (2) those who commit nondelinquent acts indicating a need for assistance or supervision (e.g., status offenders); and (3) dependent (those whose parents want to care for them but cannot) and neglected (those whose parents can take care of them but choose not to) youth. This diverse range of clientele implicates the need for a vast array of correctional options from both the public and private sectors.

Youth Shelters

Youth shelters are considered short-term, nonsecure (unlocked) facilities typically used for status offenders, such as runaways, and dependent and neglected youth. Delinquents are rarely held in youth shelter facilities. Youth shelters are best considered a "bus stop" for youth who are waiting to be reunited with their family, placed with a relative, adopted, or placed in a foster home.

Before the 1970s, there were relatively few shelter care facilities in the United States. This is because before the 1974 Juvenile Justice and Delinquency Prevention Act (JJDPA), there were few restrictions on the institutionalization of status offenders and other nondelinquent youth in secure juvenile correctional facilities. Thus, it was common to find status offenders and dependent and neglected youths alongside delinquents in state schools. Per the mandates of the JJDPA, which required the removal of status offenders and other nondelinquents from secure confinement, the need arose for shelter care facilities. Although no accurate count exists, there are numerous shelter care facilities in the United States. They are primarily considered to be local- and county-level facilities, but many are operated by nonprofit and for-profit private agencies at these same government levels.[28]

Detention Centers

Detention centers are secure, short-term facilities. They primarily hold delinquent youth in three different circumstances: (1) delinquent youth awaiting an adjudication hearing; (2) youth accused of a probation or parole violations; and (3) adjudicated delinquents who require short-term transitional placements until they are moved to a public or privately operated juvenile correctional facility.

Detention centers might best be described as the workhorse of juvenile correctional institutions, and primarily they are operated privately or at the county level. There are more than 600,000 admissions to juvenile detention each year.[29] Although most youth will be released from these facilities after a short period of time, the massive number of youth who pass through these facilities in any given year means that bed space is severely limited in many jurisdictions. Because of this need for bed space, private detention centers are numerous and fill an important gap in public facility space. Detention centers are versatile, and it is not uncommon to find state correctional agencies contracting with detention centers for bed space or "holds"—regardless whether the detention center is a public or private facility. It also is common for detention centers to receive juvenile parole violators. In these cases, parole violators may serve a short period of time in a state, county, or private detention center, instead of serving an additional term in a public or private state school.

Diagnostic and Reception Facilities

There are a number of other facilities for juvenile offenders, primarily used after their adjudication in juvenile court. Diagnostic and reception facilities are short-term secure institutions that assess state-committed delinquents to place them in the most appropriate juvenile correctional facility based on their particular needs. Usually these facilities are state operated, but this is not always the case and services can be contracted out to private entities (as is the case with the Federal Bureau of Prisons).

Stabilization Facilities

Stabilization facilities are another type of juvenile correctional facility. They are operated by public and private entities, and they are used primarily to house severely mentally ill or emotionally disturbed youth. These secure, short-term facilities typically are used for the stabilization of youth. Once stabilized, youth may be transferred to a "regular" state-operated or private juvenile correctional facility to complete their minimum commitment period. Because stabilization facilities provide specialized types of care, private agencies may operate these types of facilities, but they may be owned by the government. When states do not have an established stabilization facility for youth, inpatient hospitals usually fill the void unless a private agency with the requisite expertise is available. Indeed, most state juvenile correctional systems do not have specialized staff to deal with severely mentally ill or emotionally disturbed youth. In these situations, privately operated facilities may fill the gap.

Boot Camps

Boot camps also can be considered juvenile correctional institutions. Boot camps for juvenile offenders became a popular correctional option in the late 1980s and early 1990s. Boot camps are guided by the simple philosophy that hard work and discipline can be effective means of accomplishing rehabilitation. Boot camps may be operated by county and state correctional agencies, and a number of private organizations operate boot camps as well. Boot camps are controversial in juvenile justice, particularly when private authorities operate the boot camp. Criticisms abound that privately operated boot camps lack the necessary oversight, and this lack of oversight leads to abusive conditions. Critics claim that privately operated boot camps lack appropriate numbers of qualified staff—that many boot camp "drill instructors" are former military men and women with little to no correctional experience or training.

There have been numerous instances of abuse reported in juvenile boot camps over the last several years—from private and government-operated boot camps. In 2006, a boy was allegedly beaten to death in the Bay County boot camp in Florida, a program operated through a county contract with the state. An adolescent boy died in a motel bathtub after being committed to the privately operated America's Buffalo Soldiers Re-Enactors Association boot camp in Buckeye, Arizona. This death was only the tip of the iceberg, however. Accounts from youth indicate that staff members forced "recruits" to eat mud during "mud treatments" and forced youth to lie on their backs in a "dead cockroach" position while having muddy water poured into their mouths. Others claimed that staff members tied a noose around recruits' necks, kicked recruits, subjected them to corporal punishment, and warned them not to report the abuse.[30]

Youth Ranches and Forestry Camps

A correlate to boot camps is youth ranches and forestry camps. Although these correctional programs are not institutions per se, they are equivalent to secure confinement. Ranches and forestry camps are found in the public and private sectors. One of the most popular ranch programs in the United States is the Florida Environmental Institute (FEI) Last Chance Ranch, which handles some of Florida's most serious and violent delinquents. Ranches and forestry camps receive roughly 10 to 15 percent of all youth in residential placement. The Last Chance Ranch is funded by the Florida Department of Juvenile Justice and Department of Education, the United Way, and private donations. This program is something of a hybrid public-private juvenile correctional program, but it is managed by private authorities.

Juvenile Correctional Facilities

At the far end of the juvenile correctional system spectrum are state schools—or, as they are more commonly known today, juvenile correctional facilities. There are thousands of public and private correctional facilities for juveniles in the United States. Although public facilities are less numerous than private juvenile correctional facilities, public facilities hold roughly 70 percent of all committed delinquent offenders in the United States.[31] This suggests that public juvenile correctional facilities likely have larger populations of youth than privately operated correctional facilities. That said, the bottom line is that private facilities do hold a significant number of delinquents in residential placement.

The variety of youth involved in the juvenile justice system implicates numerous types of institutional placements. These institutional placements were described above as short or long term and secure or nonsecure. It is also the case that these placements are operated by public and private agencies. Although there is variation depending on the type of institutional placement and level of government involvement, both the public and private sectors have a part in juvenile institutionalization. Unlike the adult system, the juvenile justice system is significantly more diverse in the clientele it serves and must be more versatile.

YOUTH IN PUBLIC AND PRIVATE JUVENILE CORRECTIONAL FACILITIES

State Juvenile Justice

The most recent statistics indicate that there are roughly 1,200 public juvenile correctional facilities and nearly 1,800 private juvenile correctional facilities in the United States. In 2003, roughly 97,000 youth resided in juvenile correctional facilities—approximately 95 percent of these individuals were delinquents, as opposed to status offenders.[32]

Public juvenile correctional facilities held approximately 70 percent of all youth in residential placement and private facilities held roughly 30 percent of all youth residing in juvenile correctional facilities.[33] According to Office of Juvenile Justice and Delinquency Prevention (OJJDP), private facilities generally hold a different population of offenders than do public facilities. In general, private facilities hold a greater proportion of delinquents who have been committed to the facility by a court, as opposed to juveniles who are awaiting adjudication or disposition. Thus, public facilities appear to hold a more diverse range of youth than private juvenile correctional facilities, which appear to hold almost solely committed delinquents.

Private juvenile institutions tend to hold a smaller number of youth on average than do public facilities. Additionally, although most youth in residential placement are delinquents, the OJJDP revealed that, when status offenders are sent to a residential placement, most of them end up in a private, as opposed to a public, facility.[34] Thus, in some cases, private facilities may be receiving or able to choose a "better class" of juvenile offenders than public juvenile correctional facilities. Moreover, some research has revealed that status offenders often serve much longer sentences in private facilities than if they placed in public juvenile correctional facilities.[35] This is most likely the result of the deinstitutionalization mandates of the JJDPA of 1974, which have a lesser effect on private institutions than on public institutions for juveniles.

Federal Juvenile Justice

An oft-neglected aspect of juvenile corrections are those youth who violate federal laws and are adjudicated in federal court. Although rare, if a juvenile is charged with a federal law violation and is tried in federal court, the trial will take place in front of a U.S. District Court judge or a federal magistrate, as opposed to a juvenile court judge. If a juvenile is adjudicated in federal court, the juvenile may face many of the same sanctions that would apply at the state level, including institutionalization.

If a juvenile delinquent is institutionalized as a result of a federal offense, his or her placement would be in a state or private juvenile correctional facility contracted by the Federal Bureau of Prisons (FBOP). Because the federal government does not operate juvenile facilities, the FBOP enters into agreements with tribal, state, and local governments, and into contracts with private organizations, to provide secure and nonsecure services to juvenile offenders.

Facilities contracted by the FBOP are required to provide assessment and treatment services to committed delinquents in the same way they would to delinquents committed through nonfederal court cases. A listing of all tribal, state, local, and private juvenile facilities contracted by the FBOP in 2004 shows agreements and contracts with roughly 60 different types of secure and nonsecure facilities in all regions of the United States. According to the FBOP directory of contract juvenile facilities, roughly 21 of these facilities are privately operated.[36]

FBOP contract facilities do not hold a large number of federally convicted youth. As such, federally committed delinquents are almost always housed with state-committed delinquents. The most recent statistics indicate that the FBOP rarely holds more than 200 federally convicted juveniles at any one time across the country. Most juveniles held by the FBOP are convicted for violent offenses and most are Native American juveniles. Although minor crimes committed by Native American juveniles are handled by reservation tribal courts, serious crimes are tried in federal court, which accounts for the high number of confined Native American juveniles relative to other juveniles under federal confinement.[37]

Like other public and private facilities holding state-committed delinquents, those that hold federally convicted and committed juvenile are monitored by the FBOP. The FBOP conducts on-site visits for the purpose of evaluating the performance of the institution and adherence to service delivery.

CURRENT ISSUES IN JUVENILE CORRECTIONS

This section examines several issues and perspectives related to a discussion of public versus private operation of juvenile correctional facilities. It examines the cost issue, which may be one of the most commonly held beliefs as to why privatization is present in corrections. This section also examines other popular explanations for why privatization in corrections may be attractive. It then examines evidence on the quality of confinement for juveniles in both public and private facilities, which may be one of the major complaints against privatization in juvenile corrections. This section ends with a discussion of perspectives concerning public versus private operation of juvenile correctional facilities.

Cost

Perhaps more than any other issue, cost is considered to be one of the main reasons why private industry continues to extend into adult and juvenile corrections. A major claim of privatization is that profits can be attained because private agencies can provide the same services as a public agency but more efficiently and at a lower cost. The experience in some states suggests this cost savings has been realized.[38] Whether private agencies can do the same things that government agencies are doing, at the same or higher caliber more efficiently and less costly, however, really are unanswered questions. One reason cost remains an unanswered question is that private agencies do not always do the "same things" as public agencies. For example, private agencies may accept lower-security inmates, which tends to reduce costs. Indeed, some private juvenile correctional facilities may only accept offenders with a short time left in their commitment period, or they may have a large population of status offenders. There is a major difference in operating costs between the public and private sector if a private facility houses only lower-security offenders or the "best risks."

It is also the case that private institutions for juveniles often have no public counterpart. This is another reason why governments contract with private firms, because they have expertise or institutions the government may not have. For example, private agencies may operate specialized treatment institutions that have no equivalent in the public juvenile correctional system. Because there is not comparison institution in the public sector, it is difficult to estimate the money saved by privatization, if any.

Private agencies may offer fewer educational, vocational, and treatment programs compared with public agencies. Although there is much variation within and between states and private agencies, such differences have led some to conclude that comparing the operating costs of private and public juvenile correctional agencies is like comparing apples to oranges. Unless public and private agencies do the same things, with the same types of youth, comparisons of cost are problematic at best.

Cost savings can come in a number of ways, but when cost savings are found, it usually is not because private agencies are somehow more efficient at fundamental correctional procedure than their public counterparts. Rather, if savings from privatization in juvenile corrections are found, it has more to do with the fact that private prison employees may have reduced training requirements, which saves money. Private prison agencies may also employ nonunion employees, which can result in significant savings in salary and benefits when compared with public correctional facility employees.[39] Although there is variation among states, these two areas may result in cost savings absent the belief that private agencies are simply "more efficient."

The bottom line is that many private juvenile correctional agencies are doing different things and have different requirements than public juvenile correctional facilities, which may result in perceptions of cost savings that are not entirely accurate. Comparing the cost of private institutions with public institutions simply is not a straightforward issue. Notwithstanding the problems described, even the best evaluations of cost show that fairly nominal (if any) reductions in cost come with privatization.[40]

Why Privatization Is Attractive

Aside from the cost argument, evidence suggests that one of the major reasons why privatization is attractive in corrections is that it may be a faster way to open institutional beds than by going through the normal government process. Indeed, approval for government appropriations to design, build, and operate correctional institutions may take years. Using a private agency can result in quickly acquired beds, even if the facility has yet to be designed and built.[41] There is a belief that contracting for services and beds through private agencies is preferable in some circumstances, because private firms "are not mired in the 'red tape' that encumbers public agencies, especially in procurement and labor relations."[42]

Overcrowding is certainly a concern in adult corrections, and overcrowded facilities are prevalent in juvenile corrections as well. One comprehensive government report revealed that nearly 35 percent of state training schools for juveniles across the country were overcrowded.[43] As mentioned, overcrowded conditions are sometimes hard to fix in a short period of time. Often, lawsuits and consent decrees require that correctional systems remedy conditions of overcrowding quickly, something that depends almost entirely on legislatures. In this way, contracting with a private correctional agency is attractive for correctional systems and can open up correctional beds more quickly than government agencies.

Certain conditions of confinement as a result of overcrowding or other factors can also be addressed with privatization. Although the problematic conditions of confinement that existed in juvenile correctional facilities in the 1970s and 1980s have largely been addressed, numerous facilities still are not in minimum compliance with established standards. As a result, turning to a private correctional corporation can result in compliance with many minimum standards, especially those related to physical plant concerns. Private correctional corporations rarely "take over" existing correctional facilities, thus private facilities are newer than many juvenile correctional facilities in operation today and they usually meet minimum established standards. Indeed, one comprehensive study of 48 public and private juvenile correctional facilities revealed that the average age of private juvenile correctional facilities was just over four years, whereas the average age of public juvenile correctional facilities was almost 30 years.[44] In this way, privatization can supplement existing public juvenile correctional facilities to remedy a number of conditions.

Comparative data do not exist for private juvenile corrections, but one survey of adult privatization revealed that the primary reason jurisdictions contracted with private agencies was to reduce overcrowding in their system. Other commonly cited reasons included the ability to acquire additional beds quickly or to gain operational flexibility. Thus, although cost savings usually is cited as one of the main reasons for privatization, which is a popular belief among the general public, this survey revealed that saving money through operating costs or in construction were less frequently cited reasons for contracting with private correctional firms.[45] Again, comparative survey data concerning the ability to contract out for juvenile correctional services and facilities are not available. Whether the motivation to privative would change is unknown, but the indication is that reducing overcrowding, acquiring new beds, and remedying certain conditions of confinement are also important reasons for privatization in juvenile corrections. The findings that nearly 35 percent of state training schools are overcrowded, that public facilities on average are "older" than private institutions, and that private facilities hold nearly 30 percent of all committed juveniles explain why privatization has been attractive in juvenile corrections.[46]

Environmental Quality

Environmental quality refers to factors such as the meeting of basic needs, order and safety, programming, adherence to juveniles' rights, and numerous other dimensions.[47] This is certainly a concern for adult inmates, but many believe that environmental quality is even more important for juveniles, because they may be less able to withstand lower-quality environments than adults.

There are two schools of thought on the issue of environmental quality between public and private juvenile correctional facilities. One school of thought suggests that environmental quality in public juvenile correctional facilities will be lower than in private facilities because public facilities do not have competition. The other school of thought suggests that private juvenile correctional facilities will have lower levels of environmental quality than public juvenile facilities because private facilities operate based on profit—thus they will shortcut services and cut corners to make more money.[48]

One study examined perceptions of environmental quality as reported by more than 4,000 juvenile residents who were housed in 48 public and private juvenile correctional facilities in 19 states. The authors examined numerous indicators of environmental quality, including the following: control in the facility, activities, care, quality of life, structure, justice, therapeutic programming, and preparation for release. In addition to youth and facility characteristics, the researchers asked juvenile respondents to comment on levels of danger from staff and residents, environmental danger, risks to residents, and freedom in the facility.

The results of this survey revealed few meaningful differences in the levels of environmental quality between public and private juvenile correctional facilities. Private facilities, however, were scored more positively by juvenile residents on almost all areas of environmental quality.[49] Although the authors attribute some of these findings to the fact that private institutions for juveniles in their study were newer and held far fewer juveniles (perhaps indicators of quality), the overall finding is that private juvenile facilities do not differ in quality compared with public sector counterparts.[50]

This study suggests that quality does not necessarily have to suffer in either type of facility. The evidence concerning environmental quality is that public and private facilities may be doing similar jobs when it comes to offering a quality environment to house delinquent offenders, but the age and higher populations of public juvenile correctional facilities may have a slight impact on environmental quality.[51]

Overall Perspectives

The previous discussion suggests that there may be advantages to privatization, especially for those juvenile correctional systems confronted with the need to reduce overcrowding, acquire additional beds, meet minimum standards for facility operation, and save money. Opponents to privatization, however, argue that the profit motive of private agencies may result in corners being cut—as with inexperienced and unqualified staff, lower numbers of staff, and lower-quality services than in public agencies.[52] Although the evidence presented above suggests this may not be entirely accurate, it is a major claim against privatization.

Critics also believe that lower levels of oversight in some jurisdictions may contribute to situations of potential abuse directed toward prisoners. This criticism may have merit. In June 2004, the Louisiana Department of Corrections entered into a contract with Trans-American Development Associates (TADA) to construct, finance, and operate the Swanson Correctional Center for Youth (better known as Tallulah Juvenile Facility). Because of claims of abuse, violence, and excessive punishment, the Louisiana Department of Corrections took over operations of the facility in 1999, but TADA continued to own the facility. Experts noted that Tallulah was "a juvenile prison so rife with brutality, cronyism and neglect that ... it is the worst in the nation."[53] Eventually, the Tallulah juvenile facility was closed and converted into an adult prison.[54]

Outside of these more tangible concerns, critics of privatization argue that it is the state's responsibility to deal with its delinquents on a moral level.[55] Critics argue that rehabilitation should not be a moneymaking enterprise, given its historical focus on rehabilitation above all else. The fact that full facilities means greater profits for private agencies has led critics to conclude that private agencies actually want to keep juveniles locked up—and that this is no way to operate a system based on rehabilitation. They also argue that because cost savings rarely results from innovative programs for juveniles, rehabilitation may be lost with privatization because private facilities have no incentive to support prevention programs or other programs that would prevent the juvenile from recidivating.[56]

Despite these and other criticisms, private agencies do have something to contribute to the correctional system. At the same time, however, there are worthy arguments against privatization. Whether the extension of private agencies into a traditionally public domain is good or bad, useful or not, is not necessarily the issue at hand. The fact remains that privatization is occurring and has been for several years—and at particularly high levels in the juvenile correctional system. An understanding of why privatization has occurred in corrections, and the advantages and disadvantages associated with privatization, is important in a discussion of the public and private operation of juvenile correctional facilities.

LEGAL ISSUES AND LIABILITIES

A variety of legal issues are associated with correctional facilities, be they adult or juvenile. These issues include determining what rights, if any, incarcerated individuals retain and identifying what conditions of confinement violate the constitutional prohibition on cruel and unusual punishment.

When privatization gained momentum in the 1980s and early 1990s, there was much discussion of the legal issues associated with privatization. It was initially unclear to what degree states could delegate the task of operating correctional services and facilities (either adult or juvenile) to private entities. It was also unclear what effect privatization would have on the state's liability for unsatisfactory conditions of confinement and mistreatment of those who were incarcerated. Courts moved quickly to address these questions. First, states have the authority, under the delegation doctrine, to delegate administrative tasks (such as the operation of prisons and juvenile facilities) to private agencies, as long as the state retains some oversight of the facility.[57] Second, those housed in private facilities have the same constitutional rights they would have in a state-operated facility. This is particularly noteworthy because it means that courts do not distinguish between public and private juvenile correctional facilities when it comes to determining whether any constitutional rights have been violated. Third, and perhaps most significant for the operators of private facilities, private prison employees do not enjoy the benefit of the "qualified immunity" defense that is available to public employees.[58] This means that employees of private juvenile correctional facilities who are sued for negligent or reckless conduct cannot use this defense to escape civil liability for their misconduct.

Constitutional Rights

Cruel and Unusual Punishment

Following several U.S. Supreme Court decisions clarifying and expanding the rights of juveniles in the court system, juvenile justice reformers turned their attention to the rights of institutionalized juveniles.[59] The Eighth Amendment prohibits "cruel and unusual" punishment. Precisely what constitutes cruel and unusual punishment is the subject of much debate. For purposes of this chapter, it is sufficient to say that the ban on cruel and unusual punishment bars the use of inappropriate procedures, polices, and practices by juvenile facility personnel.

Reformers in the 1970s discovered abuses in several state juvenile systems. In Arkansas, investigators discovered that juveniles were routinely beaten and forced to engage in a variety of unsafe and humiliating activities, including eating feces and being made to oink like a pig.[60] Similar practices were uncovered in a number of other states.

Perhaps the most disturbing and horrific pattern of abuse took place in the Texas juvenile justice system. These abuses were documented in *Morales v. Turman*. The federal district court found that a number of policies and practices of the Texas Youth Council violated the Eighth Amendment prohibition on cruel and unusual punishment. The Texas system was woefully overcrowded and understaffed, and staff were poorly trained. The results were widespread abuse of juveniles in the system, overcrowded facilities that made it impossible to provide adequate security, and a lack of access to treatment programs. During the 1970s, courts found evidence of constitutional violations in several other state systems, including Rhode Island, New York, and Mississippi.[61]

Although the U.S. Supreme Court has never determined precisely what constitutes cruel and unusual punishment in a juvenile facility, it is clear that juveniles have the right to be free of cruel and unusual punishment at least to the same degree as adult inmates. State and lower federal courts that have examined the conditions of confinement in juvenile facilities have barred a variety of practices, including the use of solitary confinement, tranquilizers, and corporal punishment. Courts have imposed restrictions on the amount of force that can be used and the types of restraint devices that can be employed.

Despite the greater attention now paid to juvenile facilities by the courts, the evidence is clear that instances of abuse are still occurring. Recent investigations have found patterns of abuse in several states, including Arkansas, California, Colorado, Georgia, and Louisiana.[62] Both the U.S. Department of Justice and Human Rights Watch (an international organization) have conducted investigations of abuse in public and private juvenile facilities.

Access to Courts

The U.S. Supreme Court has never determined whether confined juveniles have a constitutional right of access to the courts, similar to the right of access enjoyed by adult inmates. Nonetheless, every state provides juveniles with a statutory right of access to the courts. The parameters of this right are not uniform, however. Some commentators have argued that because the juvenile justice system has as its primary goal rehabilitation rather than punishment, there is no need for the same access to the courts—in other words, because the juvenile justice system exists to help those in its care, those in its care won't need to go to court for protection. The lower federal courts that have considered this argument have not been convinced, in large part because decisions such as *In re Gault* (1967) made it clear that abuses could and did take place in the juvenile justice system despite its ostensible focus on rehabilitation.

Right to Treatment

The U.S. Supreme Court has held that an incarcerated adult has a right to some degree of medical care.[63] This right is not to the best medical care available. Rather, it is a right to a basic, minimal degree of medical care. The Supreme Court has never addressed the right to treatment for juveniles, but several lower courts have done so. Most of these courts have held that juveniles are entitled to a higher standard of care and treatment than adults, because treatment is more closely related to rehabilitation. Precisely what services are required is subject to some debate. For instance, in *Morales v. Turman*, the federal district court required the Texas Youth Council to meet national standards for the assessment and treatment of juveniles.

Conditions of Confinement

A comprehensive national survey of juvenile correctional facilities conducted in the 1990s identified a number of areas of concern involving the conditions of confinement. Juvenile facilities suffered from overcrowding, inadequate security, inadequate suicide prevention, and inadequate medical and mental health services.[64] Although the U.S. Supreme Court has never expressly held that juveniles have a constitutional right to particular conditions of confinement, the Court has so held in regards to adult institutions. It seems highly likely that the Court would require for juveniles at least the same minimal conditions of confinement that adult inmates receive.

Overcrowding

A report by Parent and colleagues found that approximately 35 percent of state juvenile institutions were overcrowded. Overcrowding in a facility is not unconstitutional per se. The U.S. Supreme Court held, in *Rhodes v. Chapman*, that overcrowding in an adult institution was not, in and of itself, violative of the Constitution. Rather, there must be evidence that the overcrowding negatively affects the delivery of other institutional services, such as sanitation, food service, or medical care. It is possible, however, that a court may determine that overcrowding is more damaging to juveniles than to adults, and hold that overcrowding alone is sufficient to find a constitutional violation. To date, however, no court has done so.

Suicide

Public health research indicates that juveniles are more likely to attempt suicide than adults and that institutionalized juveniles are four times more likely than juveniles in the general population to attempt suicide.[65] The latest data indicate that there are at least 17,000 instances of suicidal behavior or suicide attempts in juvenile facilities each year. Juvenile facility staff frequently lack the training necessary to accurately detect suicidal behavior, and they are often so overworked that they cannot pay close attention to early warning signs. In addition to the tragic consequences of a suicide are the related liability issues. Correctional staff and administrators who fail to prevent a suicide attempt that they should have detected may be held civilly liable for their misconduct.

CONCLUSION

For the most part, public institutions dominate the juvenile correctional system. That said, private correctional facilities are playing an increasingly important role in juvenile corrections. Critics suggest that a moneymaking enterprise should have no place in a system whose goals have been traditionally rehabilitation. History shows, however, that privatization has always had a place in the juvenile correctional system, and the larger juvenile justice system, to some degree.

Over the last several years, juvenile corrections have been characterized as a mix between public and private justice. Today, nearly 30 percent of all institutionalized juveniles are held in private facilities—a number that grows slightly each year—thus the lines between public and private justice in the juvenile justice system have been blurred. The numerous needs and diverse clientele in the juvenile justice system suggest that privatization is needed. Indeed, the juvenile justice system engages private agencies to provide a number of services, programs, and institutions that might never be realized in their absence. It is simply the case that private correctional agencies sometimes can offer something that the government cannot.

The belief that private correctional facilities can do what they want when they want is a common misperception about privatization. Although public and private juvenile correctional agencies may differ in areas, the reality is that private juvenile correctional facilities are probably not any better or worse than government-operated correctional facilities. It is simply not the case that administrators of private facilities can "run wild." Rather, private juvenile correctional facilities, depending on state laws and contractual arrangements, perhaps receive more oversight than do government agencies, and they are certainly more open to liability, given the absence of the qualified immunity defense.

There is no clear-cut answer as to whether private facilities cost more or less than government facilities. This is one of the main claims of privatization, but determining cost is a difficult if not impossible venture. Rather, there are a number of other reasons why privatization may be attractive in juvenile corrections—opening bed space, reducing overcrowding, providing more modern conditions. If private agencies are able to accomplish these tasks for governments, then they are providing an important service to juveniles who find themselves incarcerated.

The bottom line to the debate between public and private operation of juvenile correctional facilities is that each has something to contribute to the juvenile correctional process. A tremendous variation exists both within and between states as to the operation of either facility, but in many ways, their operation is similar. The mere presence of privatization in juvenile corrections suggests that it serves an important function. As a result, it is unlikely that privatization will simply go away in the near future. Consistent with its historical precedent in juvenile justice, privatization will continue to supplement the public juvenile correctional system, and in the end, it may lead to a more appropriate environment for the rehabilitation of delinquents who have reached the deepest ends of the correctional system.

NOTES

1. Clear, Cole, & Reisig, 2006.
2. Beattie, 1986.
3. Taylor, 1993; Walker, 1988.
4. Walker, 1998.
5. Armstrong & MacKenzie, 2003.
6. Stephan & Karberg, 2003.
7. Stephan & Karberg, 2003.
8. Armstrong & MacKenzie, 2003.
9. Sickmund, 2004.
10. Sickmund, Sladky, & Kang, 2005.
11. Armstrong & MacKenzie, 2003; Sickmund, 2004.
12. McDonald, 1992.
13. Joel, 1988.
14. McDonald & Patten, 2004, pp. 11–12.
15. Fritsch, Caeti, & Hemmens, 1996.
16. Marion & Oliver, 2006; Wilson, 1989.
17. DiIulio, 1988.
18. Rothman, 1971.
19. del Carmen & Trulson, 2006; Fritsch & Hemmens, 1995.
20. Fritsch & Hemmens, 1995.
21. Steiner & Hemmens, 2003.
22. Rothman, 1971, 1980.
23. Bartollas & Miller, 2001.
24. Bartollas & Miller, 2001.
25. McDonald, Fournier, Russell-Einhourn, & Crawford, 1998.
26. Building Blocks for Youth, 2006.
27. Sickmund, 2004.
28. del Carmen & Trulson, 2006.
29. Parent et al., 1994; Sickmund, 2004.
30. del Carmen & Trulson, 2006.
31. Sickmund et al., 2005.
32. Sickmund et al., 2005.
33. Sickmund et al., 2005.
34. Sickmund, 2004.
35. Shichor & Bartollas, 1990.

36. Federal Bureau of Prisons, 2004.
37. Scalia, 1997.
38. McDonald et al., 1998.
39. Marion & Oliver, 2006.
40. McDonald et al., 1998; McDonald & Patten, 2004; Pratt & Maahs, 1999.
41. McDonald et al., 1998.
42. DiIulio, 1988; McDonald et al., 1998.
43. Parent et al., 1994.
44. Armstrong & MacKenzie, 2003.
45. McDonald et al., 1998.
46. Parent et al., 1994; Sickmund, 2004; Sickmund et al., 2005.
47. Armstrong & MacKenzie, 2003.
48. Armstrong & MacKenzie, 2003; Logan, 1992.
49. Armstrong & MacKenzie, 2003.
50. See, however, Logan, 1992.
51. Shichor & Bartollas, 1990.
52. Marion & Oliver, 2006; Shichor & Bartollas, 1990.
53. Building Blocks for Youth, 2006, p. 1.
54. del Carmen & Trulson, 2006.
55. Marion & Oliver, 2006.
56. Shichor & Bartollas, 1990.
57. McDonald et al., 1998.
58. *Richardson v. McKnight*, 1997.
59. *Kent v. United States*, 1966; *In re Gault*, 1967.
60. del Carmen & Trulson, 2006.
61. Rhode Island (*Inmates of Boys' Training School v. Affleck*, 1972); New York (*Pena v. New York State Division of Youth*, 1976); Mississippi (*Morgan v. Sproat*, 1977).
62. del Carmen & Trulson, 2006.
63. *Estelle v. Gamble*, 1976.
64. Parent et al., 1994.
65. del Carmen & Trulson, 2006.

REFERENCES

Armstrong, G., & MacKenzie, D. (2003). Private versus public juvenile correctional facilities: Do differences in environmental quality exist. *Crime & Delinquency, 49*, 542–563.

Bartollas, C., & Miller, S. (2001). *Juvenile justice in America* (3rd ed.). Upper Saddle River, NJ: Prentice Hall.

Beattie, J. (1986). *Crime and the courts in England 1660–1800.* Princeton, NJ: Princeton University Press.

Building Blocks for Youth. (2006). *The privatization of juvenile corrections facilities.* Retrieved March 30, 2006, from www.buildingblocksforyouth.org/issues/privatization/facts.html.

Clear, T., Cole, G., & Reisig, M. (2006). *American corrections* (7th ed.). Belmont, CA: Wadsworth.

del Carmen, R., & Trulson, C. (2006). *Juvenile justice: The system, process, and law.* Belmont, CA: Wadsworth.

DiIulio, J. (1988). What's wrong with private prisons. *Public Interest, 92*, 66–83.

Federal Bureau of Prisons. (2004, July). *Contract Juvenile Facilities*. Retrieved April 1, 2006, from www.bop.gov/locations/cc/SOW_Secure_Juvie.pdf.

Fritsch, E., Caeti, T., & Hemmens, C. (1996). Spare the needle but not the punishment: The incarceration of waived youth in Texas prisons. *Crime and Delinquency 42*, 593–609.

Fritsch, E., & Hemmens, C. (1995). Juvenile waiver in the United States 1979–1995: A comparison and analysis of state waiver statutes. *Juvenile and Family Court Journal, 46*, 17–35.

Joel, D. (1988). *A guide to prison privatization*. Retrieved March 14, 2006, from www.new.heritage.org/research/crime/bg650.cfm.

Logan, C. (1992). Well kept: Comparing quality of confinement in private and public prisons. *The Journal of Criminal Law and Criminology, 8*, 577–613.

Marion, N., & Oliver, W. (2006). *The public policy of crime and criminal justice*. Upper Saddle River, NJ: Prentice Hall.

McDonald, D. (1992). Private penal institutions. In M. Tonry (Ed.), *Crime and justice: A review of research* (Vol. 16, pp. 361–419). Chicago: University of Chicago Press.

McDonald, D., Fournier, E., Russell-Einhorn, M., & Crawford, S. (1998). *Private prisons in the United States*. Cambridge, MA: Abt Associates.

McDonald, D., & Patten, C. (2004). *Governments' management of private prisons*. Cambridge, MA: Abt Associates.

Parent, D., Leiter, V., Kennedy, S., Livens, L., Wentworth, D., & Wilcox, S. (1994). *Conditions of confinement: Juvenile detention and corrections facilities*. Washington, D.C.: U.S. Department of Justice, Office of Juvenile Justice and Delinquency Prevention.

Pratt, T., & Maahs, J. (1999). Are private prisons more cost-effective than public prisons? A meta-analysis of evaluation research studies. *Crime & Delinquency, 45*, 358–371.

Rothman, D. (1971). *The discovery of the asylum*. Boston, MA: Little, Brown and Company.

Rothman, D. (1980). *Conscience and convenience: The asylum and its alternatives in progressive America*. Boston, MA: Little, Brown and Company.

Scalia, J. (1997). *Juvenile delinquents in the federal criminal justice system*. Washington, D.C.: U.S. Department of Justice, Bureau of Justice Statistics.

Shichor, D., & Bartollas, C. (1990). Private and public placements: Is there a difference? *Crime & Delinquency, 36*, 289–299.

Sickmund, M. (2004). *Juveniles in corrections*. Washington, D.C.: U.S. Department of Justice, Office of Juvenile Justice and Delinquency Prevention.

Sickmund, M., Sladky, T., & Kang, W. (2005). *Census of juveniles in residential placement*. Washington, D.C.: U.S. Department of Justice, Office of Juvenile Justice and Delinquency Prevention.

Steiner, B., & Hemmens, C. (2003). Juvenile waiver 2003: Where are we now? *Juvenile and Family Court Journal, 54*, 1–24.

Stephan, J., & Karberg, J. (2003). *Census of state and federal correctional facilities, 2000*. Washington, D.C.: U.S. Department of Justice, Bureau of Justice Statistics.

Taylor, W. (1993). *Brokered justice*. Columbus, OH: Ohio State University Press.

Walker, D. (1988). *Penology for profit*. College Station, TX: Texas A&M University Press.

Wilson, J. (1989). *Bureaucracy*. New York: Basic Books.

CASES CITED

Estelle v. Gamble, 429 U.S. 97 (1976).

In re Gault, 387 U.S. 1 (1967).

Inmates of Boys' Training School v. Affleck, 346 F. Supp. 1354 (Rhode Island, 1972).

Kent v. United States, 383 U.S. 541 (1966).

Morales v. Turman, 383 F. Supp. 53 (E.D. Texas, 1973).

Morgan v. Sproat, 432 F. Supp. 1130 (S.D. Mississippi, 1977).

Pena v. New York State Division of Youth, 419 F. Supp. 203 (S.D. New York, 1976).

Rhodes v. Chapman, 452 U.S. 337 (1981).

Richardson v. McKnight, 521 U.S. 399 (1997).

CHAPTER 10

The Future of Delinquency Prevention and Treatment

Ronald Burns

Client RC-183 please step forward. Please place your body into the scanner and look into the screen. Thank you. Now, observe the consequences of your actions as they appear on the screen. Pay particular attention to the impact you've had on the victim and their family. Your physiological responses to the victims' reactions are being measured and appropriate treatment will be rendered. Now, please step away from the scanner and proceed to Floor 29 where Dr. Elms will administer your treatment in the form of electromagnetic radiation and implant adjustment. Thank you.

The above scenario may seem far-fetched, but just consider the societal changes we have experienced in the past 20 years, particularly with regard to our responses to crime, delinquency, and justice. Computers in police cars, electronic monitoring devices, and computer simulations used as evidence in courtrooms may have seemed far-fetched to earlier generations, however, they are now ingrained in our juvenile and criminal justice systems.

To comment on the future of delinquency prevention and treatment requires diligent consideration of numerous issues, not the least of which is the methods by which we forecast the future.[1] In looking toward the future, researchers often use quantitative and qualitative research methods, as well as the Delphi technique and the creation of scenarios. A brief version of the latter approach introduces this chapter. Greater confidence is attained by using multiple approaches, similar to the manner in which criminologists have greater confidence in discussing crime trends using data from the Uniform Crime Reports and National Crime Victimization Surveys.

Forecasting the future requires consideration of temporal and spatial issues. Futurists may comment on issues expected to occur 5, 10, 50, or even 100 years from now. To be sure, there are no restrictions on how far into the future one can look, but the confidence level generally decreases as one looks further into the future. For instance, we have greater confidence in the weather forecast for tomorrow than we do in the forecast for five days from now. Spatial issues concern, among other issues, the scope of the issue under observation. For instance, one could comment on future events and developments at the international, national, state, county, local, neighborhood, or individual levels. Put simply, forecasting the future is a vital, although challenging, task.

Contributing largely to the challenges of forecasting the future is the uncertainty of human behavior. Although futurists apply scientific approaches, one can never be certain how, why, or when particular behaviors affect society. Consider the impacts of the terrorist attacks against the United States on September 11, 2001. Now, consider how futurists have had to revise their earlier projections in light of those events. Although some may have projected the vulnerability of the United States to such attacks, it is unlikely that many forecasted such drastic changes, for instance, with regard to homeland security, particularly as it relates to air travel and the restructuring of our federal law enforcement agencies.

This chapter addresses the future of delinquency prevention and treatment. Disbursed throughout are quantitative analyses that look to the future of delinquency prevention and treatment, and comments by leading forecasters who seemingly have their fingers on the pulse of what we can expect with regard to these issues. These comments are offered in light of qualitative changes that have occurred and those that are taking place.

CONTEXTUALIZING DELINQUENCY PREVENTION AND TREATMENT

Examination of the future of delinquency treatment and prevention requires at least some consideration of what constitutes delinquency prevention and treatment, and a review of historical developments and current trends within juvenile justice and delinquency.

Delinquency Prevention

Prevention has been, and continues to be a vital component of most efforts to confront delinquency. The long-standing belief that young people are more impressionable than adults has resulted in greater prevention efforts being directed toward youths than toward adults. It is felt by many that preventing involvement in delinquency is more effective than "correcting" or "fixing" misguided youths. The belief that "you can't teach an old dog new tricks" provides the impetus for many delinquency prevention programs and strategies.

Jackson and Knepper identify five delinquency prevention strategies, including specific and general deterrence (e.g., Scared Straight programs);

diversion from formal processing; intervention (e.g., education campaigns such as D.A.R.E. and McGruff); the public policy approach (e.g., curfews, restrictions on firearm purchases); and the public health model, which targets preventing youth from engaging in negative behavior and encourages positive behavior.[2] Each of these strategies promotes various programs and methods to proactively approach delinquency, to stop it before it occurs or becomes (increasingly) problematic. Jackson and Knepper note that "[d]elinquency prevention is not about finding a miracle cure for youth misbehavior," adding that "[d]espite about 25 years of federal prevention efforts, no single prevention program has been found to inoculate young people from breaking the law."[3]

Delinquency Treatment

Delinquency treatment is concerned with rehabilitating young offenders—that is, identifying the underlying causes of delinquency and implementing appropriate methods of correction. Treatment programs are typically based on "the assumption that delinquent behavior is a manifestation or symptom of some other deeper problem" in which symptoms are identified, diagnoses are made, and treatment is pursued.[4] Treatment programs typically follow psychiatric or psychological approaches, although the medical model is evident in some treatment programs, particularly those involving alcohol or drug abuse.[5] Treatment programs are found in both community and institutional settings, and can be used in conjunction with punitive approaches.

Historical Developments and Current Trends

Although the history of delinquency and responses to it are well documented,[6] a brief discussion is warranted to look toward the future. Bartollas highlights the historical periods regarding juvenile justice within the United States, beginning with the Colonial Era (1636–1823), and its emphasis on families being responsible for correcting the actions of their children.[7] The House of Refuge period (1824–98) emphasized the institutionalization of juveniles, while the Juvenile Court period (1899–1966) provided youthful offenders access to a court system designed to meet the specific needs of wayward juveniles. The Juvenile Rights period (1967–75) provided juveniles greater due process rights in the courts, while the Reform Agenda period of the mid- to late-1970s stressed diversion from the juvenile justice system for status offenders and nonserious delinquents. The 1980s brought increased social control over juveniles and experienced a move away from the reform efforts of the 1970s, a trend that continued through the 1990s and is evident today. Gang crime, crimes associated with crack cocaine, gun crime, and media sensationalism of juvenile crime contributed to the radical shift in philosophy when responding to delinquency.

This brief history helps sets the stage for an examination of the future of delinquency treatment and rehabilitation. To begin, a notable pattern exists with regard to developments in juvenile justice and societal changes in general. The United States initially was an agrarian society, thus there were no programs or institutions for juveniles, because there was little government involvement in family life. Accordingly, families were expected to confront problem children internally. As industry evolved and large cities emerged, wayward juveniles became more visible in society, which ultimately encouraged government involvement in the form of institution-alization. From a futurist's perspective, one could have anticipated such changes given historical developments in society in general.

Other periods of juvenile justice developments reflect events that shaped society as a whole. For instance, the Juvenile Rights period occurred at a time in U.S. history when many groups were fighting for civil rights (e.g., Native Americans, prisoners, African Americans), while the Reform Agenda period occurred during a time when the adult criminal justice systems were promoting community corrections. The shift toward punitiveness and getting tough on juveniles that began in the 1980s and continues today is reflective of, among other things, a more conservative U.S. popu-lation, the enhanced use of incarceration for adult offenders, and greater emphasis on retribution and deterrence in the adult justice system.

FACTORS INFLUENCING DELINQUENCY TREATMENT AND PREVENTION

Futurists often observe particular social forces, or what are considered drivers of the future. Among the prominent drivers of futures research are demography, economics, crime factors, technology, and public opinion. Regarding delinquency treatment and prevention, demographic projections help justice officials and policy makers anticipate population growth (or decline) and the characteristics of those changes. In turn, we can speculate whether or not we have available treatment slots for the forecasted num-ber of juveniles in need. From a prevention perspective, we can examine where the greatest changes are expected to ensure that proper prevention methods are available. Justice officials and policy makers must consider short- and long-term changes in demographics. Recent data from the U.S. Census indicate increased percentages of minority groups in society, thus the need to emphasize multiculturalism in all aspects of justice and to rec-ognize and respond to the disproportionate percentage of minority youth involved in the juvenile justice system.

Economic factors play a significant role in crime and justice. Forecasters undoubtedly must keep an eye on economic trends to effectively anticipate future trends and changes. Put simply, a strong economy typically decreases the likelihood of crime and delinquency. A weak economy has the opposite effect. Economic trends could be used to anticipate an increased presence of juveniles in the justice system, in turn commanding an increased need for rehabilitation opportunities and prevention efforts if, indeed, they are part of society's plan of attack. Poverty is a strong predic-tor of involvement in our justice systems, and involvement in our justice systems is a strong predictor of further involvement in our justice systems.

These factors alone provide ample guidance for any futurist concerned with delinquency prevention and rehabilitation. Understanding that most crime is financially motivated provides guidance for treatment and prevention efforts, as evidenced by the number of programs offering opportunities for education, job skills, and financial management. Economic factors affect delinquency and criminal behavior, and perhaps equally important, funding for juvenile justice, in general, which could result in fewer or greater opportunities for prevention and rehabilitation efforts.

An often-overlooked component of researching crime and delinquency in society is the generalization often given with regard to the terms "crime" and "delinquency." For instance, stealing a bicycle and unlawfully killing someone are distinct behaviors, yet they can be lumped together under the term "crime." In other words, the qualitative nature of illegal behaviors is notably important in the discussion of the future of delinquency prevention and treatment. Accordingly, crime factors certainly influence projections of the future. Understanding what to expect with regard to the qualitative nature of delinquency inherently affects the quantity and quality of treatment and prevention opportunities needed and provided. One merely needs to observe recent, punitive societal reactions to gang crime, gun crime, and drug-related crimes to understand how the nature of these crimes affects societal response. Particularly, concern for juvenile violence has led to greater emphasis on punitive responses to juveniles in general.

With an eye to the future, one must consider the increased presence of international and electronic opportunities for crime and delinquency and the need for prevention and treatment responses. Although it may be premature to direct our prevention and treatment efforts toward preventing international forms of delinquency, we would be foolish to believe that traditional forms of delinquency (i.e., street crimes) will remain our only concern in the future. In other words, the technology age is upon us and with it comes increased opportunities for delinquency and corresponding treatment and prevention needs. Young children and young adults alike are growing up in a society that relies heavily on technology and automation. As society changes, so, too, do forms of crime and delinquency. Furthermore, as crime and delinquency change, so does the need for innovative forms of prevention and treatment. As suggested in the opening scenario, technology is expected to become increasingly ingrained in responses to crime and delinquency. Electronic monitoring is but one example of how technology has been implemented in our justice systems.

Shifts in public opinion undoubtedly influence future events. Societal concern about crime and justice beginning in the 1980s largely contributed to more punitive responses to crime and delinquency. Public concern for juvenile violence led to policy shifts directed away from the historical rehabilitative ideals of juvenile justice toward a more punitive approach. Juvenile boot camps as a form of punishment and rehabilitation became increasingly popular with politicians and the public alike beginning in the 1980s. Boot camp programs seemed to be ideal options because they offered a noticeably obvious form of punishment (e.g., the drill instruction) tempered with rehabilitation (e.g., instilling discipline). They provided an apt transition from a time when we focused on juvenile rehabilitation to a period when we focused on punishment. Similarly, the series of school shootings beginning in 1997 led to enhanced social control directed toward elementary and high school students, as the public and politicians voiced their concern for seemingly unsafe schools,[8] and recent responses to the threat of terrorist attacks have resulted in greater concern for public safety and increased social control.

Several prominent researchers offered their views of what lies ahead for tomorrow's youth. Stephens, a futurist, noted a series of issues currently affecting attempts to properly guide at-risk youth, including the increasing gap between the wealthy and the poor, a growing number of single-parent households, reduced accountability for children as more families require both parents to work, an expanding gun culture, and increased negative attitudes about today's youth evidenced by the increased number of children being processed in adult courts. These obstacles provide direction for potential efforts to redirect wayward youth.[9]

Toward the end of the twentieth century, Ohlin identified several challenges associated with the future of juvenile justice policy and research. Particularly, he cited needed efforts to confront the alienation of youth; build community resources; allocate greater and more effective use of federal, state, and local government resources; provide enhanced employment and education opportunities for youth; temper society's seemingly distorted fear of juvenile crime; and create cooperation among research centers that would provide more effective guidance with regard to policy-making efforts.[10] It could be argued that an increasing concern for getting tougher on delinquents has resulted in few accomplishments with regard to Ohlin's noted areas of concern. Perhaps the future will bring about greater consideration of the suggestions made by Stephens and Ohlin. Perhaps it won't. I prefer to remain optimistic.

THE FUTURE OF DELINQUENCY TREATMENT AND PREVENTION

So, what lies ahead for delinquency prevention and treatment? Among the many challenges in looking to the future is timing. Many forecasts identify impending changes with regard to various social phenomena, although the timing of those changes are, in many cases, difficult to determine. In light of such factors as economics, changes and proposed changes in the juvenile and adult justice systems, demographics, crime trends, technology, and public opinion, the following discussion is organized into short-, mid-, and long-term projections of the future of delinquency treatment and prevention. Because of the notable impacts associated with the possible elimination of juvenile courts, an examination of the future of the juvenile court system sets the stage for this discussion. Although refraining from specifics, this account of what we can expect in the future guides us with regard to policy making, technology, and the expected roles of the general public in delinquency treatment and prevention.

The Future of Juvenile Courts

The future of delinquency prevention and treatment is undoubtedly influenced by numerous factors, not the least of which is the future of the juvenile court system. In light of the recent shift away from the rehabilitative ideals on which the courts were founded and toward a more punitive approach, it is suggested by some that a juvenile court system distinct from the (adult) criminal court system is unnecessary. Thus, there would be one justice system that processes all cases involving adults and juveniles.

Abolitionists argue that elimination of juvenile courts would result in resource savings, reduced financial costs of justice, and greater continuity of services.[11] Eliminating juvenile courts, it is argued, would provide juveniles greater due process rights and address concerns that interpretations of terms such as "delinquency" and "adolescence" are outdated.[12] Feld believes that the juvenile court system is fundamentally flawed in that it attempts to incorporate social services in a judicial setting, adding that social welfare should not be an overriding concern of the legal system. In turn, he argues, juvenile courts should be eliminated and youthfulness should be a mitigating factor as juveniles are processed in what is currently the adult court system.[13]

Arguments against the abolition of juvenile courts include historical beliefs that children are less responsible than adults for their behavior, and they maintain a greater likelihood of rehabilitation than adults.[14] Preservationists believe failures in the juvenile courts are attributed to problems associated with implementation, not the structure of the courts. Furthermore, they argue that the court works for most juveniles who enter, and criminal courts would not be more effective.[15]

Eliminating the juvenile court system would likely encourage a more punitive response to delinquency and a more limited concern for prevention and treatment. The limited focus of concern on prevention and treatment, and the emphasis on incapacitation, deterrence, and retribution, currently recognized in the adult system would likely become the general practice with regard to juveniles who enter the courts. This projection is based on the increasing percentage and number of juvenile waivers to adult court. In itself, eliminating the juvenile court system is a statement that juveniles should be processed in a manner similar to adults. Suggesting that juvenile courts will merge with adult courts is, however, a bit premature. To undo the accomplishments of more than 100 years of development in the juvenile courts seems too radical a change in the short term, particularly in light of the bureaucratic staying power of existing (and large) government institutions.

Jackson and Knepper offer alternatives for the abolition of juvenile courts, including an enhanced version of the current family courts; family bankruptcy courts to facilitate government intervention when families recognize imminent problems with their children; and increased multicourt youth justice that replaces the traditional juvenile court system with specialized court systems (e.g., teen courts, community courts, gun courts, drug courts, etc.).[16] Incorporation of these alternatives seem more likely to occur than does the abolition of a distinct juvenile court system, especially when one considers the investments made in the juvenile courts and the long-standing belief that juvenile offenders are distinct from adult offenders.

To be sure, the future of delinquency prevention and treatment will be influenced by changes in the structure and processes of the existing juvenile court system. Of course, other factors will also play a role in shaping where and how we proceed in the future. Benekos and Merlo state, "In the early decades of the twenty-first century, the juvenile justice system will devote increasing attention to at least five issues: gangs, disproportionate minority representation, comparative juvenile justice, the death penalty, and juveniles incarcerated in adult institutions."[17] They add that "competing ideologies and politicized public policies"[18] will guide the future of juvenile justice, because no particular approach will displace the others. Specifically, they argue that we can expect a continued combination of prevention, education, and treatment; balanced and restorative justice; and punishment, retribution, and adultification. The following chronologically based sets of expectations provide more general outlooks of what we can expect with regard to delinquency prevention and treatment.

Short-Term Expectations

What can we expect in the next 5 to 10 years of delinquency prevention and treatment? Recent trends indicate enhanced punitiveness directed toward delinquents with a corresponding decrease in rehabilitation and prevention. The recent increase in the rate of violent offenses, which occurred after a relatively consistent decrease in crime beginning in the mid-1990s, has been attributed to increased juvenile delinquency.[19] It has been noted that (1) a declining economy; (2) an increasing number of offenders returning from prison and seeking the services of juveniles who are less deterred by the justice system; and (3) society's continued concern for terrorism (which requires substantial resources, thus leaving limited funding for delinquency treatment and prevention) have contributed to increased juvenile involvement in violent crime.[20]

The risk factors associated with a declining economy, limited treatment and prevention funding, and increased numbers of "uncorrected" former inmates are apparent. Society's existing efforts to crack down on crime, particularly juvenile violence, are evident in the increasing frequency with which juveniles are transferred to the adult court. Thus, in the short term, one could expect greater efforts to punish unruly youth. Crime and delinquency are cyclical, meaning that the decreases we have recently experienced will likely be countered by increases. If increased punition was the *modus operandi* during periods characterized by decreasing crime rates, it is expected that efforts to get even tougher on crime and delinquency will be imminent during periods of increasing crime.

Getting tough on crime and delinquency brings a corresponding lack of funding for prevention and treatment. Similar to major corporations, municipalities must work within the confines of financial budgets, and more generally, with limited resources. Getting tough is expensive, but it conjures perceptions among the public that something is being done. Treatment and prevention are uncertainties, meaning that we cannot be certain that the funding directed toward the prevention of youth violence and attempts to "correct" unruly youths is being put to good use. Getting tough also generates uncertainties. In light of decreasing budgets, largely in response to an overriding concern for homeland security, government officials are tasked with determining where resources will be allocated. Treatment and rehabilitation are often seen as being soft on crime. In a time of perceived crises, it is not the American way to be soft. Thus, it is anticipated that increased funding will be directed toward punishing juveniles at the expense of treatment and prevention. We should not expect, however, the funding discrepancy to be as drastic as it is at the adult level.

We will continue to recognize juveniles as "correctable" and impressionable in the sense that we can prevent their involvement in crime and "fix" those who have ventured down the wrong paths. In discussing the future of juvenile justice, Jackson and Knepper note, "[d]espite the overall emphasis on accountability, prevention will continue to be a theme"[21] in years to come. They also identify community involvement as a "pervasive theme" in future juvenile court practices. Their statement is echoed by Benekos and Merlo who state, "[e]ven though 'get-tough' political rhetoric and adultification legislation has characterized juvenile justice in the last 15 years, the juvenile justice system will continue with its mission to help youthful offenders and reduce delinquency."[22]

Mid-Term Expectations

Following a period of continued and likely enhanced crackdown on juveniles, we can expect enhanced community involvement with the treatment and prevention of youth crime, assisted by technological developments. This projection is offered in light of the somewhat apparent pattern of practices in the adult criminal and juvenile justice systems. Specifically, it seems that practices in the juvenile justice system reflect what happens in the adult system; however, there is a delay in developments in the juvenile system. In other words, juvenile justice practices seemingly shadow those in the adult system, although there is a time lag. For instance, consider the delay between the establishment of a juvenile court system. Consider the delay in providing due process for troubled youth. Furthermore, consider the delay in getting tough on juvenile offenders. We have been getting tough on adult offenders for more than two decades, but the punitive approach toward juveniles has occurred more recently. This apparent congruence between the two systems provides support for the aforementioned projected short-term goal of getting tougher on juveniles and for the notion that increased community support to address delinquency treatment and prevention are anticipated after a period of increased punitiveness.

Similar to the manner in which many police departments have adopted a community-oriented philosophy that relies heavily on police interaction with the community, particularly with regard to crime prevention, it is expected that communities will become increasingly active in confronting delinquency and its prevention. Many communities are currently active in issues related to delinquency; however, the anticipated short-term shift toward increasingly getting tough on delinquents will leave limited resources for prevention and treatment programs. Thus, the community, after some time, will recognize the need for its input and efforts.

Society is slowly coming to grips with the fact that our justice systems are primarily reactive and provide limited crime prevention. That is, we generally believe that responding to crime is the primary means to stop crime. As more individuals recognize the limitations of our justice system to respond to criminal behavior (many crimes go unreported, many reported crimes go unsolved, recidivism rates are discouraging), it is anticipated that notable grassroots efforts will be made in support of community delinquency prevention and rehabilitation. Dawson aptly notes that "[a]n integral part of any juvenile justice system is a network of private, charitable, or religious institutions, facilities, and programs."[23] Hahn echoes this statement in suggesting that "[c]ommunities can do a great deal to provide front-line prevention of juvenile violence and delinquency."[24]

Stephens emphasizes the need for greater community involvement to prevent and respond to delinquency. Encouraging mentoring for all children, establishing community-school partnerships to offer before- and after-school tutoring, setting up peer counseling hotlines, and developing community-oriented proactive policing programs that stress prevention are among the elements of Stephens's comprehensive plan to address youth at risk. His refreshing suggestions demonstrate the feasibility and importance of using resources that are available outside of formal, justice-based institutions.[25]

Aside from the powerful effects of the various means of informal social control, the community has much to offer with regard to delinquency prevention and treatment. Among the options available to respond to delinquency include diversion from the system, probation, intensive supervision, restorative justice efforts, restitution, community service, work programs, family group conferencing, teen court, and electronic monitoring. This is not a comprehensive list of available options to confront delinquency, and innovative approaches are certainly in the works and will emerge in the future. Of particular importance, this list of options includes only one example of technology-based assistance for at-risk or troubled youth (i.e., electronic monitoring). The future undoubtedly will bring about a series of technology-based alternatives.

This projection involving greater community involvement may seem outlandish given recent claims that people today are more socially isolated than in years past.[26] However, no magic bullet is being overlooked in making this projection. In other words, historically, we have relied on our justice systems and the public to confront crime and delinquency. The limited accomplishments of our justice systems demonstrate that support from the public is vital. Developments in the area of community policing, community justice, and restorative justice provide optimism for claims of greater community involvement in the future of delinquency prevention and treatment.

One of the more positive contributions of community policing efforts is the involvement of the police in current and anticipated crime and delinquency prevention efforts. Efforts to prevent delinquency are apparent in various community policing programs, for example, in the U.S. Department of Justice's Youth-Focused Community Policing initiative, which focuses on establishing and strengthening police-community relationships to address delinquency prevention, intervention, and enforcement. In his insightful book, *Police for the Future*, Bayley highlights the need for greater police crime prevention and offers a blueprint for police practices to become more proactive,[27] while Hahn more generally addresses the need for a more proactive response to crime and delinquency in the entire justice system.[28] In light of the inherent limitations of our justice systems, we can expect greater community policing efforts to proactively confront delinquency.

We can also expect greater community involvement in the treatment of troubled youth. For instance, Clear and Cadora discuss community justice as an alternative approach to addressing crime and delinquency. Following this approach, areas with a high concentration of crime are targeted for attempts to strengthen informal systems of social control. They cite the emphasis on informal social control, proactive approaches to crime and delinquency, problem-solving, and partnership development with residents, businesses, and various social services as key components of community justice.[29] According to Bilchik, restorative justice, with its "focus on crime as harm, and justice as repairing the harm, offers a vision that elevates the role of crime victim, yet views victim, offender, and community as equal customers of juvenile justice services and as important, active coparticipants in responding to juvenile crime."[30] Both community justice and restorative justice require substantial input and accountability from the general public. Efforts to involve the community in delinquency prevention and treatment do exist today. It is projected, however, that we can expect greater community involvement in delinquency prevention and treatment.

Long-Term Expectations

As mentioned, the confidence levels in forecasts of the future diminish as one projects further into the future. Nevertheless, a conservative forecast of the future suggests that in 25 to 50 years technology will play an increasingly significant role in delinquency treatment and prevention. Again, it is difficult to forecast long-term changes with great levels of confidence; however, recent technological developments point toward automated prevention efforts and therapeutic responses. One could dismiss as science fiction the opening scenario of this chapter, which involves, in part, a technological application of behavior modification with a dose of technology-based reality therapy. But today's science fiction could be tomorrow's reality. One merely needs to compare today's world with society as it existed 25 years ago to appreciate the forcefulness of technological advances. We would be foolish to believe that we have "maxed out" with regard to technological development. Recall the earliest computers, or the early, text-based version of the Internet. Now, consider the evolution of both the computer and the Internet. We should remain optimistic that similar, major developments will occur as technology continues to evolve and we direct our efforts to such issues as delinquency prevention and treatment.

The long-term future may include the use of a variety of behavior-regulating implants as an accepted practice in delinquency prevention and treatment. Stephens notes that such controversial implants could be applied as a form of birth control, to control behavior, to monitor one's health, to ensure proper functioning of one's brain, and even to assist individuals with learning deficiencies.[31] Although the development of implants continues, society must come to terms with the ethical considerations inherently associated with their use.

Technology offers optimism for delinquency prevention and treatment. In light of the entrepreneurship and creativity apparent in society's recent technological transformation, it is projected that the energies and resources that thus far have been put into developing marketable, recreational goods and services will eventually be recognized for their potential application to delinquency prevention and treatment. In other words, society will increasingly seek, and develop, technology-based programs, simulators, virtual realities, assessment centers, correctional facilities, and the like to reduce the burden on human efforts to prevent and confront delinquency and to provide more effective responses to wayward youth.

Researchers continually stress the need to identify particular programs to meet needs of particular youths. It is possible that, in the future, full-body scans and measured physiological and mental responses could facilitate the identification of appropriate technology-based prevention programs or rehabilitative efforts. Or, perhaps, technological advances could be used to address some of the social issues that contribute to delinquency, such as poverty or broken homes. The success of future efforts to prevent or treat delinquency depends largely on our level of optimism. Successful visionaries look at how they can make things happen, not why they can't. We must remain vigilant to incorporate technological advances into our efforts to address delinquency. And it is anticipated that we will.

CONCLUSION

I find forecasting the future to be an extremely worthwhile and enjoyable practice, and I make all efforts to share forecasting techniques with my students. The utility of forecasting the future is evidenced in this discussion of anticipated changes with regard to delinquency prevention and treatment. The enjoyment stems from the inherent lack of pressure in being correct. Although not to dismiss the practice of forecasting the future as a pseudo-science (as it certainly is not), one merely needs to watch the local weather forecast on the evening news to understand the difficulties of understanding and forecasting what will happen from one day to the next. Weather forecasters spend many hours looking at weather models within local regions to give us the "five-day forecast." Consider how many times you have wondered why meteorologists can't get it right. Well, it's simple. It is difficult to understand what is going to occur in the future, even despite the availability of advanced scientific tools. The temporal and spatial variables influencing forecasts of the future, as well as noted drivers of the future, become increasingly prominent when we discuss such macrolevel issues as crime, national security, and delinquency treatment and prevention.

Another utility of futurist research involves the opportunity for optimism. In their look toward the future of juvenile justice, Benekos and Merlo offer optimism in light of decreasing crime rates, which results in, among other things, issues other than crime attracting and receiving public and political attention. This optimism is generated by increasing evidence of effective intervention strategies and prevention programs, public support for delinquency prevention and treatment programs, and the development of alternative forms of juvenile justice.[32]

We can look at increasing crime trends (should they occur) and forecast gloom and doom for the coming years. Such information, however, can be used more productively by spurring us toward thoughtful creativity and consideration of alternative approaches to crime and delinquency prevention and treatment. Forecasters create scenarios of what the future may look like, which should stimulate strategically designed plans that could enable our world to resemble a fictitious society.[33] In other words, we could diagram the ideal society in, say, 20 years from now and work backward. How do we get there from here? One merely needs to observe the evolution of computers and the Internet to understand the importance of having a vision and remaining optimistic.

Stojkovic and Klofas note that futurists must confront three substantial issues in looking to the future. First, they must give due consideration to the past and the present. Second, they must scientifically project from the past toward the future. Third, futurists must question their "own role in creating (the) future rather than passively accepting it."[34] The impetus is not only on futurists to shape the future, but also on all of us to play a role. Among other things, remaining optimistic and recognizing that the future is not predetermined should encourage us to assume a more proactive role in efforts directed toward the future of delinquency prevention and treatment.

NOTES

1. Cole, 1995.
2. Jackson & Knepper, 2003, pp. 316–324.
3. Jackson & Knepper, 2003, p. 337.
4. Bynum & Thompson, 2005, p. 440.

5. Bynum & Thompson, 2005.
6. Rosenheim, Zimring, Tanenhaus, & Dohrn, 2002; Wolcott, 2001.
7. Bartollas, 2003, pp. 16–20.
8. E.g., Burns & Crawford, 1999.
9. Stephens, 1997.
10. Ohlin, 1998.
11. Dawson, 1990.
12. E.g., Jackson & Knepper, 2003.
13. Feld, 1997.
14. Dawson, 1990.
15. Jackson & Knepper, 2003.
16. Jackson & Knepper, 2003.
17. Benekos & Merlo, 2005, p. 31.
18. Benekos & Merlo, 2005, p. 36.
19. E.g., Johnson, 2006.
20. Johnson, 2006.
21. Jackson & Knepper, 2003, p. 387.
22. Benekos & Merlo, 2005, p. 37.
23. Dawson, 1990, p. 148.
24. Hahn, 1998, p. 59.
25. Stephens, 1997.
26. McPherson, Smith-Lovin, & Brashears, 2006; Putnam, 2000.
27. Bayley, 1994.
28. Hahn, 1998.
29. Clear & Cadora, 2003.
30. Bilchik, 1997, p. ii.
31. Stephens, 1997.
32. Benekos & Merlo, 2005, pp. 21–22.
33. Burns, 1998; Clear, 1995; Cole, 1995.
34. Stojkovic & Klofas, 1995, pp. 282–284.

REFERENCES

Bartollas, C. (2003). *Juvenile delinquency* (6th ed.). Boston: Allyn and Bacon.
Bayley, D. H. (1994). *Police for the future.* New York: Oxford University Press.
Benekos, P. J., & Merlo, A. V. (2005). Reaffirming juvenile justice: Strategies for the future. In R. Muraskin & A. R. Roberts (Eds.), *Visions for change: Crime and justice in the twenty-first century* (4th ed., pp. 17–42). Upper Saddle River, NJ: Prentice Hall.
Bilchik, S. (1997, August). Foreword. *Balanced and restorative justice for juveniles: A framework for juvenile justice in the 21st century.* Washington, D.C.: Office of Juvenile Justice and Delinquency Prevention.
Burns, R. (1998, November/December). Forecasting Bollinger: Methods for projecting the future of jails. *American Jails,* 55–56.
Burns, R., & Crawford, C. (1999). School shootings, the media, and public fear: Ingredients for a moral panic. *Crime, Law and Social Change, 32*(2), 147–168.
Bynum, J. E., & Thompson, W. E. (2005). Juvenile delinquency: A sociological approach (6th Ed.). Boston: Allyn and Bacon.
Clear, T. R. (1995). Ophelia the CCW: May 11, 2010. In J. Klofas & S. Stojkovic (Eds.), *Crime and justice in the year 2010* (pp. 205–223). Belmont, CA: Wadsworth.

Clear, T. R., & Cadora, E. (2003). *Community justice*. Belmont, CA: Wadsworth.

Cole, G. F. (1995). Criminal justice in the twenty-first century. In J. Klofas & S. Stojkovic (Eds.), *Crime and justice in the year 2010* (pp. 4–17). Belmont, CA: Wadsworth.

Dawson, R. A. (1990). The future of juvenile justice: Is it time to abolish the system? *Journal of Criminal Law & Criminology, 81*(1), 136–155.

Feld, B. (1997). Abolish the juvenile court: Youthfulness, criminal responsibility, and sentencing policy. *Journal of Criminal Law and Criminology, 88*(1), 68–136.

Hahn, P. H. (1998). *Emerging criminal justice*. Thousand Oaks, CA: Sage Publications.

Jackson, M. S., & Knepper, P. (2003). *Delinquency and justice*. Boston, MA: Allyn and Bacon.

Johnson, K. (2006, July 13). Police tie jump in crime to juveniles. *USA Today*, p. 1A.

McPherson, M., Smith-Lovin, L., & Brashears, M. E. (2006). Social isolation in America: Changes in core discussion networks over two decades. *American Sociological Review, 71*, 353–371.

Ohlin, L. E. (1998). The future of juvenile justice policy and research. *Crime & Delinquency, 44*(1), 143–153.

Putnam, R. D. (2000). *Bowling alone*. New York: Simon & Schuster.

Rosenheim, M. K., Zimring, F. E., Tanenhaus, D. S., & Dohrn, B. (Eds.). (2002). *A century of juvenile justice*. Chicago: University of Chicago Press.

Stephens, G. (1997). Youth at risk: Saving the world's most precious resource. *The Futurist, 31*, 31–37.

Stojkovic, S., & Klofas, J. M. (1995). Preparing for the year 2010. In J. Klofas & S. Stojkovic (Eds.), *Crime and justice in the year 2010* (pp. 281–296). Belmont, CA: Wadsworth.

Wolcott, D. (2001). "The cop will get you": The police and discretionary juvenile justice, 1890–1940. *Journal of Social History, 35*(2), 349–371.

CHAPTER 11

Projecting Juvenile Populations: A Forecasting Model

Pablo E. Martinez

Although there is great public consensus about the need to punish offenders, prevent crime and protect citizens, there is great variation in thoughts about just which offenders should be locked up and for how long. A limited number of beds are available at any given time and officials are under pressure to save detention space for the most dangerous offenders and those who are most likely to recidivate. Because those most likely to commit offenses at a greater rate are not always those who are violent, we often engage in difficult choices about sentencing and the release of offenders into the community.

Officials often rely on forecasters to help them in the decision process. As facilities become overcrowded, there are only three basic solutions. Political as well as economic consequences must be weighed to decide whether (1) to build more detention space, (2) to release more offenders earlier on parole, or (3) to take fewer new youth into the confinement system, reserving beds for only those who are highest risk. Before building or engaging in any long-term strategy, it is important to determine what the population might look like down the road and what the implications or consequences of any path chosen right now might be.

For example, researchers in California used forecasting to determine the impact that the new three strikes law, and its lengthy sentences, would have on the prison population. Information about the number of two-strike offenders currently in the system as well as the number of one-strike offenders, all of whom could potentially become three-strike cases, had to be analyzed to determine not only the rate at which existing offenders might become eligible for three strikes, but also the rate at which new offenders would enter the system and gain strikes.

The business of forecasting is a difficult task and perhaps more so in the criminal justice field. Projection numbers are used for several purposes. The first is to inform the public about the upcoming problems of the system. Rather than being anecdotal, media accounts of individual cases, these projections must be developed from accurate interpretations of valid and reliable indicators. Otherwise, people can become unnecessarily alarmed or fearful, as when political columnist DiIulio predicted inaccurately that a wave or juvenile superpredators would be seen in the system.

The second purpose of forecasting is to project costs and appropriations for operations and capital investment (building new facilities). Finally, forecasting is used to analyze the impact of proposed legislative changes.

Depending on the purpose, more sophisticated tools may be required to arrive at projections. When projections are needed to make a statement to the public, interest groups, or the press regarding the future number of youthful offenders under the control of the justice system, a statistical line-fitting technique may be sufficient. When projections are needed for budgets and appropriations, more information is necessary. Typically, this will require accurate information regarding the number of offenders coming into the system, and the number of offenders leaving the system, as well as the time they remain under the jurisdiction of the system.

If the projected numbers are used in a legislative impact analysis, the model needs to be able to break down the populations more clearly, for example, into different groups by offense type, length of sentence, or criminal record.

FACTORS AFFECTING FUTURE JUVENILE OFFENDER POPULATION

The future size of the juvenile offender population is affected by at least three major factors:

- Variables that affect crime, such as the state's population in specific age groups
- Socioeconomic indicators such as employment and income
- Changes in policy (sentencing), for example, more tough or lenient punishments

The size of the population can be obtained by using projections of the population for the state, which are produced by the Bureau of Census or a local affiliate such as a population research center at the state level. Relatively valid and reliable socioeconomic indicators (such as unemployment rates) are much harder to obtain. Long-term forecasting of unemployment is not reliable. Policy changes are difficult to quantify. Most frequently, the researcher assumes a status quo scenario, which means that policy will remain constant, something that never happens. Despite these difficulties in obtaining the elements necessary to forecast accurately, the more detail the model provides, the more useful the projection will be. If elements are quantified, they can be monitored, and such information is useful to explain why projections might turn out to be either too high or too low. Unfortunately, this is information that can be provided only after the fact.

Forecasting in the criminal justice field is not an exact science, but rather a combination of science and art. As a science, the forecaster uses statistical techniques to analyze historical trends and identify predictors. As an art, the forecaster uses his or her best professional judgment to make adjustments to the results of statistical analysis. In some instances, forecasters must use their best judgment and forecasting knowledge to provide all the necessary elements in the model. For instance, a forecaster must make an assumption about sentencing practices in the use of average sentences for projection models. Actual sentencing practices may turn out to be higher or lower than the forecasters' best estimate.

Forecasting Teams and the Role of Assumptions

Projections are the result of statistical analysis to determine trends and relationships. In this process, decisions must be made about what direction to take when the data indicators are not clear. These decisions are known as "assumptions of the model," and they represent basic assumptions that the model uses to project numbers. Although the forecaster can make such decisions, the best approach is to create an assumptions team to ensure that many different views and ideas are incorporated. This team model is being used in many locations. In Colorado, for instance, it is known as the Juvenile Corrections Population Forecasting Advisory Committee, established by Executive Order in 1998.[1] This type of team is composed of individuals who have an interest in the projection, such as the directors or representatives of agencies that are affected by the projection, members of the Legislative Budget Board, legislative aides to the members of the Criminal Justice committees in the House and in the Senate, and staff from the governor's office. In Oregon, the governor appoints the members, but in other states they may be part of the forecasting working group.

The forecasting working group determines those issues that are not clear-cut, for example, should the average length of stay (ALS) that is used to project the population under supervision be the same as the most recent year, or should it be the average for the last couple of years? Additionally, agency officials are encouraged to indicate whether there are any recently implemented policy changes that would change how long offenders remain confined or that would affect the failure rate of probationers. These procedures not only insulate the forecaster, but also give interested parties a sense of ownership over the results. This may help people obtain needed information for future projections. Additionally, people are more likely to use forecasts when they participated in the process. The most effective system is one in which the same set of numbers are used by all policy makers and interested parties. Whatever level of sophistication, the most credible systems are those for which one set of numbers is used for all levels of forecasting.

In this chapter, a methodology is presented that can produce projections (or forecasts) of juvenile correctional client populations. This model can be used to request budget allocations, to answer questions, and to explain policy implications. A model based on this methodology was developed by the author of this chapter for Texas and has been used by the Criminal Justice Policy Council for more than a decade to forecast juvenile correctional population for the state.[2] Mears evaluated the model and published a report as part of the Assessment of Space Needs Project and concluded that—

> The Texas forecasting process is grounded in (the) notion of credibility and the importance of the interactive processes. Forecasts are empirically based, but they also are informed by a multidimensional process for generating continuously updated projections of future correctional populations.[3]

The chapter concludes with a discussion of how to produce the best policy scenario while protecting the forecaster and creating an environment of credibility for the projection. It is a total system model. In other words, the model considers the group of the population at risk and uses probabilities to determine the flow of juveniles through the different decision points of the criminal justice system.

A Disaggregated, Macrosimulation Model

The model presented in this chapter simulates the way juvenile offenders are processed by the system. It uses probabilities to determine how many offenders advance to the next stage of the system and, once confined in a correctional facility, uses survival rates to calculate remaining populations.

To produce a model that is useful for policy analysis, detailed information is needed. A flow chart of the total system is useful to visualize data needs. Figure 11.1 illustrates a flow chart of the juvenile justice system. The major purpose of the flow chart is to visualize how the system works and to identify the type of data that are needed to produce a projection.

REFERRALS AND PROBATION SUPERVISION

Projecting Juvenile Referrals

Inputs into the system come from two sources: (1) new referrals to the Juvenile Probation system (newly convicted offenders); and (2) violators of court orders (probation or parole). These two numbers need to be projected.

Projecting New Referrals

Who is referred to the juvenile probation system? To answer this question an examination of Figure 11.2 is extremely useful. Although Texas law

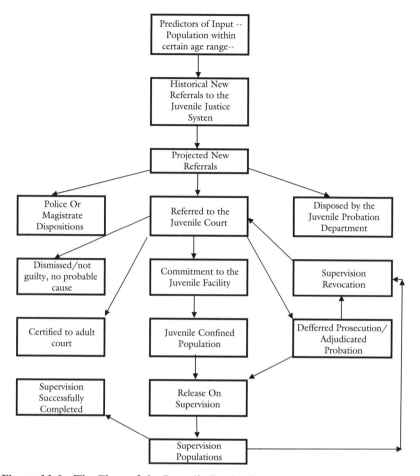

Figure 11.1. The Flow of the Juvenile Justice System

is used as an example, experts have pointed out that legislation regulating juvenile procedures in this country are fairly consistent.[4] Jurisdictional differences across the country regarding who is considered a juvenile would affect
these numbers. In Texas, a juvenile is considered anyone less than 17 years of
age. In other words, if someone is 16 years, 11 months, and 29 days old and
commits a criminal offense, he or she is under the jurisdiction of the juvenile
system unless certified as an adult. If the criminal offense were committed on
or after the offender's 17th birthday, then he or she is under the jurisdiction
of the adult system and prosecuted in the adult court. Normally, children
referred to the juvenile system are not younger than 10 and, in most states,
no older than 16 years of age. Figure 11.2 shows the arrest rates per
100,000 people by age for the years 1995 and 2004 for Texas.[5]
    Figure 11.2 also illustrates what is known in the criminal justice field as
the crime curve in the disproportional contributions to crime by the various age groups.[6] The figure shows that, when comparing 1995 to 2004,

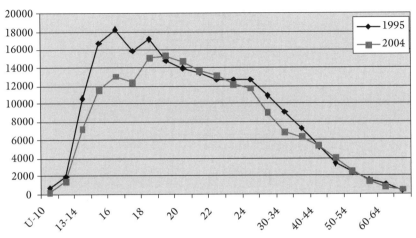

Figure 11.2. Texas Arrest Rates

there has been a decrease in the arrest rate of individuals between the ages of 13 and 16. It is this decline in the arrest rate that creates difficulty in producing projections. It is difficult to project when there is no "stability" in the system (that is, stability in the arrest rate for the ages in question). As a matter of fact, efforts constantly are made to curb crime, and if successful, rates should reflect the success of programs. But crime is not the only reason why offenders end up in the juvenile justice system. Children end up in the system for status offenses when their parents can not properly supervise them; these children are known as "children in need of supervision" (or CINS). Because status offenders are not formally arrested, projections of the juvenile system must use "new juvenile referrals," instead of arrests, to determine the number of referrals into the system. Figure 11.3 presents the number of Texas juvenile referrals by type from 1997 to 2003 (the latest year for which numbers are available).[7]

The data show that both types of referrals (new arrests and status offender referrals) have been declining. Conversely, violations of probation (court orders) have increased. As mentioned earlier, the number of new entries into the juvenile justice system is the first to be projected. This number includes delinquent and CINS referrals.

A statistical analysis can be used to determine the relationship between population and referrals. This methodology consists of finding the best-fitting straight line for a set of data. The best-fitting line is the one that comes closest, on average, to all of the data points. Although this can be done manually, a statistical tool known as linear regression is available in many statistical packages, including Excel, and it produces the best-fitting line. That statistical tool was used to analyze the Texas population between the ages of 10 and 16, including all referrals, delinquents only, and delinquents plus CINS (but not probation violators).

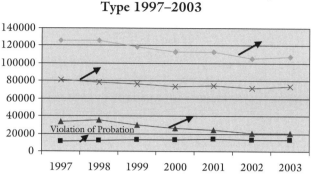

Texas
Number of Juvenile Probation Referrals by
Type 1997–2003

Figure 11.3. Texas Juvenile Referrals

The summaries of the three models are presented in Table 11.1. The data show that if total referrals were to be used, an adjusted R-square value of 0.9061 or 90.61 percent of the variances in the total referrals can be attributed to changes in the population of 10 to 16 year olds. When only referrals for delinquent acts are entered, the value drops significantly, and we can account for only 73.73 percent of the variance in referrals using the same age cohort. Conversely, when delinquent behavior and CINS were added together, about 90.62 percent of the changes in the referrals can be explained by the changes in the age cohort between 10 and 16. The results also show that the relationship between the population cohort and delinquent/CINS referrals is negative. During the most recent past, although the population of that age cohort has increased, referrals have declined. Although this may not seem to make sense, it is likely to occur during periods following major legislative changes.

The question is whether this equation should be used to predict the future. The answer might be that the forecaster should use it as long as he or she carefully monitors the population and adjusts the forecast accordingly. For instance, note from Figure 11.3 that in 2003 the number of

Table 11.1.
Model Summaries

Model summaries				
Dependent Variable	R	R Square	Adjusted R Square	Std. Error of the Estimate
All Referrals (a)	0.9600	0.9217	0.9061	2491.447
Delinquent Only (b)	0.8837	0.7810	0.7373	1606.172
Delinquent and CINS (c)	0.9601	0.9219	0.9062	2758.565
Independent variable: population ages 10 to 16				

Table 11.2.
Coefficients for Regression Equation

Model		Coefficients[a]				
		Unstandardized Coefficients		Standardized Coefficients		
		B	Std. Error	Beta	t	Sig.
1	(Constant)	235260.8	17239.717		13.646	.000
	Pop 10 to 16	−.052	.007	−.960	−7.683	.001

[a] Dependent Variable: Delinquent and CINS

referrals increased. If, after carefully monitoring over the next six months, it appears referrals are going to increase, the forecaster can take out the years before the decline (negative relationship) and rerun the regression. Frequently what happens is that legislative changes affect the input (referrals) for a short period of time, but once the full impact of the law has taken place, the trend returns to the direction it had been going before the legislative change. In other words, the impact of changes in law frequently has a delayed impact on what may happen anyway.

Another issue to consider is the fact that this model is based on seven data points (seven years). This is a good way to start if no other data are available. The *projection*, however, should not be longer than the number of years or months for which historical data are available. In the case of this example, a projection of up to seven years is acceptable.

To project future new referrals, we use the state's projected population for individuals between 10 and 16 years old. The data are obtained from the population research center, and the values of slope (−0.052) and the constant (235260.8) are derived from the regression equation, which are found in the Statistical Package for the Social Sciences (SPSS)[8] output for this type of analysis (Table 11.2). The projected numbers of referrals that result by using this methodology are presented in Table 11.3. The data show the projected population of 10 to 16 year olds and the projective juvenile referrals (delinquent and CINS combined).

Table 11.3.
Projected Number of Referrals

Projected Texa Juvenile Referrals (Delinquent and CINS) 2004 to 2006

Year	Projected Population 10–16	Projected Juvenile Referrals
2004	2795613	90925
2005	2845041	88373
2006	2887637	86173

Projecting Court Order Violations

The premise used to forecast revocations is based on empirical findings that not all offenders who are placed on juvenile probation successfully complete the probationary period. Many of these offenders do not comply with the conditions of supervision or commit a new offense. As a consequence, they reappear in front of a judge and end up as referrals. This section deals only with offenders who have to appear in court as a consequence of not abiding by the rules of probation, including committing a new criminal offense.

The model uses survival techniques to determine how many court order violations (COVs) return to court. The projection can be made by year or by month, depending on the level of aggregate data available. It is advisable to use monthly data if possible. If the data are reported yearly, the resulting projection can be disaggregated by month. The data needed include (1) number of new juvenile referrals (delinquent and CINS), and (2) the number of offenders referred for COV by month or by year. Using yearly data, Table 11.4 presents the projection for COVs. Microsoft® Excel or a comparable electronic sheet is needed to determine COVs.

To better understand the contents of Table 11.4, a good understanding of the columns and rows headings is necessary:

- Column A, Row 7: Year for which the actual number of delinquent and CINS referrals are available.
- Column B, Row 7: Actual number of delinquent and CINS referrals. Notice that numbers in bold type for years 2004 to 2006 are projections derived in the previous section of this report.
- Row 1, Columns A and B: The heading YEAR indicates labels for which year the values in the rows below apply.
- Row 2, Columns A and B: Actual COV. In this row, the actual number of COVs are entered for the respective year (Columns C to I), the most recent year for which there are actual data (in this case 2003).
- Row 3, Columns A to E: The heading is Projected COV. Columns F to M contain the projected number of COV for each year of the projection. The values in each of these cells are the summation of the values found under each column from Rows 9 to 18. Bolded numbers indicated that they are projections (Columns J to M).
- Row 4, Columns A to E: The heading is Difference–Actual vs. Projected. This row calculates the deviation of the projections from the actual numbers. A negative sign indicates the model is overprojecting.
- Row 5, Column B: The Heading is Adjusted Failure Rate. This row gives the actual failure rate for a particular year after an adjustment is made. Column A gives the amount of adjustment that is applied to the three years of the follow-up period.
- Row 5, Columns C to E: These columns give the actual failure rate for each of the three years. Column F gives the total for the three years (in this case, it is 0.1383 or 13.83 percent). This failure rate changes from

Table 11.4.
Projection for COVs

Projection of Juvenile Referrals for Court Order Violations (C.O.V.)

	A	B	C	D	E	F	G	H	I	J	K	L	M
1		Year	1997	1998	1999	2000	2001	2002	2003	2004	2005	2006	2007
2		Actual C.O.V.	10821	11964	12635	13111	13664	13397	13273				
3		Projected C.O.V.				15238	14463	13980	13269	13112	12737	12482	12138
4		Difference—Actual vs. Projected				−2127	−799	−583	4				
5		0.728 Adjusted Failure Rate	0.0728	0.0364	0.0291	0.1383							
6		Initial Failure Rate	0.1	0.05	0.04	0.19							
7	Year	Delinquent & CINS Referrals											
8	1997	115311		8395	4197	3358							
9	1998	113644			8273	4137	3309						
10	1999	106361				7743	3872	3097					
11	2000	100035					7283	3641	2913				
12	2001	99470						7241	3621	2897			
13	2002	92513							6735	3367	2694		
14	2003	94065								6848	3424	2739	
15	2004	90925									6619	3310	2648
16	2005	88373										6434	3217
17	2006	86173											6273
18													

one year to another. In Table 11.4, the number appearing for 2003 is the result of using the failure rate of 13.83 percent.

- Row 6, Columns A and B: The heading is Initial Failure Rate. This row contains the failure rate that was used when the model was initiated. The values in Columns C to E are the failure rates to start the model. These are based on previous analyses of this type of data that indicated that, after three years, a violation order would be filed for about 19 percent of the cases placed on probation. Information from any jurisdiction can be used, even if it is from a different state. It will not affect the model results because adjustments are made to those numbers to reflect the reality of a particular jurisdiction. Also, a three-year follow-up is used because a more prolonged period would require following adult offenders, and it would add error to the calculation. Column E contains the total failure rate for the three years (in this case, 19 percent).

When the simulation is done for each year, the failure rate is adjusted until it is equal or close to the actual number. The adjustment is made by changing the value in cell 5A. For the year 2003, the value in that cell is 0.728, which can be translated to indicate that, in 2003, the failure rate was 72.8 percent of the value that was used when the model was initiated.

Changing the adjustment factor for each year until it matches the actual number provides a quick and clean way to calculate failure rates of a program and tells us whether the failure rate is changing. Table 11.5 was constructed using that information, and it tells us that, since 2000, the failure rate of juvenile probationers has been increasing continuously. This validates what was observed under referrals (refer to Figure 11.3) for court order violations, which showed that COV referrals were increasing while delinquent and CINS referrals were decreasing. If the delinquent and CINS referrals have decreased, but the COV has increased, then it follows that the failure rate of juvenile probationers must be increasing. The

Table 11.5.
Failure Rate

Juvenile Probation Failure Rate by Years Under Supervision for 2000 to 2003			
	Year 1	Year 2	Year 3	Total
2000	6.25	3.13	2.5	11.88
2001	6.88	3.44	2.75	13.07
2002	6.98	3.49	2.79	13.26
2003	7.28	3.64	2.91	13.83
2004	7.28	3.64	2.91	13.83
2005	7.28	3.64	2.91	13.83
2006	7.28	3.64	2.91	13.83

results of the simulation show that, indeed, the failure rate has been increasing. Returning to the discussion of rows and columns in Table 11.4, we continue with failure estimates for each cohort.

- Row 8 to Row 17, Columns D to M: These provide the expected number of failures of a given cohort for each of the three years that are being followed. The number is derived by multiplying the number of placements that correspond to that particular row (for 1997, the placements were 115,311) by the failure rate of the first year (0.0728) (Row 5, Column C).

To facilitate this calculation, a one-year lag is given. In other words, those placed in 1997 began failing in 1998, which is the main reason for suggesting monthly data. A one-month lag controls better for the error introduced when yearly data are used. The number resulting from the calculation is 8,395 (found in Row 8, Column D). Row 1, Column D indicates it is the year 1998. This indicates that, out of the 115,311 juvenile offenders referred to probation in 1997, a total of 8,395 received COV orders during the first year after referral (1998). For the second year, the same procedure is followed except that now it is multiplied by the failure rate for year two (0.0364) and the number 4,197. Out of the total 1997 referrals, 4,197 violations were filed during the second year after referral. This procedure is followed for each year. The total number of projected COV referrals is calculated by adding the numbers in each column and that number should correspond to the appropriate year found in Row 3.

To have a complete projection, three numbers must appear in the column. Column E, Rows 8 and 9, has two numbers. Therefore, the projected number for 1999 is incomplete, which also explains why Rows 3 and 4, Column E, are empty. When all the actual numbers of referrals have been used in the model, and the failure rate for each year calculated, then the projection can be made.

The main question is what failure rate should be used to project the future. The information from Table 11.5 is useful for that decision. Table 11.5 shows that the failure rate has been increasing since 2000, the first data point for this model. The researcher can take three avenues:

- Use the most recent failure rate for the period of the projection
- Analyze the change over time and use a continuous increase
- Increase the failure rate for one or two years more and then use the last year's projected failure as a constant for the rest of the projection (no change)

Any of the three scenarios can be equally useful as long as it is specified which scenario is chosen. In the example given, the most recent actual failure rate from Table 11.4 was used, which produces a 13.83 percent failure rate after three years.

Projecting Total Referrals

As indicated earlier, the total referrals are composed of delinquents and CINS, plus those who come in front of court for COVs. Using the information provided in Tables 11.3 and 11.4, the total projected referrals can be calculated. This is presented in Table 11.6.

Notice that there are two numbers. One represents the referrals that will go through referral to juvenile probation, with some of them going to court; the other includes all referrals, including those disposed by police or magistrate. The forecaster may want to make an adjustment up or down, based on his or her expertise with the system, because the regression equation indicates that only 90 percent of the variance is explained by the relationship between the population cohort and the new referrals. For this example, an adjustment was not made to the projection.

PARTITIONING THE NUMBER OF REFERRALS

Not all the referrals end up being processed through the system. Historical information on the percentage of cases falling under each category is used to determine how the projected numbers of referrals filter down into the system. This is provided in Table 11.7 using information for years 2000 to 2003.

The information in Table 11.7 provides the means to determine how many of the referrals will end up in actual supervision placement, which is needed to calculate the number of juveniles under community supervision. It also shows the categories of disposition and the percentage for each type during the four-year period. What is most interesting from the forecaster's view is the little variance in those percentages. The percentage of cases that are dealt with by the magistrate or police officer, which means that they were "warned and released, handled in justice or municipal courts," ranges between 32.25 percent in 2000 and 36.29 percent in 2003. This type of disposition is also known as "informal" disposition. The number dismissed, consolidated, or withdrawn has ranged between 17.87 and 19.16 percent. The percentage for commitments to the Texas Youth

Table 11.6.
Total Referrals

Texas Projected Juvenilel Referrals by Type 2004–2006			
Year	Delinquent and CINS	COV	Total Referred to Juvenile Probation	Total Referrals[*]
2004	90925	13112	104037	148624
2005	88373	12737	101110	144443
2006	86173	12482	98656	140937

[*]Includes police or magistrate dispositions

Table 11.7.
Filtered Referrals

Disposition Type	Year			
	2000	2001	2002	2003
Total Referrals	100	100	100	100
Police or Magistrate Disposition	32.87%	32.25%	35.72%	36.29%
Remaining for Further Disposition	67.13%	67.75%	64.28%	63.71%
Dismissed, not guilty no probable cause, transferred or consolidated	19.16%	19.04%	17.75%	17.87%
Supervisory Caution	16.80%	17.21%	15.63%	15.01%
Deferred prosecution by prosecutor or court	12.35%	13.57%	13.56%	13.85%
Adjudicated probation	16.71%	16.14%	16.66%	15.68%
Committed to Texas Youth Commission	1.57%	1.50%	1.59%	1.50%
Certified as adult	0.12%	0.08%	0.13%	0.08%
Total Disposed	66.71%	67.54%	65.31%	64.00%

Commission (TYC) has ranged between 1.5 and 1.57 percent during the four-year period.[9] Therefore, this shows that there is certain stability in these percentages. If the forecaster distributes the projected referrals using the most recent distribution of cases, the results are not going to greatly deviate from the actual numbers. The projected total referrals for 2004 to 2006, by disposition type, are presented in Table 11.8.

Projecting Juvenile Probation Population under Supervision

The methodology used to produce the projected supervision population is basic. It does not disaggregate but requires the calculation of the historical turnover rate of the population, which also may be known as the ALS of the cohorts who are place under community supervision. This methodology is not policy sensitive, but it does produce a projection. It is a useful methodology given that detailed data from the Juvenile Probation Department regarding the population under supervision are not accessible. Table 11.9 was constructed using the Excel program to produce the population projection. The data needed to produce the projection are historical population under supervision and number of probation placements. As mentioned earlier, monthly data are better than yearly data, but in this example, yearly data are used.

Following is a summary of Table 11.9:

- Row 1: The year for the variable is being projected.
- Row 2: Population under Supervision. Historical data of juveniles under supervision at the end of the year are indicated in Row 1.

Table 11.8.
Projected Total Referrals by Disposition Type

	Actual	Projected		
Disposition Type	2003	2004	2005	2006
Total Referrals	100	148624	144443	140937
Police or Magistrate Disposition	0.3629	53936	52418	51146
Remaining for Further Disposition	0.6371	34362	33396	32585
Dismissed, not guilty no probable cause, transferred or consolidated	0.1787	26565	25818	25191
Supervisory Caution	0.1501	22310	21683	21157
Deferred prosecution by prosecutor or court	0.1395	20729	20146	19657
Adjudicated probation	0.1468	21823	21209	20694
Probation Supervision Total	**0.2954**	**43897**	**42662**	**41626**
Committed to Texas Youth Commission	**0.0180**	**2675**	**2600**	**2537**
Certified as adult	0.0008	123	119	116
Total Disposed	0.6400	95117	92441	90197

Caption above table: Projected Total Referrals by Disposition Type

- Row 3: Projected Population under Supervision. There are the only data for years 2004 to 2006.
- Row 4: Difference. In this table, that row is blank but when actual data are reported, it is entered in Row 2, under the appropriate year, and the difference between the actual and the projected rate is calculated to assist the forecaster in monitoring the model's results.
- Row 5 (Column A): Year refers to the years for which there are historical (Column B, Rows 6 to 11) or projected placements (Column B, Rows 12 to 14) to juvenile supervision. The placements used here are not the same as referrals. The placements refer to dispositions that ordered supervision (deferred or adjudicated probation).
- Row 5 (Column C): The heading for the ALS under supervision. This is given for each year starting with Rows 6 to 10. The values presented in Rows 11 to 14 are projected. In reality, this value measures the turnover rate of the population under supervision.

The ALS is calculated based on the previous year placements and supervision. If the population were the same as the previous year's placements, then the ALS would be 12 months. Given that the juvenile population under supervision (Row 2) in Texas is less than the previous year's supervision placements (Column B), the ALS is less than a year. To calculate the historical ALS, it is necessary to take the population under supervision for a given

Table 11.9.
Projected Texas Juvenile Population under Supervision, 2004–2007

	A	B	C	D	E	F	G	H	I	J	K	L	M	N
1	Year -------------------->			1998	1999	2000	2001	2002	2003	2004	2005	2006		2007
2	Population Under Supervision --->			39718	39249	39145	39490	38558	38999					
3	Projected Population Under Supervision------>									38974	37250	36202		35323
4	Difference													
5	Year	No of Placements	ALS											
6	1998	50925	9.2487		39249									
7	1999	48524	9.6806			39145								
8	2000	48998	9.6714				39490							
9	2001	49616	9.3255					38558						
10	2002	49793	9.3987						38999					
11	2003	49761	9.3987							38974				
12	2004	47560	9.3987								37250			
13	2005	46222	9.3987									36202		
14	2006	45100	9.3987											35323
15														

Projected ALS

Projected

Projected

year, divide that number by the previous year's number of supervision placements, and then multiply it by 12. Once the historical data are exhausted, then the forecaster uses the projected supervision placements (see Table 11.8) and makes a decision about which ALS to use.

Examining the result of Table 11.9, note that the actual ALS has remained relatively constant during the past two years. In this situation, it is advisable to use the most recent month for the projection period. The population under supervision appears in Table 11.9 as a diagonal line, beginning at the top left and moving to the bottom right. For the year 2004 and beyond, that number must be projected. To project the population under supervision, the number of supervision placements for the previous year is divided by 12 (because the projected number is for a full year) and multiplied by the projected ALS (Column C, Rows 11 to 14). The projected numbers are then logged in Row 3, Columns J to N.

Projecting the Confined Population

The natural flow of this projection model is the ability to produce a disaggregated projection model for confined population, in this case for the TYC. It is disaggregated by offenses that affect length of stay. That is, the facility classifies offenders based on the type of offense for which they were adjudicated and that classification determines the minimum and maximum time they spent in the facility. The following data elements are needed to complete this part of the model:

- Projected commitments (this was calculated in the previous section of this chapter): A breakdown of the commitments to the facility from the previous year by offender types
- The distribution of time served for juveniles released the previous year by offender types
- The population of the institution (in this case TYC) at the end of the most recent year
- The distribution of time served by offender type for those children at the institution at the end of the most recent year

In the first section of this chapter, we explained how to obtain the projected commitments (see Table 11.8). The other data elements can be obtained from the institution. For this example, actual data will be used when available; however, in some instances (e.g., distribution of time served), the data are created.

Projecting the Population from Commitments

Offender Type

The offender type categories are related to the severity of the offense and each group differs in the amount of time served in custody. Sentenced offenders are a special category. They are sentenced with a determinate

Table 11.10.
Projections by Offender Type

Projected TYC Commitments by Offender Type				
Offender Type	2003	2004	2005	2006
Total Commitments	2511	2675	2600	2537
Sentenced	7.00%	187	182	178
Type A Violent	6.00%	161	156	152
Type B Violent	24.00%	642	624	609
Chronic-Serious	2.00%	54	52	51
Controlled substance dealer	1.00%	27	26	25
Firearms	3.00%	80	78	76
General	57.00%	1525	1482	1446

sentence given by the judge. When the offender reaches a certain age, they are transferred to an adult prison and, when released, they will be subject to adult parole. All the other offender types have an indeterminate sentence. The judge commits the offender to the TYC and, once there, they are classified according to their offense type, which directs the amount of time they will serve in the facility. The general offender category is the least serious, and it includes offenders who do not fall into the other categories.

Data from the TYC show the commitments by offender type. This information is transformed into ratios. Then, using the projections of commitments to the TYC previously presented, projections by offender type are made using the most recent ratios. This information is presented in Table 11.10.

Deriving Survival Rates

To project population and releases, it is necessary to calculate how long offenders remain in custody. The number of releases (using case data) is needed to calculate the survival rate of the offender in the institution. For illustration, the general offender who serves the least amount of time in a facility is used. If in the most recent year 1,500 general offenders were released from the TYC, and the time served is as depicted in Table 11.11, then that information can be used to calculate survival rates, which also is done in Table 11.11. The number of offenders released by month is calculated using a frequency distribution of time served in months for the general offender. The frequency tables provide the percentage and the cumulative percentage. The calculated survival rate is 100 minus the cumulative percentage, and it represents the percentage of offenders who are still confined after a specific number of months served. Looking at Table 11.11, it can be said that 50 percent of offenders who come to the TYC on any given date are still in confinement after the sixth month. Tables like this are constructed for each offender type and can be used to determine release

Table 11.11.
Time Served

Time Served of General Offenders Released from TYC and Calculated
Survival Rate

Time Served (months)	No. of Offenders	Percentage	Cummulative Percentage	Survival Rate
1	0	0.00%	0.00%	100.00%
2	150	10.00%	10.00%	90.00%
3	0	0.00%	10.00%	90.00%
4	225	15.00%	25.00%	75.00%
5	0	0.00%	25.00%	75.00%
6	375	25.00%	50.00%	50.00%
7	0	0.00%	50.00%	50.00%
8	375	25.00%	75.00%	25.00%
9	0	0.00%	75.00%	25.00%
10	0	0.00%	75.00%	25.00%
11	225	15.00%	90.00%	10.00%
12	150	10.00%	100.00%	0.00%

dates for offenders who come to the TYC at a specific time, as presented in
Table 11.12.

The model produces monthly projections. Because projected commitments are produced yearly, it is necessary to separate them by month and
by type of offender using the information provided in Table 11.10. General offenders account for about 57 percent of all commitments. For the
year 2004, that is estimated to be about 1,500 offenders. The variation of
monthly commitments to juvenile facilities is the result of the number of
working days in a month as well as vacation and holiday time. The best
way to divide the yearly projection into months is to examine the previous
year's placements by month and apply that proportion to each month of
the projection. Table 11.12 presents the projected population from intakes
for general offenders. This table refers to offenders who came into the system after the projection began.

Table 11.12 shows that the projection begins on September 2003.

- Row 1 contains the label indicating the month and year of the projection
- Row 2 contains the survival ratios for the general offender group
  obtained from Table 11.11
- Row 3 stores the projected population

For the first month of the projection, the projected population is 123,
the same as the number of general offenders received during that month
(Column C, Row 7). In other words, no one is released during the first

Table 11.12.
Projected Release Dates

	A	B	C	D	E	F	G	H	I	J	K	L	M	N	O	P	Q
				Projected Population from General Offenders' Commitments to TYC													
				Sep-03	Oct-03	Nov-03	Dec-03	Jan-04	Feb-04	Mar-04	Apr-04	May-04	Jun-04	Jul-04	Aug-04	Sep-04	Oct-04
1	Month			Sep-03	Oct-03	Nov-03	Dec-03	Jan-04	Feb-04	Mar-04	Apr-04	May-04	Jun-04	Jul-04	Aug-04	Sep-04	Oct-04
2		Survival		1	0.9	0.9	0.75	0.75	0.5	0.5	0.25	0.25	0.25	0.1	0	0	
3		Projected Population		123	238	344	428	520	582	649	684	722	754	777	793	790	790
4		Actual Population															
5	Projected Releases																
6	Month	Monthly Percentage	Monthly Commitments														
7	Sep-03	0.082	123	123	111	111	92	92	62	62	31	31	31	12	12	0	0
8	Oct-03	0.085	128		128	115	115	96	96	64	64	32	32	32	13	13	0
9	Nov-03	0.079	119			119	107	107	89	89	59	59	30	30	30	12	12
10	Dec-03	0.076	114				114	103	103	86	86	57	57	29	29	29	11
11	Jan-04	0.082	123					123	111	111	92	92	62	62	31	31	31
12	Feb-04	0.082	123						123	111	111	92	92	62	62	31	31
13	Mar-04	0.085	128							128	115	115	96	96	64	64	32
14	Apr-04	0.085	128								128	115	115	96	96	64	64
15	May-04	0.086	129									129	116	116	97	97	65
16	Jun-04	0.083	125										125	112	112	93	93
17	Jul-04	0.088	132											132	119	119	99
18	Aug-04	0.087	131												131	117	117
19	Sep-04	0.082	122													122	109
20	Oct-04	0.085	126														126
21	Nov-04	0.079	117														
22	Dec-04	0.076	113														
23	Jan-05	0.082	122														

month. By September 2004 (Row 3, Column P), the projected population is 790. Row 4 is included to enter the actual population when it becomes available, which helps the forecaster monitor the model's results. This feature allows the forecaster to identify the components of the model that need correction in future updates. Row 5 contains the Projected Releases. This is calculated by taking the previous month's population, subtracting the population of the month for which releases are being projected, and adding the most recent intakes (commitments).

Column A, starting with Row 7, contains the months for which projected placements are available. In this case, projections are available through 2006, but the table ends in January 2005. Column B, starting with Row 7, contains the percentage of a yearly commitment to the juvenile facility, which comes during the indicated month (Row A). In Column C, starting with Row 7, the projected number of monthly general offender commitments is indicated. Columns D to Q, staring with Row 7, show what happens to each monthly cohort who comes into the system. The monthly placement (Column D) is multiplied by the survival ratio (Row 2, starting with Columns D to O). When the survival ratio is 1.0, the releases from that group are 0, which is the ratio for each month during which the cohort first arrives to the facility. As the survival ratio decreases, the number of releases increases. When the survival ratio reaches zero, no one from that cohort remains in the institution.

This procedure is completed for each offender group committed to the institution. At the end, the resulting population from each offender group is added to produce the total population resulting from new commitments to the system. Likewise, a release from each offender group is added to produce total releases.

Calculating Remaining Population

When a projection begins, the population of the facility is composed of offenders who have just come into the institution and have served little time, while others have served enough time to be released shortly. This section of the model shows how to project the releases of those offenders who were already confined in a facility at the beginning of the projection. As in the previous section, the general offender group is used to illustrate the process. This is presented in Table 11.13. Because most of the headings in this table are the same as in Table 11.12, only those headings that are different are explained.

In Column C, Row 6, Number of Offenders refers to the general offenders who were confined at the end of August 2003 by the amount of time they had been confined in the facility. A total of 126 offenders were in the facility who had served one month (Column B, Row 7) and 12 offenders had served 12 months (Column B, Row 18). A total of 750 general offenders were confined at the end of August 2003 (Column D, Row 3). The cohort of 126 offenders who had served one month was the only intact cohort (i.e., it included 100 percent of those who came in). All other cohorts had lost some offenders because of releases.

Table 11.13.
Projected Offender Releases

Projected Population from General Offenders Already Confined in TYC as of 8-31-2003 (Beginning of Projection)

#	A	B	C	D	E	F	G	H	I	J	K	L	M	N	O	P	Q
1		Month		Aug-03	Sep-03	Oct-03	Nov-03	Dec-03	Jan-04	Feb-04	Mar-04	Apr-04	May-04	Jun-04	Jul-04	Aug-04	Sep-04
2		Survival		1	0.9	0.9	0.75	0.75	0.5	0.5	0.25	0.25	0.25	0.1	0.1	0	0
3		Projected Population		750	629	526	425	336	246	184	120	88	57	25	13	0	0
4		Actual Population															
5		Projected Releases		0	121	103	101	89	90	62	64	32	31	32	12	13	0
6	Original Cohort	Time Already Served (Months)	Number of offenders														
7	126	1	126	126													
8	121	2	109	109	113												
9	130	3	117	117	109	113											
10	132	4	99	99	98	91	95										
11	124	5	93	93	99	98	91	95									
12	130	6	65	65	62	66	65	61	63								
13	128	7	64	64	65	62	66	65	61	63							
14	64	8	16	16	32	33	31	33	33	30	32						
15	64	9	16	16	16	32	33	31	33	33	30	32					
16	92	10	23	23	16	16	32	33	31	33	33	30	32				
17	100	11	10	10	9	6	6	13	13	12	13	13	12	13			
18	120	12	12	12	10	9	6	6	13	13	13	13	13	12	13		
19	0	13	0	0	0	0	0	0	0	0	0	0	0	0	0	0	
20	0	14	0	0	0	0	0	0	0	0	0	0	0	0	0	0	0
21	0	15	0	0	0	0	0	0	0	0	0	0	0	0	0	0	0
22	0	16	0	0	0	0	0	0	0	0	0	0	0	0	0	0	0
23	0	17	0	0	0	0	0	0	0	0	0	0	0	0	0	0	0

To properly use the survival ratios (Row 2), the original cohort in each group has to be restored. This is calculated by dividing the number confined on each month served by the survival ratio for the number of months that the cohort has been confined. For instance, Column C, Row 12, shows that on August 31, 2003, there were 65 juvenile offenders confined who had served a total of six months. The corresponding survival ratio for a six-month period is 0.5 (Column I, Row 7). Dividing 65 by 0.5 equals 130, which is the estimated total number of offenders who came to the TYC when the 65 still confined arrived. It indicates that 65 of that cohort have been released. To produce the remaining population, the original cohort is multiplied by the corresponding survival ratio. Thus, for September 2003, the original cohort of 126 (Column A, Row 7) is multiplied by 0.9 (Column E, Row 2) and that produces the remaining population of 113, which is now logged in Column E, Row 8. This indicates that 113 offenders have served two months (Column E, Row 8). To calculate the remaining population, the values found within each column, staring on Row 7, are added. In the case of September 2003, the total population in Column E equals 629. Therefore, 629 offenders remain from the 750 that were confined at the end of August 2003, and, therefore, 121 offenders were released during that month (Column E, Row 5). This procedure is repeated for each offender group and each offender group occupies a separate worksheet of the workbook.

Projecting Total Population and Total Releases

The procedure to calculate the total projected population consists of completing the different worksheets for the intakes and producing a projected population from intakes. The next step is to complete all worksheets related to the population that was already confined when the projection produces a total population for the confined population. The third step is to add these two totals together to produce the total projected population. This is calculated in Table 11.14 for the general offender, and a space is provided to enter the numbers for the other offender types. The population from intake should increase, while the population from the confined group should decrease.

The same procedure indicated above for total population applies when determining the projected total releases. This is presented in Table 11.15. The releases from the confined group should be high at the beginning of the projection, while releases from the intake group start low and gradually increase in number.

CONCLUSION

Forecasting is an attempt to create estimates of future data for decision makers. In that process, there are three critical components: (1) making reasonable assumptions, (2) making decision makers understand the region of error in the forecast estimates, and (3) being careful not to focus on

Table 11.14.
Total Populations and Total Releases

Month and year	Projected Population of TYC 2004 to 2006 by Offender Type												
	Sep-03	Oct-03	Nov-03	Dec-03	Jan-04	Feb-04	Mar-04	Apr-04	May-04	Jun-04	Jul-04	Aug-04	Sep-04
From Confined Population													
Sentenced													
Type A Violent													
Type B Violent													
Chronic-Serious													
Controlled Substance Dealer													
Firearms													
General	629	526	425	336	246	184	120	88	57	25	13	0	0
Total	629	526	425	336	246	184	120	88	57	25	13	0	0
From Intakes													
Sentenced													
Type A Violent													
Type B Violent													
Chronic-Serious													
Controlled Substance Dealer													
Firearms													
General	123	238	344	428	520	582	649	684	722	754	777	793	790
Total	123	238	344	428	520	582	649	684	722	754	777	793	790

(continued)

Table 11.14. (*continued*)

Month and year	Sep-03	Oct-03	Nov-03	Dec-03	Jan-04	Feb-04	Mar-04	Apr-04	May-04	Jun-04	Jul-04	Aug-04	Sep-04
Total Population													
Sentenced													
Type A Violent													
Type B Violent													
Chronic-Serious													
Controlled Substance Dealer													
Firearms													
General	752	764	769	763	766	766	768	772	778	779	789	793	790
Total	875	1002	1113	1191	1286	1349	1417	1457	1500	1533	1566	1586	1580

Projected Population of TYC 2004 to 2006 by Offender Type

211

Table 11.15.
Projected Total Releases

	Projected Releases of TYC 2004 to 2006 by Offender Type												
Month and year	Sep-03	Oct-03	Nov-03	Dec-03	Jan-04	Feb-04	Mar-04	Apr-04	May-04	Jun-04	Jul-04	Aug-04	Sep-04
From Confined Population													
Sentenced													
Type A Violent													
Type B Violent													
Chronic-Serious													
Controlled Substance Dealer													
Firearms													
General	121	103	101	89	90	62	64	32	31	32	12	13	0
Total	121	103	101	89	90	62	64	32	31	32	12	13	0
From Intakes													
Sentenced													
Type A Violent													
Type B Violent													
Chronic-Serious													
Controlled Substance Dealer													
Firearms													
General	0	12	13	30	31	61	61	92	92	92	109	114	124
Total	0	12	13	30	31	61	61	92	92	92	109	114	124

(continued)

Table 11.15. (*continued*)

Month and year		Sep-03	Oct-03	Nov-03	Dec-03	Jan-04	Feb-04	Mar-04	Apr-04	May-04	Jun-04	Jul-04	Aug-04	Sep-04
Projected Releases of TYC 2004 to 2006 by Offender Type														
Total Releases														
Sentenced														
Type A Violent														
Type B Violent														
Chronic-Serious														
Controlled Substance Dealer														
Firearms														
General		121	116	114	119	120	123	126	123	123	124	121	127	124
Total		121	128	127	149	151	183	187	215	215	217	231	241	249

sensational implications of the estimates. The first component requires a reasonable view and understanding of the system processes involved in the outcomes to be predicted. The second component is necessary because of a tendency to fixate on the numbers, and the third component is necessary because of the nature of sensationalism, which can overshadow the major part of a forecast while smaller subestimates have greater error. The model and techniques presented in this chapter are an effort to achieve these three components in a reasonable way, with reasonable assumptions.

We need to forecast system inputs and outputs in a systematic and objective way. Otherwise, the juvenile system's traditional swings based on public and political reactions to relatively rare events will continue to rule decision making. The problem with such decision making is that the system is continually required to respond and adjust to events that actually have little impact on system processes or outputs. Meanwhile, the very adjustments themselves tend to affect both, frequently in a negative way. Objective forecasting can give us a better approach to estimating what effects changes on the system will have and a way to deflect gut-level decision making.

NOTES

1. Executive Order No. 98–06.
2. Criminal Justice Policy Council, 2002.
3. Mears, 2002, p. 14.
4. Zimring, 1998.
5. Based on data from the Texas Department of Public Safety, 1995, 2004.
6. Blumstein, 1995.
7. Data are from the Texas Juvenile Probation Commission, 1997 to 2003.
8. The SPSS is a widely used computer program, particularly in government agencies and academic institutions.
9. Texas Youth Commission, 2005.

REFERENCES

Blumstein, A. (1995, August). Violence by young people: Why the deadly nexus? *National Institute of Justice Journal*, pp. 2–9. Washington, D.C.: National Institute of Justice.

Criminal Justice Policy Council. 2002. *Adult and juvenile population projections.* Austin, TX: Criminal Justice Policy Council.

Executive Order No. 98–06. (1998). Governor's Office, State of Colorado. Denver, CO.

Mears, D. P. (2002). *Forecasting juvenile correctional populations in Texas.* Washington, D.C.: Urban Institute, Justice Policy Center.

Texas Department of Public Safety. (1995).

Texas Department of Public Safety. (2004).

Texas Juvenile Probation Commission. (1997 to 2003).

Texas Youth Commission. (2005). *Commitment profile.* Retrieved July 19, 2006, from www.tyc.state.tx.us/research/profile.html.

Zimring, F. (1998). *American youth violence.* New York: Oxford.

Index

About the Editors and Contributors

Marilyn D. McShane is a trustee-at-large member of the executive board to the Academy of Criminal Justice Sciences. She and Frank Williams have recently published the textbook *Step By Step Through the Thesis Process: A Resource Guide*. Their *Criminological Theory* book is in its fourth edition with the same publisher.

Frank P. Williams III is professor emeritus at California State University. He is author of *Imagining Criminology* and coauthor of four editions of *Criminological Theory*. He is also coauthor of the soon-to-be-released textbook *Step by Step Through the Thesis Process: A Resource Guide*.

Gordon Bazemore is professor of criminology and criminal justice and director of the Community Justice Institute at Florida Atlantic University. His recent publications appear in *Justice Quarterly, Youth and Society, Crime and Delinquency, The Annals of the American Academy of Political and Social Sciences, The Justice System Journal*, and the *International Journal of Victimology*. Dr. Bazemore has completed two books, *Restorative Juvenile Justice: Repairing the Harm of Youth Crime* (coedited with Lode Walgrave) and *Restorative and Community Justice: Cultivating Common Ground for Victims, Communities and Offenders* (coedited with Mara Schiff). He is currently principal investigator of two national projects: a study of restorative justice conferencing funded by the National Institute of Justice and the Robert Wood Johnson Foundation, and a national action research project funded by the Office of Juvenile Justice and

Delinquency Prevention to pilot restorative justice reform in several juvenile court jurisdictions.

Barbara Belbot is an associate professor of criminal justice at the University of Houston Downtown. She has a doctorate in criminal justice and a Juris Doctor. She writes extensively in the area of prisoners' rights and is currently studying prison reform movement organizations.

Ronald Burns is coauthor of *Environmental Crime: A Sourcebook* along with Michael Lynch and has recently published the textbook *The Criminal Justice System.* He is the Southwest Region representative to the executive board of the Academy of Criminal Justice Sciences and recently completed his term as president of the Southwestern Association of Criminal Justice.

Julie Kiernan Coon is an assistant professor of criminal justice at Central Connecticut State University. She earned a doctor of philosophy in criminal justice from the University of Cincinnati in 2005. She served as a project director on a National Institute of Justice–funded research project examining the role of law enforcement in schools. She is also in the process of writing a book about the use of security technology in U.S. public schools.

Craig Hemmens holds a Juris Doctor from North Carolina Central University School of Law and a doctorate in criminal justice from Sam Houston State University. He is a professor in the Department of Criminal Justice at Boise State University. He has published nine books and more than 100 articles on a variety of criminal justice-related topics. His publications have appeared in *Justice Quarterly,* the *Journal of Criminal Justice, Crime and Delinquency,* the *Criminal Law Bulletin,* and the *Prison Journal.*

Leslie A. Leip is an associate professor of public administration at Florida Atlantic University. Her research has focused on evaluations of public and nonprofit programs, specifically programs for juveniles. Dr. Leip's most recent publications appear in *Notre Dame Journal of Law, Ethics and Public Policy, Justice Quarterly, Public Administration Review, Western Criminology Review, The Journal for Juvenile Justice and Detention Services,* and *Criminal Justice Policy Review.*

Pablo E. Martinez is assistant professor of criminal justice at Texas State University–San Marcos. He has close to 30 years of experience in the development of forecasting simulation models for adult offenders. He developed models for Texas, Kentucky, and Colorado, and was a consultant for the states of Oklahoma and Hawaii. In the juvenile forecasting area, he developed a model for the state of Texas. His forecasting methodology will be published by the *Prison Journal* in a forthcoming issue. He is the author of numerous technical reports published by the Texas Department of Criminal Justice and the Texas Criminal Justice Policy Council.

Jennifer L. McGivern is a doctoral student in sociology at the University of Washington, with a specialization in criminology. She plans to explore the role of social networks in restorative justice for her dissertation.

Edward J. Schauer was instrumental in the recent development of the Texas Juvenile Crime Prevention Center, the College of Juvenile Justice and Psychology, and the first doctoral program in juvenile justice, all at Prairie View A&M University. His research interests include black male success, women's issues in criminal justice, and sex trafficking and prostitution. He has taught critical thinking in the Academy for Collegiate Excellence and Student Success (ACCESS)—an award-winning summer academic enrichment program. He has been continually involved with University College, a residential learning community for freshmen. He received his doctorate from Sam Houston State University.

Ila J. Schauer is an academic advisor with University College, the residential learning community for freshmen at Prairie View A&M University. For the past six years, she has mainly advised African American males—most of whom have become academically successful. She has experience in social work, having worked for several years in children's protective services in Louisiana. In addition to her professional advisor duties, she also serves as training coordinator for the Advisement Center at PVAMU, and chairs the First Generation College Student Interest Group for the National Academic Advising Association. She earned her master of education degree in counselor education from Sam Houston State University.

Pamela J. Schram is associate professor in the Department of Criminal Justice at California State University, San Bernardino. Her major research interests include corrections and juvenile justice with an emphasis on gender and race/ethnicity. Her research and scholarship have included evaluating drug treatment and life skills programs in correctional settings, multijurisdictional drug task forces, and an intervention program for juveniles.

Randall G. Shelden is a professor of criminal justice at the University of Nevada-Las Vegas, where he has been a faculty member since 1977. He is the author or coauthor of 10 books, including *Criminal Justice in America: A Sociological Approach*; *Girls, Delinquency and Juvenile Justice* (coauthored with Meda Chesney-Lind), which received the *Hindelang Award* for outstanding contribution to Criminology in 1992 and currently in its 3rd edition); *Youth Gangs in American Society* (coauthored with Sharon Tracy and William B. Brown, in its third edition); *Controlling the Dangerous Classes: A Critical Introduction to the History of Criminal Justice*; and *Criminal Justice in America: A Critical View*. His most recent book is *Delinquency and Juvenile Justice in American Society*. He is also the author of more than 50 articles in academic journals and book chapters on the subject of crime and justice.

Beau Snell received his master's degree in social work from Carroll College in Helena, Montana. He is currently director of Montana Youth Homes, a private nonprofit organization serving troubled youth in western Montana.

Clete Snell is graduate coordinator at the University of Houston-Downtown. He is author of *Peddling Poison: The Tobacco Industry and Kids* and of *Neighborhood Structure, Crime, and Fear of Crime*.

Lawrence F. Travis III is a professor of criminal justice at the University of Cincinnati. He has directed a number of local, state, and national research projects, including a national study of the role of law enforcement in public schools. He has published five books and monographs and more than 70 articles and book chapters on a range of criminal justice topics.

Chad R. Trulson is an assistant professor in the department of criminal justice at the University of North Texas. He has published articles in numerous professional journals and recently coauthored *Juvenile Justice: The System, Process, and Law with Rolando v. del Carmen*. His current research examines racial desegregation in prisons, and recidivism and institutional misconduct among state-committed delinquents.

Elizabeth M. Wheaton holds a master's degree in international business and trade from Grambling State University and a master's degree in economics from Temple University. She plans to complete her doctorate in economics at Temple University in December of 2006. Her research interests include child labor and the worldwide marginalization of children.